CREATIVE ARTS

IN COUNSELING AND MENTAL HEALTH

SAGE | 50 YEARS

SAGE was founded in 1965 by Sara Miller McCune to support the dissemination of usable knowledge by publishing innovative and high-quality research and teaching content. Today, we publish more than 850 journals, including those of more than 300 learned societies, more than 800 new books per year, and a growing range of library products including archives, data, case studies, reports, conference highlights, and video. SAGE remains majority-owned by our founder, and after Sara's lifetime will become owned by a charitable trust that secures our continued independence.

Los Angeles | London | New Delhi | Singapore | Washington DC

CREATIVE ARTS

IN COUNSELING AND MENTAL HEALTH

Editors

PHILIP NEILSEN
Queensland University
of Technology

ROBERT KING
Queensland University
of Technology

FELICITY BAKER
University of
Melbourne

⑤SAGE

Los Angeles | London | New Delhi
Singapore | Washington DC

$\textsf{SAGE}$

Los Angeles | London | New Delhi
Singapore | Washington DC

FOR INFORMATION:

SAGE Publications, Inc.
2455 Teller Road
Thousand Oaks, California 91320
E-mail: order@sagepub.com

SAGE Publications Ltd.
1 Oliver's Yard
55 City Road
London EC1Y 1SP
United Kingdom

SAGE Publications India Pvt. Ltd.
B 1/I 1 Mohan Cooperative Industrial Area
Mathura Road, New Delhi 110 044
India

SAGE Publications Asia-Pacific Pte. Ltd.
3 Church Street
#10-04 Samsung Hub
Singapore 049483

Copyright © 2016 by SAGE Publications, Inc.

Printed in the United States of America

ISBN 978-1-4833-0285-0

This book is printed on acid-free paper.

Acquisitions Editor: Kassie Graves
Editorial Assistant: Carrie Montoya
Production Editor: Libby Larson
Copy Editor: Cathy Kottwitz
Typesetter: C&M Digitals (P) Ltd.
Proofreader: Theresa Kay
Indexer: Kathleen Paparchontis
Cover Designer: Janet Kiesel
Marketing Manager: Shari Countryman

MIX
Paper from responsible sources
FSC
www.fsc.org
FSC® C014174

15 16 17 18 19 10 9 8 7 6 5 4 3 2 1

Brief Contents

Detailed Contents

4 Visual Art: Principles and Evidence Base for Art Therapy   28

Claire Edwards, Tom O'Brien, and Robert King

5 Visual Arts: Multidisciplinary Day Program in Practice for Young People With Severe Mental Health Problems   48

Sandra Drabant and Robert King

8 Creative Writing: A Practice-Based Account of Designing and Facilitating Life-Writing Workshops for a Group With Severe Mental Illness   87

Philip Neilsen and Robert King

9 Music Therapy and Mental Health Recovery: What Is the Evidence?   95

Claire Stephensen and Felicity Baker

12 The Evidence Base for Dance/Movement Therapy in Mental Health: Moving the Body of Knowledge 136

Sherry W. Goodill

13 Applied Theater for Mental Health: Literature Review and Evidence-Based Research 148

Andrea Baldwin

14   Respect Yourself Drama Education Program in Practice   167

Andrea Baldwin

15 Digital Storytelling for the Self-Advocacy of Marginalized Identities: Theory and Practice 177

Sonja Vivienne

Acknowledgments

The editors would like to thank the many people who have taught us about the role of the arts in counseling and mental health, through generously sharing their creativity and learning experiences towards recovery.

We would also like to thank our research assistant Eloise Cowie for her valuable contribution.

SAGE and the editors would also like to thank reviewer Jane Webber, Kean University, for her valuable feedback.

CHAPTER 1

Introduction

Robert King, Felicity Baker, and Philip Neilsen

We know that not everyone reads the introduction to a book, but if you are the kind of person who likes to read the introduction, here is what you can expect. We will try to explain why we think that engagement in the creative arts promotes recovery of mental health. To do this, we will have to explain what we mean by creative arts, what we mean by recovery, and what we mean by mental health. We will also have to provide you with something of a theoretical framework or explanatory model and have reference to some of the empirical evidence that is discussed later in the book. We will also give you a sense of the contents of the book and share with you some of our expectations and fantasies about who you, the reader, might be.

This book begins with the proposition that there is something therapeutic about engagement in the creative arts. There are of course lots of other forms of creative activities—such as building useful things, gardening, and nurturing animals—that have therapeutic benefits; however, our interest is in the creative arts—by which we mean activities such as art making, music making, drama, dance, and creative writing. These activities might be described as forms of self-expression, but we think they are more than this. We think that what makes them therapeutic is not just that they give expression to the person but that they are also artistic performances that are occurring through other relational experiences with the recipient—the viewer, audience, listener, or reader. In other words, while creativity is often an individual act, it is not the act of an individual in a void but always performed within relational experiences.

At first glance, the proposition that creative activity is therapeutic might seem a little counterintuitive. After all, words like *poet* and *tormented* seem to have a natural affinity. Jackson Pollock, Sylvia Plath, Syd Barrett, and Eric Satie were among many successful creative artists whose mental health was suboptimal. It is even possible that a little madness, or at least the ability to experience things differently to most other people, assists creativity. However, the possibility that creative people are more emotionally unstable than the rest of the population (and we are far from sure this is the case) does not mean that it is the creative activity that destabilizes. More likely, the creative activity is a stabilizing force for people who otherwise would be much less able to manage in life.

In any case, a focus on famous and successful artists would be misleading. This book is about ordinary people and their struggles with anxiety, mood disturbance, substance use, and psychosis. It is mostly about their work with therapists and the role that creative activity plays in these struggles. We have adopted the widely used term *recovery* instead of *struggles*. *Recovery* is a positive term that evokes the restoration of lost capacity, whereas *struggles* can sometimes be futile. Recovery can be misunderstood as it can have the connotation of restoration of full health. However, in the context of mental health, it often means learning to live with persistent symptoms and may be more concerned with the restoration of identity, the establishment of meaningful social connections, and the development of a belief that life can be worthwhile rather than with the complete elimination of illness.

This book is not just about people who have a diagnosed mental illness. We are also interested in people whose well-being has been compromised by severe physical illness or social disadvantage. In other words, we are interested in how creative activity can promote well-being.

We wrote this book for therapists (and people training to become therapists), but we hope it will also be of interest to others. We suspect that many readers will be specialists who are working or training in areas such as art therapy, music therapy, or drama therapy. However, we have a much wider audience in mind. We hope that the book will inspire therapists—such as nurses, social workers, psychologists, occupational therapists, and the small army of support workers and counselors who do not have formal professional designations—to encourage and support their clients to explore their creativity. We also hope that people who are searching for ways to overcome their personal difficulties or better manage difficult emotional states will read this book and be stimulated to try for themselves one or more of the creative arts.

So why are we confident that engagement in creative arts will assist your clients (if you are a therapist) or yourself? We have both a theoretical framework and an increasing body of empirical evidence. The empirical evidence is mostly linked to specific creative arts interventions (especially music therapy and art therapy) and you will find detailed discussions of this evidence in later chapters. In the introduction, we will confine ourselves to some more general observations about the status of the evidence. We think we can offer you a theoretical framework that has application to the therapeutic impact of all forms of creative activity, so we will outline this first.

A THEORETICAL FRAMEWORK FOR CREATIVE ARTS IN RECOVERY

We think that creative activity promotes mental health because of a combination of factors and not because of any single factor. The factors or components that are likely to contribute are

- behavioral activation,

- self-efficacy/mastery,

- overcoming experiential avoidance,

- strengthening of personal identity, and

- social connectedness.

We will consider each in turn, but before doing so, we think it is important to emphasize that we are not suggesting that all will operate in equal measure for any specific person. In some cases, just one or two may be present. However, all have the potential to contribute. They are also interlinked. While they are presented here as discrete factors, in practice changes in one often have implications for others. For example, behavioral activation can impact on social connectedness. However, it is not unreasonable to think of these factors as having at least some characteristics of a hierarchy with behavioral activation as the most basic step toward recovery and social connectedness as the ultimate aim of recovery.

Behavioral Activation

Many forms of mental illness, but in particular depression, tend to deactivate the person both mentally and physically. The result is extended periods of time spent sitting or lying, brooding or ruminating, but achieving very little. This becomes a self-perpetuating cycle, whereby inactivity results in feelings of inadequacy and guilt that further depress the person. Additionally, disuse of mental and physical capacities leaves the person with reduced capacity for activation, even if the mood lifts a little. Activation reverses this cycle. As the person starts to engage in meaningful activities, confidence begins to develop and physical and mental capacity starts to grow. Much of the early work in creative arts therapy is concerned with activation. Art therapists sometimes engage clients in simple squiggle games, where the aim is not to give expression to feelings or create anything but simply to get the person moving. Likewise, early work in music therapy is often concerned with *musiking*— making music within a relational experience. Readers with an interest in exploring this component of the model further are recommended to look at the work of Neil Jacobson and others in his Seattle group who were able to show that behavioral activation alone was a highly effective treatment for depression.

Self-Efficacy/Mastery

Mental illness commonly impacts on motivation as well as impairing basic cognitive functions such as attention and concentration. The result is that many people affected by mental illness experience reduced efficiency and capacity when performing a range of activities. Over time, this diminishes confidence and self-belief and can lead to a generalized loss of self-efficacy.

People who engage in creative arts therapies often discover they are more capable than they imagined—in activities for which they thought were usually reserved for those with special talents. Discovering their own creative capacity challenges their generalized lack of self-belief and helps people focus on what they can do rather than on what has been lost or diminished. As a result, they are more willing to try things and more likely to approach challenges with a sense of possibility rather than with the expectation of failure. Readers interested in learning more about self-efficacy are recommended to look at the classic work of Albert Bandura as well as more recent work in the positive psychology tradition.

Experiential Avoidance

There is a substantial body of theory and evidence to suggest that emotional difficulties are often associated with the avoidance of difficult or painful experiences. It is not surprising that people avoid these kinds of experiences, but the problem is that avoidance is not an effective strategy for managing them. There are two reasons for this. First, avoiding experiences associated with past trauma or that provoke social anxiety does not offer the potential to resolve them. In fact, it means that the opportunity for learning to deal with situations that are emotionally challenging is diminished and the difficulty is likely to persist. The second reason is that the process of avoidance often has further adverse impacts such as social isolation or nonspecific anxiety or depression.

Creative arts may provide people with a means of approaching and engaging with pain or difficulty in an indirect manner. It allows for a gradual approach and sometimes a symbolic, rather than direct, processing of experience. It is thus less threatening than a head-on confrontation with a problem but still a means by which the person can engage with, rather than avoid, the issues. This is akin to what Freud meant when he referred to creativity as a means by which unconscious conflicts can be sublimated rather than repressed. Further, many contemporary practices that draw on philosophies of empowerment, equity, human rights, and resource-oriented practices completely avoid the notion of "healing" and view cultural participation as a medium to reconnect those who have been excluded from social participation due to mental illness with sociocultural community practices. Readers interested in learning more about experiential avoidance and its consequences are encouraged to explore the work of Steven Hayes and acceptance and commitment therapy, which developed as a result of this work.

Personal Identity

Personal identity is a term used to describe how we view ourselves. It represents what we know, understand, and feel about ourselves and is most actively shaped during our adolescence. However, it is continually transformed throughout life as we encounter new experiences and events that threaten our self-concept and leave people questioning who they are as people. In other words, self-concept is not fixed and unchanging but a dynamic process shaped by the world around us, the people we interact with, and life events. People's self-concept is comprised of six domains—the personal self, social self, family self, academic/vocational self, moral self, and physical self—that impact the roles they take in various contexts within their environment. People with a low self-concept are doubtful about their own worth.

Because mental illness can have a pervasive impact on functioning and role performance, it can often compromise one or more components of identity and self-concept. People often identify themselves by occupational role, family role, or role in community activities. When people find themselves unable to manage these roles as a result of mental illness, there is a risk that their sense of identity will be compromised and, instead, the disability narrative becomes the dominant narrative in their lives. This is what Erving Goffman referred to as *spoiled identity*, and it results in diminished self-esteem, lowered expectations, and eventually loss of hope.

Engagement in creative arts can foster the development of an identity and strengthen the self-concept that is independent of illness. Where appropriate and safe for the artist, creative arts therapists may facilitate public performance, exhibition, or publication of artistic works, in part because this provides community endorsement of an emerging identity as a musician, artist, or writer. This is particularly effective if engagement with the community is not strongly linked to having a mental illness. This is not to say that public display or performance is always a good idea. Any artistic communication can involve some sharing of self, and sometimes this may mean sharing personal experience of mental illness. It is important that the artist or performer understands this and the implications for loss of privacy and potential exposure to stigma. The therapist has a responsibility to weigh the potential benefits of wider distribution of the work with the potential risks. Aside from the classic work by Goffman, readers who want to learn more about identity and mental illness are encouraged to explore more recent work by Paul Lysaker and his colleagues.

Social Connectedness

Chronic mental illness often leads to social isolation. This perpetuates mental illness since isolated people do not experience the sense of community and support that connected people experience. Social isolation occurs as a result of a combination of the previously outlined factors. People affected by mental illness often lose confidence interacting with others because of a sense that other members of the community look down on them (stigma) or that they are not worthy of participating in the community (self-stigma). Social isolation also occurs because of reduced opportunity for interaction with other people. This is often exacerbated by unemployment, which is high among people affected by mental illness because of loss of efficiency. Employment is important to most people not just because it yields an income but also because it typically engages people in meaningful interaction with others.

Participation in creative arts activities can be solitary but it often takes place in groups. Some creative arts such as choral singing, ensemble music, dancing, and theatre are inherently social activities. However, even more solitary activities such as writing or painting can occur partly through workshops, readings, and exhibitions that bring people together to share and try out ideas and techniques or to show completed work to others and the public. Furthermore, creative arts activities often lend themselves to natural transitions from rehabilitation settings to community settings. People with mental health problems may become sufficiently interested in and confident with creative arts in a rehabilitation setting to engage with community groups engaged in similar activities.

A NOTE ON THE EVIDENCE BASE FOR CREATIVE ARTS IN RECOVERY

This book has reference to many kinds of evidence from anecdotal and personal accounts to meta-analyses of randomized controlled trials (RCTs). We think that the evidence base for the effectiveness of music therapy in recovery is strong. The reason for this is that there are sufficient RCTs to create confidence that people who participate in music therapy experience improvements in their mental health and well-being that are not experienced by those who are randomly assigned to a control group. These benefits are robust across a range of populations, age groups, and mental health problems. As Claire Edwards's chapter shows, the evidence base for art therapy is also quite strong. There are fewer well-designed studies for art therapy than is the case with music therapy, but there are enough RCTs showing benefits to warrant the presumption that art therapy is broadly equivalent in effect to music therapy. There are fewer well-designed studies investigating the effectiveness of other kinds of creative arts therapies, which means that we need to be a little cautious about benefits. However, because creative arts interventions tend to have broadly similar characteristics, we think it more likely than not that these too will eventually have a strong evidence base.

When considering the effectiveness of creative arts therapies, it is worth bearing in mind what we know about the effectiveness of the so-called talking therapies, which have been investigated very rigorously over an extended period of time. Whereas it was once thought that the specific characteristics of these therapies were critical to the outcome and that some kinds of talking therapy were more effective for some kinds of problems than others, it is increasingly clear that this is not the case. Rather, verbally mediated therapies are broadly equivalent and contemporary therapies tend to be as effective as older therapies. Furthermore, recent research developments suggest that the relationship between a therapy and a disorder is much less specific than might be expected. While some therapies might have advantages with respect to particular problems, the relative advantage—even with specific problems—tends to be small.

What this means is that all therapies, whether talking therapies or arts-based therapies, probably achieve their effects through broadly similar mechanisms of change, even though they have specific characteristics. In other words, it is likely that they all impact on one or more of the five theoretical factors outlined previously. Furthermore, the interconnectedness of these factors implies that having an impact on one will inadvertently flow through to others. When it comes to understanding the potential effectiveness of arts-based therapies, we should expect that they are broadly equivalent to talking therapies.

It does not follow, however, that they are interchangeable with talking therapies. We think that creative arts therapies have some specific advantages that give them distinctive utility. Many people with mental health problems have difficulty talking about their problems or emotions. This may be because they are children, because English is not their first language, because they are inhibited or fearful, because it is too painful to share their story, or because they have cognitive limitations. Arts-based therapies provide an access point for such people. There are also people who are quite capable of engaging in verbally mediated therapy but who especially enjoy or value creative activity.

However, we are not suggesting that arts therapies should replace talking therapies, more that they can work in partnership to increase the potential for improved quality of life and maintenance of managed symptoms. At the same time, we believe that creative arts therapies are effective in promoting recovery and provide a pathway to recovery that is distinctive and, for some people, essential.

WHAT YOU WILL FIND IN THIS BOOK

In this book you will find a range of perspectives on the role of creative arts in recovery. The book describes six creative art forms and their use as a therapeutic medium—visual art, writing, music, drama, dance and movement, and contemporary and mixed media. There are some chapters dedicated to describing the body of evidence to support the therapeutic effects of the art form and other chapters that describe how the interventions are applied in practice. What is further unique to this book's comprehensiveness is that it contains some personal accounts by people who explain how creative arts have helped them.

If you are the kind of person who reads a book right through, rather than selecting chapters or sections of interest, you will notice that there are stylistic variations throughout the book. This partly reflects the different writing styles of the various authors who have contributed. However, it also reflects variations in content. Our accounts of the implementation of creative arts interventions are designed to help practitioners see how it can be done. The focus is on description of the intervention and exploration of responses of participants. By contrast, when we attempt to provide a summary of the evidence base for creative arts interventions, there is much more formal analysis and greater risk that the content will seem a little dry to the casual reader. We live in a world in which the practice and evidence base are increasingly interlinked, so we make no apology for including reasonably scholarly outlines of the evidence base in a book that is primarily designed for practitioners. However, we do acknowledge that there are consequences for continuity of style.

ABOUT THE AUTHORS

The authors are a diverse group of people. While most are currently living in Australia, some trained or worked in the United States or the United Kingdom. Some are people with personal experience of mental illness and a personal understanding about how creative activity contributes to recovery. Others are therapists who have spent much of their lives designing and implementing creative arts activities and programs for people with mental illness. Some are researchers with an interest in program evaluation. Some would identify primarily as creative artists. Most fall into more than one category. What we share in common is a conviction about the value of creative arts—which is why we have come together to create this book. We hope you enjoy the book and find it helpful.

CHAPTER 2

Lived Experience

Writing and Recovery

Robert King (with J. R. Scott and Jane Boggs)

I think that writing novels . . . is in many ways an act of self-therapy. Undoubtedly, there are those who have some kind of message and write it in a novel, but in my case at least, that is not how it works. Rather, I feel like I write novels in order to find out what kind of message is in me to begin with. In the process of writing a story, these kinds of messages just suddenly float up from the darkness.

(Haruki Murakami, as cited in Dil, 2007, p. 36)

This chapter provides a window into the lived experience of people whose creative writing forms part of their experience of recovery from mental illness. We learn about the experience of a group of people who participated in a creative writing workshop and meet a couple of poets. The first part of the chapter contains my[1] observations and reflections on a writing workshop provided by an agency that provides rehabilitation services for people recovering from mental illness. The second part of the chapter consists of some notes on what it means to write by people recovering from mental illness. These people are not professional writers. They are, prior to now, unpublished. However, they do not necessarily write for themselves alone. Like most writers, they can be a little hesitant about exposing their work, but I try to explain why I think they write with a reader (not just themselves) in mind.

Before we meet these people, I would like to introduce you to Haruki Murakami. Murakami is a professional writer. In his own country of Japan, he is a celebrity. Every time a new novel is released, queues form outside the bookshops the night before it comes on sale. While he is not such a celebrity outside of Japan, his work is translated and widely read and appreciated around the world. Each year, when the Nobel Prize season comes around, his name is prominent in the speculations about possible recipients of the prize for literature. In other words, he is a rather unusual writer in that he has managed to achieve both popular success and critical acclaim.

So what makes Murakami relevant in a chapter that explores writing as part of the recovery journey of people struggling with mental illness? The answer is to be found in the quote that starts this chapter and in a rather extraordinary doctoral thesis by Jonathan Dil and in some of Dil's subsequent work. Murakami once described his work as self-therapy. It is probably not the main reason why he writes. However, there is something about writing that brings him into contact with aspects of himself that he would otherwise not know about. Furthermore, there is something about this encounter that is important and somehow therapeutic.

> I think that human existence is like a two-storied house. On the first floor is where everyone gets together to eat, watch television, and talk. On the second floor is where you have your private room and sleeping quarters. You go there to be alone, read books, and listen to music. You then have the basement. This is a special place where many different things are stored. While not a room you use everyday, it is nevertheless a place you sometimes go to zone out. It is my opinion, however, that beneath this basement exists another one. This place has such a special door and is so difficult to find that usually you cannot enter, and many people never find it. If by some chance you do suddenly enter, however, what you find is darkness.

> (Haruki Murakami, as cited in Dil, 2007, p. 37)

This darkness is a place well known to people who live with depression and other forms of mental illness. Indeed, *darkness* is a word used by J. R. Scott in his poem "Involuntary," which you will encounter later in this chapter. It is a disturbing place and, for a person struggling with mental illness, a place that is not entered by choice. As Murakami goes on to explain, the writer is in a different position from the person cast into darkness by mental illness.

> I think a writer is someone who can do this deliberately. I believe that a writer's primary source of power comes from their ability to open that secret door, enter that darkness, see what they need to see and experience what they need to experience, come back, close that door, and return to reality.

> (Haruki Murakami, as cited in Dil, 2007, p. 37)

The point of difference is that the writer chooses to open the secret door, whereas the person experiencing mental illness often just finds herself or himself in the dark place. The link with Murakami is that the act of writing can also help find the way out of the dark place. Furthermore, having a reader in mind means that the journey is not quite as lonely. It is not a requirement to be successful as a writer. The success is that the work of writing allows a person to explore this place on her or his own terms and, as Murakami puts it, to return to reality.

A WRITING WORKSHOP

My colleague, Philip Neilsen, describes his writing workshop in Chapter 8 of this book. Philip and I collaborated in the development of the workshop. His job was to run the workshop and mine was to learn about the experience of people who participated in the workshop.

To do this, I attended for a couple of sessions. I observed the participants and I mingled during the break. I listened to the fragments of writing they shared with the group and to the questions and comments they made during the workshop. After the workshop I contacted most of them by phone to find out how they had experienced the workshop and what made it valuable or otherwise. The main themes are reported elsewhere (King, Neilsen, & White, 2012). I will confine myself in this chapter to a few observations and thoughts that occurred to me about what writing meant to participants and what the workshop meant to them.

The participants were people engaged in a program of psychosocial rehabilitation with a nongovernment organization. They were all being treated for a mental illness. We did not formally inquire about the diagnosis as it was not relevant to the workshop. However, their disorders were sufficient to prevent them from participating in regular work, and the profile of service users includes people with diagnoses of schizophrenia, bipolar disorder, personality disorder, and more severe and chronic depression and anxiety. What brought them together was a shared interest in writing. Some wrote poetry, some diaries or journals, and one had written a very substantial narrative about her life and illness.

Philip is a successful writer who has published poetry, short stories, and novels. The workshop was designed along the lines of a mainstream writing workshop and was promoted as such. It was not promoted as a rehabilitation activity even though it was provided in a rehabilitation center. The focus was on the craft of writing rather than the content. When I spoke with participants during and after the workshop, it was clear that this was important, especially for those who saw themselves as writers who were affected by mental illness and not as people with a mental illness who also wrote. It was clear that some participants were really interested in improving the style and structure of their writing. They made active use of the worksheets and exercises Philip provided and worked on their sentences and paragraphs. Even for those who were less concerned with style, the focus of the workshop allowed them to engage with an identity that was not bound to the illness and for which the illness was not an impediment.

It was also clear when I spoke to participants that Philip's standing as a professional writer mattered to them. There were two reasons for this. The first was that it meant he had credibility as a teacher. He shared his own experience of development as a writer, and participants could see how the things he had learned had enabled him to become more effective and successful. This made them receptive to disciplines and approaches that might otherwise seem a bit dry or remote from self-expression. The second was that they viewed Philip as a kind of celebrity. People recovering from mental illness often feel marginalized, especially if they are unable to work. The fact that someone successful in the field was working with them made them feel worthwhile, especially because he was not condescending and treated them as fellow writers. This was a recurrent theme when I phoned people and asked them what they remembered of the workshop.

When Philip and I planned the workshop, we were cognizant of the philosophy and orientation of the host organization, which had a very positive and strengths-focused approach to rehabilitation. The writing exercises Philip developed invited people to reflect on personal experience but on lighter, everyday, or positive experiences. Some were happy to work within this framework, but I was struck by how many ignored the recommendations and instead focused on more negative or difficult experiences. Some participants brought writing they had produced prior to the workshop. This also focused on the experience of mental illness.

It seemed to me that most participants wanted to use writing not to escape from their mental illness but instead to engage with it and explore it. This was not quite what we had expected but, at the same time, was not entirely surprising. The Scottish poet Roddy Lumsden (2011) famously observed, "A poet confessing to mental illness is like a weightlifter confessing to muscles." This is saying not just that poets often have experience of mental illness but that the experience of mental illness is essential to the production of poetry.

I am sure that there are poets who have not experienced mental illness and some poets, like Les Murray, are more ambivalent about the relationship between their mental illness and their creativity. Murray said, in an interview for the Australian Broadcasting Commission (2009), "I don't like [mental illness] as a muse. I tried not to write about it. But finally if you're sick enough you'll use whatever tools you've got." It is not entirely clear whether Murray sees poetry as a tool to deal with mental illness or mental illness as a tool to produce poetry, but I think he means that poets have to work with their experience. For some reason, there is an affinity between mental illness and poetry (and other forms of creative writing). Mental illness played a central part in the experience of the participants in our workshop, so we should not be surprised that this experience was central to much of their writing. Roddy Lumsden also said in a 2009 interview in *The Scotsman* (Mansfield, 2009),

> I've always thought it's very important that if you're lucky enough to be in one of the only jobs where mental illness is not a stigma, you should stand up and say, "Look, this is something lots of people go through." I don't feel uncomfortable with people knowing those things about me.

When I talked with workshop participants to learn about how they experienced it, a lot of the comments were as might be expected. They found it to be a safe and supportive environment, they appreciated the practical tips and suggestions that Philip provided, and they enjoyed finding out about what others were doing. What came across more strongly than I had expected was their connection to Philip. At some level, this should not be surprising as he was warm and engaging and shared a lot of himself and his work in his interactions with the group. However, there was something in their responses that went beyond appreciation of a very skilled and experienced teacher. There was a mixture of surprise and pleasure that they were taken seriously as writers, that their work was worthy of improving. It was as if Philip was inviting them to join the guild of writers and that with that invitation came the possibility of an enrichment of identity. I got the sense that prior to the workshop most participants took writing seriously and understood how important it was personally but that during the course of the workshop they glimpsed the possibility that their work could connect them to a wider public.

There were two themes in their responses to my questions that alerted me to this way of experiencing the workshop. The first was that they experienced Philip as being different from what they expected. They expected that, since he was a well-published and successful writer, there would be a marked separation between him and themselves. I had the sense that such a separation would not have bothered them, as they saw themselves as people who were already different as a result of their mental illness. However, the absence of separation—which was often reported as noncondescension—opened them to the possibility that an identity as a writer could jostle with an identity as a person struggling with mental illness. The second is that they began to understand that writing is more than a mode of self-expression. It is also a craft that requires an understanding of principles and procedures and careful work in the selection and organization of words, revision of sentences, and development of storylines. In particular, I got the sense in the way that they talked about the workshop that they understood, in a way they had not before, that this work—the slog of writing—was the key to transition from a purely personal process to an effective engagement with the world of readers.

Of course, each participant experienced the workshop a little differently and explained his or her response to it in distinctive ways. However, it was clear to me that what most surprised and impressed participants was that it was an invitation from one writer to another.

CLUBHOUSE WRITERS

Clubhouses are an international network of member-based organizations that provide support and psychosocial rehabilitation for people affected by mental illness. They have a strong ethos of peer support and engagement with the community through work. I have had a long association with clubhouses, and so, when I was seeking some voices of writers who lived with mental illness, I put out a call to members in clubhouses with which I had been associated in Australia and the United States. The following are a couple of responses from members who wanted to share something about what makes writing important to them in their struggle with mental illness.

J. R. Scott

J. R. Scott is a member of the Stepping Stone Clubhouse in Brisbane. He was one of the first to offer a contribution. He wrote to me as follows:

> Writing poetry has become an important part of what I consider to be my emotional immune system. The toolbox I utilize to minimize episodes of depression and to draw from when confronted with one. It has evolved into my closest ally as a truth bearer of identity and emotions. This realization is the result of a long journey taken over a very short period of time.

> It began with me being admitted to a psychiatric hospital after an attempted suicide. The only recollection I have of that day was the sadness I felt for having failed in my attempt to kill myself. I was lost, distressed, and alone and having to confront the situation I was now in. Doctors, nurses, social workers and psychiatrists all having a prod and a poke with what seemed like a never ending list of questions. Silence and solitude was all I wanted, and retreating behind the

curtain to my bed was where I found it. I would communicate with the staff when need be but only on a superficial level. My true feelings I kept to myself.

At some point during my stay, I began scribbling those feelings into notebooks. On my bed, sheltered behind the curtain with my thoughts, I would write with no particular outcome in mind except perhaps to pass some time. Eventually, I had pages of words with feeling and emotion but no direction. This was when I decided to try and put my thoughts into some sort of literary form. I chose poetry.

I had never read much poetry, but I was familiar with how powerful it could be in conveying emotion. How it should be structured and all other technical aspects I had no idea of. All I wanted was some way to expel my emotions freely.

When I started spending more time in the common areas of the hospital, though still keeping to myself, I would always carry my notebook with me and would spend hour on hour sitting in the courtyard writing. It was around this time that I had a significant setback in my recovery.

While I was not interacting with the staff or other patients voluntarily, I was still very observant of what was happening around me. No longer sheltered in my room behind a curtain, I was seeing a world of despair. The lost hope in the eyes of those around me. I was overwhelmed with the feeling that lives were being saved, but to what end? To continue existing, moving between the entries and exits of the infamous revolving door. I fell into a deep despair. My only consolation was being able to expel my feelings, without judgment, into my notebook. The result was my first poem, titled "Involuntary." It was the result of expressing my feelings without any predisposed thought pattern or goal.

In essence, it was me at that particular point in time. And this is it:

Involuntary

Senses collecting the grey of the day,

Surrendering time to the eroding decay,

A voice from the lost

Heard far not near,

Redemption! Redemption!

Yesteryear.

Embrace me warm sun

Falls deaf lonely tears,

The edge calling closer,

Brings with it no fears;

Into the darkness

No gracious goodnight,

A silent salvation—

Goodbye to the light…

This poem may or may not be many things, but the one thing that it is, is honest. It is a reflection of where I was at a particular point in my life. Revealing my sadness, my despair, and my suicidal thoughts. It has also been, however, the most significant tipping point in my recovery to date. I became aware that writing, for gratification's sake and not literary performance, allowed me to live my thoughts without judgment. To express my angers, frustrations, and desires in a consoling manner.

I began to write at every opportunity without any outcome in mind except to write honestly. Curiosity also took hold and I began to research poetry and poets. Reading the poetry of others has also had a positive impact on my recovery. When I can't find solace in my own words, I often find it in the writings of others.

My passion for writing, and in particular poetry, continues. No longer is it only a tool that is helping me in my recovery, but I have discovered that it is overwhelmingly a part of who I am, and it is playing an important role in my acceptance that depression is also a part of who I am. This self-acceptance is what is allowing me to move forward in reclaiming my life.

Writing poetry is still very much a private passion. I have shown my work to several family members, friends, and those involved in my recovery but have not taken it to a wider audience through poetry groups, writing clubs, or Internet forums. My goal for my writing is to continue to do it as honestly as I can and perhaps publish a chapbook of my work in the near future.

Jane Boggs

Jane is a member of the Genesis Clubhouse, in Worcester, Massachusetts. Jane wrote:

I feel I must write, for I feel like I'm "bursting," in a way. I want to share in some way what I feel. Yet I cannot write with concentration and true feeling unless I am alone. Maybe this sounds like a contradiction. I feel "safe in a way" and yet, I want to communicate so much.

I feel I have something I can say. I feel like part of the world—the world I see. So writing is truly a saving thing to me—a refuge of sorts. It frees me to be a part of life.

Jane also sent a poem:

Message of the Morning

All the cares that so concern—that fret so—have given in to the soft, moist of the morn.

Everything seems to sparkle and shine. The trees reach up so clearly and distinctly—

I cannot battle the gentleness that is there—it dominates and enfolds me in such a way

It banishes all other.

I breathe this, the morn—and see simple, so—"kind" things.

The shadows give way to the brightness, reluctantly it seems—but inevitably.

My heart seems to rise a bit along with the sun, and the newborn world seems almost

To begin a dance of sorts.

As the shadows give way to the brightness, I feel almost an

Invitation to a sort of freedom.

In the darkness of the night, I know I must remember this—

"the message of the morning"

It is clear that for both J. R. and Jane writing serves two purposes. In part, it provides a means of processing and dealing with painful or frightening experiences that are associated with mental illness. In J. R.'s case, it is the feelings of despair that result from involuntary treatment and in Jane's case, feelings of anxiety. In each case, the poem emerges to provide comfort, to place an otherwise unbearable experience in a larger perspective. However, there is something beyond this private source of comfort. As Jane explained so eloquently, there is also a desire to communicate, to offer the work in the hope that it will also resonate with a reader. J. R., too, expresses a desire for connection—at first indirectly through exploring the work of other writers but, perhaps, later through sharing his work with a wider public.

In his poem "Involuntary," J. R. Scott processes an especially difficult moment in his life. Not only is he struggling with depression but he is also detained against his will in a psychiatric unit. He was socially withdrawn and at risk of retreating further into a passive state of despair that he saw in others around him. However, rather than do this, he engaged with his feelings and observations and used poetry to describe them. Having reference to the framework we outlined in the introduction to this book, I would say that this was an activating experience and an experience that allowed a degree of mastery. The production of the poem meant that he was no longer just a passive victim of his situation. It also caused him to begin to think of himself as something other than a person with a mental illness. It was the beginning of an identity as a writer. In his personal account, we see him contemplating a more developed social expression of this emerging identity.

As I see it, this reaching out to a wider world through writing, as described by J. R. Scott and Jane Boggs, gives expression to the hope that the writer is not alone in a personal torment but that there is something universal in the experience, which means that mental illness is not a state of absolute otherness. Joanie Eckert, another clubhouse member, explained it like this: "I have found strength in writing my story and sharing it with the community to help bridge the stigma against mental illness: that there is hope for everyone." As Lacan (1975–76) explained in his commentary on James Joyce, the act of writing connects the writer to the universe of signifiers that he termed "the Other." It is not a guarantor of recovery, but it opens up the possibility.

CONCLUSION

In the introduction to this book, we provided a theoretical framework for understanding how the creative arts can contribute to a person's journey of recovery. We argued that creative activity has the potential to activate a person, promote self-efficacy and mastery, help overcome experiential avoidance, strengthen personal identity, and contribute to social connectedness. The reports and experiences discussed in this chapter illustrate how writing specifically can assist the recovery process. We can see instances of each of the five means by which creative activity contributes to recovery in the accounts of professional writers, the reports of people who participated in a writing workshop, and the personal accounts of people who are not as yet professional writers but who are writing as part of their transition from a state that is dominated by the experience of mental illness to a state where mental illness forms just part of their experience and identity.

This does not mean that writing, or any other creative activity, is a panacea or even an alternative to the various medical and psychological treatment that have been developed to help people manage the symptoms of mental illness. Writing does not get rid of depression or anxiety. At best, it can reposition the person in relation to these kinds of experiences. As Roddy Lumsden explained, many writers have an ongoing struggle with symptoms of mental illness. However, there is no shame in that.

NOTE

1. Robert King is the author of this chapter except for the specific and clearly identified contributions by J. R. Scott and Jane Boggs.

REFERENCES

Australian Broadcasting Commission. (2009, October 8). Les Murray and the black dog. *The Book Show*. Retrieved from http://www.abc.net.au/radionational/programs/bookshow/les-murray-and-the-black-dog/3083662#transcript

Dil, J. (2007). *Murakami Haruki and the search for self-therapy* (Unpublished doctoral thesis). The University of Canterbury, Christchurch, NZ. Retrieved from http://ir.canterbury.ac.nz/bitstream/10092/1004/1/thesis_fulltext.pdf

King, R., Neilsen, P., & White, E. (2012). Creative writing in recovery from severe mental illness. *International Journal of Mental Health Nursing, 22*(5), 444-452. doi:10.1111/j.1447-0349.2012.00891.x

Lacan, J. (1975–6). Seminaire XXIII (Le Sinthome) (J. A. Miller, Ed.). *Ornicar, 6-11,* 1976–77.

Lumsden, R. (2011). *Roddy Lumsden is dead.* Hull, East Yorkshire, UK: Wrecking Ball Press.

Mansfield, S. (2009, March 12). Roddy Lumsden interview: Poetry, Kate and me. *The Scotsman*. Retrieved from http://www.scotsman.com/news/roddy-lumsden-interview-poetry-kate-and-me-1-1029476

Murray, L. (2011). *Killing the black dog: A memoir of depression.* New York, NY: Farrar, Straus & Giroux.

CHAPTER 3

Lived Experience

Visual Art and Music in Recovery

Patricia Strobel, Tom O'Brien, and Ann Bermingham
(introductory and concluding remarks by Robert King)

This chapter is something of a continuation of the previous chapter. Like the previous chapter, it explores the experience of people engaged in creative activity with a view to better understanding the relationship between creative activity and recovery from mental illness. As with the previous chapter, we hear from these people in their own words as they describe what creative activity means to them.

However, there are two important differences. First, there are differences with respect to the kind of creative activity. The previous chapter was concerned with writing, especially—but not exclusively—poetry. This chapter is concerned with visual art making and music. The second point of difference is the perspectives of the people engaged in creative activity. In the previous chapter, the focus was on the perspective of people struggling with mental illness. In this chapter, we hear the voices of three people whose work involves helping people who are recovering from mental illness. Each person provides a distinctive perspective on the role of creative activity in their own lives and in their work.

Patricia Strobel is a visual artist who runs a community arts group. Prior to her own experience with mental illness, she had enjoyed a successful life with a business and a family. In her essay, she describes a transformative journey that led her to where she is now—using her passion for art to work with people whose lives are dominated by mental illness. She also explains how artwork helped her to survive the challenges to her identity when she was treated for a mental illness herself.

Tom O'Brien is a social worker and psychotherapist with a long history of work with people, especially children and their families, affected by mental illness. Like Patricia, Tom has enjoyed a successful career and family life. Unlike Patricia, he has not had to deal with the personal experience of hospitalization because of mental illness. However, he started his career working in one of the major institutions, once called asylums, and he has worked in close proximity with people experiencing severe mental illness throughout his career. In his essay, Tom describes how, late in his professional life, he entered the world of art making, with consequences that surprised him and those around him.

Ann Bermingham is a social worker and musician. She has been the musical director of the Richmond Fellowship Choir since 2009. Richmond Fellowship Queensland (RFQ) is a nongovernment organization that provides support and psychosocial rehabilitation services for people with mental illness. RFQ formed the choir in 2005 to provide an opportunity for performance for people who love music. In her essay, Ann explains how the choir evolved and how she sees its role in the lives of its members.

At the end of the chapter, I[1] offer a few concluding thoughts, returning to the theoretical framework introduced in the introduction to this book and developed in the preceding chapter.

PATRICIA STROBEL

I do remember a time when I was carefree with no sign or knowledge of depression, but that was way back before I was nine years old. Running through the bushland, climbing trees, and feeling free as a bird. Rainy days were spent painting and drawing. I was a tomboy and loved it. I loved school, too; I found it challenging and exciting.

Then everything changed. Adults became the enemy to be avoided at all costs. "No more playing games. Children are like wild horses—they are of no use until their spirit is broken," I was told at the age of nine. A teacher set out to break my spirit, forcing me to skip a grade at school, resulting in my schoolmates being in a grade behind me and in a different playground as well. I learned the true meaning of the words *hate, helplessness,* and *loneliness.* Assault and abuse was a daily routine for one long year.

There were a few things she could not take away from me. One was my inner being, where I dwelled most of the time for comfort, and the other was art. I still have pieces of art that I created around that time. They are dear to me. I have come to learn to manage my depression, but that took many, many years to accept and learn. I should seek "recovery," I was told by the medicos. *Recovery* to me meant I would be back feeling the way I felt as a child. Free and happy. Being a person who is known as stubborn and persistent, I decided I would find the secret to recovery, and once found, I would use it to fix myself.

So having married, raised two children, and run my own businesses throughout my life, I was at a stage where I at last had the time to chase and solve the mystery of recovery and thus be cured.

I set myself to learning all the various types of therapy—herbs, books, dance, drumming, yoga, meditation, and so on, and dozens of self-help books. But I was puzzled to find they did not work for me. So, off I went to see a GP because I was not sleeping and just wanted a sleeping pill, because I reckoned that if I could only get a good night's sleep I would then have a clear mind to find that elusive answer. Suddenly, my GP had me sent off to psychiatrists, who sent me off to the hospital, plied me with drugs of many varieties until I was now quite unsure of who or what I was, or even where I was.

While in the hospital, my art remained with me and thankfully so did my inner being (albeit a bit quirky because of the drugs). I created art at a rate of knots, even painting murals on the walls of one of the consulting rooms in the hospital. This cost me $80 for the room to be repainted! While in the hospital I met a wonderful doctor, who seemed to actually want to listen to me. I held him in deep suspicion for a very long time, trying to figure out his angle. This was the very first time in my life anyone had ever asked me how I felt. Hard to believe, but true. I still see him monthly to this day, and I know he will always listen to me.

Once released from the hospital, having still not discovered "recovery," I decided that it must be hidden among the teachings of psychology, so I enrolled for a university degree with the intention of doing visual arts, while also doing a few psychology subjects to enable me to unveil the secret through scholarly learning. Although I had been forced to leave school at 15, that was not going to stop me from getting a degree, so I applied and was accepted into a university.

Over the next six years, I completed a bachelor of arts degree on campus, graduating with a double major in psychology and human behavior. I was very determined to solve this mystery. I believe that nothing is impossible if you have the determination and willingness to put in time and effort. Having graduated, and thoroughly enjoying the process of learning, there was something very crucially important that I had learned by the time I graduated.

This was the fact that for me and most others with depression and PTSD—there is no recovery, and chasing after it had left me

Figure 3.1 This painting is called *Frenzy*, and I painted it while in the hospital suffering from depression. There was a group of patients racing up and down the corridor outside of my room, which made me irritated, and it felt to me that they were in a frenzy.

Source: Patricia Strobel.

feeling a failure for not achieving it or succeeding in finding it. Indeed, this futile search had actually exacerbated the depression. I also learned that the real key to feeling better is to take management of my own illness. To be patient with myself when I am in the depths of depression. To lay low when I am in the throes of anxiety or migraines until I feel better. To take time out when I need it, no matter what others think. Then to press on when I am ready.

Self-management is the key to getting on with life while living with depression. My self-management plan works for me most of the time, but it will be different for different people. Part of my management plan is to take time out one day a week to do art because it calms me. When I am feeling really bad I rest. When I am feeling creative I get lots of stuff done.

Figure 3.2 This painting, which I called *Loneliness*, was also painted in the hospital. I felt lost in space and no one knew where I was.

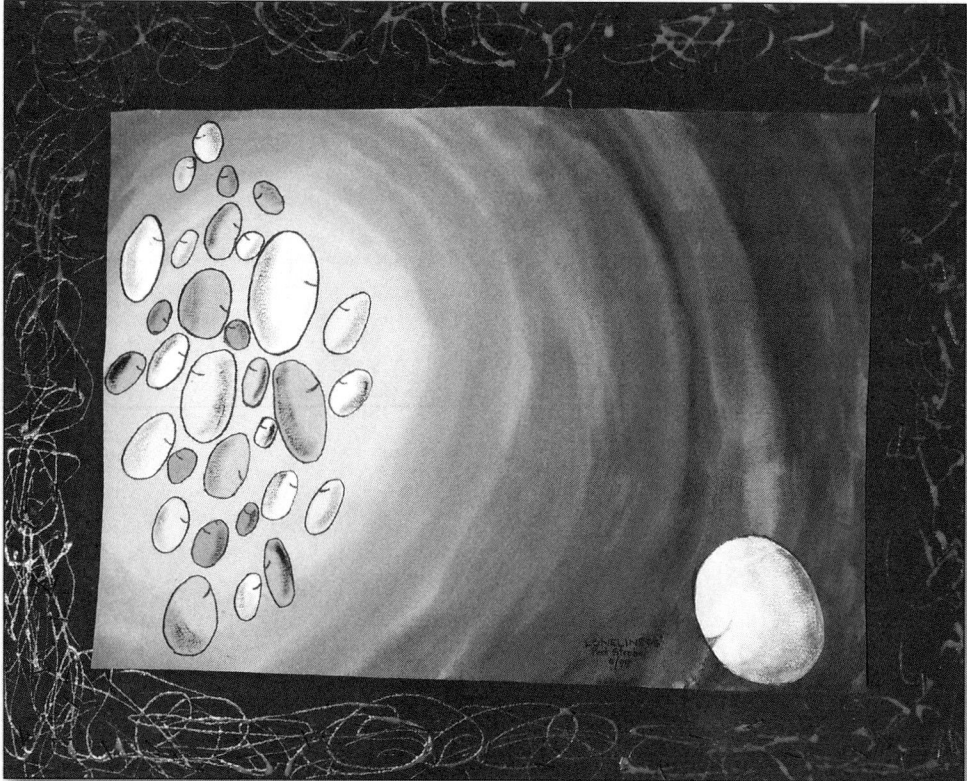

Source: Patricia Strobel.

I am the secretary and cofounder of a community art group, which I began seven years ago. I started the group because I believed that mental illness is best managed when one feels in control and has friends and activities (such as art) to immerse oneself in. I also believe that art groups that label themselves "mental illness art groups" or similar are detrimental to the people who wish to attend them by forcing them to label themselves rather than immerse themselves in the mainstream community. No one wants to tell their friends around the dinner table that they are off to their mental illness art group in the morning.

I called my group Community Arts For Everyone Inc., with the word *Everyone* a critical element. I have found over the past seven years that members of my group do not think of themselves as being ill, they just think of themselves as people who enjoy doing art in a friendly atmosphere with other people and find it therapeutic, which helps them to manage other aspects of their day-to-day lives.

Members come from all walks of life, some go on to further education, some to take up jobs. Most say that art group day is the thing that keeps them going. Some members of the group do not have mental health issues at all, some are caregivers, some are young mothers needing some time out, and some are older people. All need social interaction, positive regard, and a feeling of self-worth. I never ask, nor do many tell me if they have or do not have any mental health issues. They make friends among other members in a most natural way.

Members of the group must present at least one art-related short workshop per year to the rest of the group. I have found that this rule has resulted in the most unlikely people doing the most amazing job of presenting their workshop. We help them to organize it and they see how others present theirs. This aspect results in a huge boost to their self-esteem and confidence, which in turn helps them to feel more confident about being proactive in managing other areas of their life, including their illness and personal relationships.

Members must be responsible for themselves or bring a caregiver along to be responsible and help in running the group, cleaning up, and other tasks. We allow people to come along as visitors

Figure 3.3   This was painted sometime after my experience with hospitalization, when I was feeling settled and calm and really enjoyed the opposing angles of the birds' beaks and legs, which to me meant balance and symmetry.

Source: Patricia Strobel.

until they feel they are ready to join in. We keep the cost down to an affordable level by getting small grants to pay for rent, art materials, and the like. I try to pass on what I have learned and learn lots from others in the group—not always related to art, I must say. Sometimes I have no energy to give effort to anything; that's when I rest.

I guess I live my life in spurts of energy and creativity followed in a cycle with clusters of depression and migraines. But that's OK, because now I know I have not failed to find "recovery." It was never there anyway, but I sure wish someone had told me that earlier in my life. I believe the word *recovery* should be replaced with the word *self-management*.

TOM O'BRIEN

I'm over 60 years old, color-blind, can't draw (and while I'm in confessional mode, can't sing or dance and have no rhythm to boot), have no spiritual beliefs, and have no professional training in art therapy. Doesn't sound like the makings of an enthusiastic advocate for art therapy and other creative arts therapies.

I'm a clinical social worker with nearly 40 years of experience of work in mental health settings both in Australia and in the United Kingdom. I have an active practice in psychoanalytic therapy with adolescents and adults and an intensive formal training that emphasized the centrality of words, or their absence or misuse, as the focus of the clinical encounter. Images from dreams or fantasies, from either patient or therapist, are valued but expected to be worked on through the medium of words. My work in a child and youth mental health service was, however, one that encouraged the use of play, image creation, and communication through their interaction.

I fell in with the art therapists over 15 years ago, impressed with their capacity to work with children and young people. Seeing art (and creative arts) therapists transform uncommunicative adolescents willing to give "name, rank and serial number only" into imaginative and purposefully engaged clients was exciting and rewarding. I wanted to know more. We discussed the need for a local training program for art therapists and I linked the art therapists with my University of Queensland colleague, Robert King. Hard work and creative thinking led to the development of the master of mental health—art therapy program in 2004 and, in an even more "creative" move, I became the coordinator of that degree. I was bestowed with the honorific "Honorary Art Therapist" and exposed to bucket loads of clay, glue, and pastels. Ten years later, the degree thrives under the leadership of real art therapists.

So How Has This Privileged Exposure to Art Therapy Changed Me?

My clinical practice with adults and young people as individuals, families, and groups is forever changed. I don't often reach for the pencils and the pad but I am more open to hearing visual or spatial references in their words. Metaphor, images, reverie, half-glimpsed forms are followed, played with, and explored. The research findings that "all (therapies) have won and all shall have prizes" (Luborsky, Singer, & Luborsky, 1975) has gained new power for me as I see the creative arts therapies transform lives. In an unexpected twist, I have even developed more regard for talking type therapies more distant from my own psychoanalytic therapy.

Being allowed or forced to sit in workshops and be exposed to and by art materials and practices has given me some insight into both the techniques and the thinking process of "real" artists. I've always been a cultured fellow going along to galleries and exhibitions, being moved and sometimes excited by art activities and products, knowing what I liked, but with limited capacity for access to the thinking and experience of the art practitioner. Now I seek out artwork that moves me and I engage with it. I try to understand how and why the artist has made choices in the piece. I play with it, allow it to affect me, and I value the complex emotional experience. I have increased the quantity of my interaction with art but, more importantly, the quality of that experience.

My art practice skills remain rudimentary, and I'm still color-blind, but I have developed some personal art practice. I play with materials, images, and personal experiences to create pieces that help me explore something and attempt to engage others. My technical limitations restrict my capacity to fully engage the imaginative possibilities, but what I can produce gives me personal rewards and, from time to time, interests others.

In 2009, I created a work called *Memento mori*. The title is a Latin phrase that can be translated as "be mindful of death," "remember that you are mortal," and "remember you must die." This work reflected on death and the transient nature of our life. It consisted of rows of Tibetan prayer flags. I used these flags because I love them and their colors flying in the breeze. They make me smile whenever I see them. I wrote words on the reverse of each flag in black permanent marker. These words are from a list of 50 words or phrases that are meaningful to me as a part of a reflection on death and impermanence. Some are drawn from cultural associations and others from my own personal story.

In the years since 2009, my mother (aged 84 years) and my father (aged 92 years) have died. I was very sad about their deaths. I still am sad from time to time as I get reminded of them from a photo glimpsed or some memory revived. *Memento mori* now hangs in my house. Making it, seeing it, having it as part of my life helps me to remember my parents for their contribution to our lives rather than only remember their death. It also gives me pleasure that a creative activity of mine works!

My enhanced clinical practice, personal interest in engaging with art, and my own art practice are rewards for my active embrace of art therapy. My wife and colleague,

Figure 3.4   *Memento mori.*

Source: Tom O'Brien.

Mary O'Brien, speaking on the occasion of one of my "zero birthdays" said, "I thought I knew him pretty well after nearly 40 years, but his active engagement with art over the last years came as something unexpected but very good." I can only agree.

ANN BERMINGHAM

I have a degree in social work and worked in that capacity for about ten years, before deciding to see if I could bring my lifelong musical passion to a central focus in my life rather than a hobby. My first and last social work positions were in mental health—in the state's major psychiatric institution where I met Kingsley (CEO of RFQ) and later at a community psychiatry service.

I have been working as a musician since 1989, and over that time, leading community choirs has grown to be the major part of my work. At the time the group formed, I was, by coincidence, performing in *Barking Mad—The Musical*. This show was created by a musician friend out of her experience of living with mental illness and toured from Southern Queensland to Tasmania over several years.

The RFQ Choir first met in August 2003, practicing and performing for two years before moving to the Twelfth Night Theatre between 2006 and 2008 under the musical direction

Figure 3.5   The RFQ Choir performing.

Source: Ann Bermingham.

of Gail Wiltshire. In 2009, the choir recommenced under my direction and continues today. There is significant continuity of membership. About five of the choir members who now attend were at the first meeting back in 2003, most have been coming for three or more years, four came for the first time in 2013, and one member joined two weeks before our performance at RFQ's 2013 end-of-year celebration.

In earlier times, the RFQ end-of-year performance was often our only one. However, since 2012 the choir also performs at several annual Mental Health Week celebrations. I think performing for audiences is enjoyed and desired by many choir members.

I have always regarded music making, and singing in particular, as our birthright and as something that is intrinsic to us as human beings. I came to this choir expecting that the group would develop in its own unique way, as all choirs do, and that my assignment was to create a space in which collective and individual musical expression could flourish and evolve.

As I reflect on the RFQ Choir, I'm struck more by its similarities to other choirs that I lead and know about rather than its differences. My experience of the group is that there is a strong sense of community and mutual respect, a willingness to express opinions and to let go of them, a capacity for collaboration in musical decisions, and an openness to individual difference and to newcomers.

For me, the challenges are also similar—to find repertoire that people enjoy, that is appropriate for the level of musical skill in the group but also stretches their capacity. Certainly the feedback from choir members at the end of last year reflected universal issues.

What is different about the RFQ Choir from my other experiences is the mix of staff and clients. The fact that in rehearsal this is largely irrelevant is a testament to RFQ's culture and of the individuals involved. I feel very fortunate that the relationships forged between me and senior staff and management over the years are based on a shared vision about the group and honest and respectful communication.

I can't speak about what individuals get from the group. What I see is that people will often come along, even when they're having a tough day, and will then feel safe to participate to whatever level that they can manage. I feel proud that this is what we have created together.

CONCLUSION

In the introduction to this book, we identified five ways by which creative activity can promote and support recovery from mental illness:

- Behavioral activation
- Self-efficacy/mastery
- Overcoming experiential avoidance
- Strengthening of personal identity
- Social connectedness

By way of concluding this chapter, I would like to briefly return to each and show how the accounts provided by Patricia, Tom, and Ann testify to these processes.

The theme of behavioral activation is especially strong in Patricia's and Ann's accounts of their work and experience. Both Patricia's community arts group and the RFQ Choir require commitment and engagement from participants. As Ann very eloquently put it, "What I see is that people will often come along, even when they are having a tough day." A tough day for a person dealing with mental illness often means feeling withdrawn and lacking in energy and motivation. The choir is a commitment and members come to realize that engaging in activity, even (or perhaps especially) when they would prefer not to, is a step toward recovery. Giving voice or working on a painting enlivens the mind and assists the person to make contact with a source of energy that was otherwise unavailable.

The theme of self-efficacy and mastery is especially strong in Tom's essay. Tom was surprised and delighted to discover that he had talents he was unaware of. The realization that he was able to make art added another dimension to his life and to his sense of himself. In this respect, Tom is different from Patricia and Ann who were talented in their fields from a young age. However, he is probably similar to many who undertake creative arts therapies, believing at the time that they lack talent and capacity. The discovery of a hidden talent is an important part of recovery because it opens up a world of possibilities. Life no longer feels fixed and predetermined. There may be many other possibilities for achievement and self-realization.

It is clear that overcoming experiential avoidance is an important part of Patricia's community art group. The workshop, in which she requires every participant to contribute, is a major exercise in self-disclosure. Of course, it is mediated by the artwork, and participants can share as little or as much personal information as they wish. However, simply sharing a creation requires some confrontation with and acceptance of the experience behind the creation. I was also very affected by Tom's account of his *Memento mori*. As he explained it, this work provided him with a means of reflecting on his experience of loss and even reminding himself of people who are very important to him instead of avoiding feelings that must be painful. The artwork provided him with a means of processing his emotional experience so that he could fully register it rather than avoid it.

Identity is a central theme in Patricia's essay. She very clearly describes a dramatic shift in identity from a successful businesswoman and mother to a patient requiring hospitalization. As I understood her essay, her artwork both sustained her through a period of fractured identity and led her back to an experience of herself as a competent person able to help others. It also helped her to achieve a more stable identity in that she stopped looking for "recovery," which might be understood as an idealized but unrealistic state, but instead found satisfaction in who she is and what she is able to do with all the various limitations that we (collectively as human beings) are bound to accept.

Social connectedness is the most central theme of Ann's essay but is also important in Patricia's account of the community art group. The RFQ Choir is a means by which people connect with each other through a shared activity that each feels individually good about. Both Ann and Kingsley emphasized that the choir is not a rehabilitation activity, although this may be a benign side effect. The choir performs in a range of settings and provides its members with a point of connection with the wider public and not just with other members of the choir. I noted Patricia's observation that some members of her art group did not have a mental illness. It seems to me that when the focus is on creative activity, the presence or absence of a mental illness is a secondary issue because people are coming together to do something that matters to them and not because they have a mental illness. This is when connectedness supports the development of an identity that is not shaped primarily by the experience of illness.

NOTE

1. Robert King wrote the introduction and conclusion to this chapter. Most of the chapter consists of specific and clearly identified contributions by Patricia Strobel, Tom O'Brien, and Ann Bermingham.

REFERENCE

Luborsky, L., Singer B., & Luborsky, L. (1975). Comparative studies of psychotherapy: Is it true that "everyone has won and all must have prizes"? *Archives of General Psychiatry, 32,* 995–1008.

Visual Art

Principles and Evidence Base for Art Therapy

Claire Edwards, Tom O'Brien, and Robert King

ABSTRACT

This systematic review examines the current state of art therapy outcomes research and evaluates the overall efficacy of art therapy. The review identified 29 published art therapy outcome studies that met specified inclusion criteria. The researchers calculated the effect sizes of the studies that were included. The review found an average effect size of 0.82, which suggests that art therapy is at least as effective as other forms of psychotherapy.

BACKGROUND

Art therapy is a psychotherapeutic modality, which utilizes the creative process to encourage healing and personal growth (Malchiodi, 2003). There is increasing pressure on health and allied professionals, including art therapists, to utilize *evidence-based* therapeutic interventions. Although this term may be subject to interpretation, there is a general understanding that certain types of evidence are more privileged, and carry more weight, in a range of clinical settings. Evidence from studies using quantitative methods, in particular randomized controlled trials, is generally viewed as the gold standard for research methodologies (Gilroy, 2006). In the United States, the Task Force on the Promotion and Dissemination of Psychological Procedures was established in 1993. This task force "required the presence of two independent, randomised clinical trial studies that demonstrated the superiority of the treatment over a placebo, non-treatment or an alternative treatment procedure" (Burleigh & Beutler, 1997, p. 375).

Art therapy remains a fringe profession in many countries and does not have widespread acceptance as a health discipline despite having been established in the 1940s (Malchiodi, 2003). This is attributable, at least in part, to the slow development of an evidence base for effectiveness. It is not surprising that an evidence base is only now beginning to emerge. Art therapy is practiced by therapists who have a background in visual art and postgraduate art therapy training that does not usually involve training in methods widely used in health outcome research (Kaplan, 2001; Rosal, 1989). Training aside, the interests and expertise of most art therapists centers on art making and therapeutic engagement with clients. It is, therefore, understandable that many are either hostile toward research or, if not hostile, at least avoid doing research (Edwards, 1996; Metzl, 2008). McNiff (2004) summed up the attitudes of many, stating, "I regard this quest for statistical proof of efficacy as redundant: I already know that art heals—and everyone else does too" (p. 288).

Notwithstanding limited interest in, if not downright negativity toward, outcome research among individual art therapists, there has been recognition within the profession of art therapy that an absence of outcome evidence imposes limitations on the development of the profession and on the deployment of art therapists in health settings. This reality has been the impetus behind previous attempts to identify and report on evidence for effectiveness, which are outlined below. Because many of the barriers to research referred to previously have equally impeded outcome research in other expressive therapies, some of these have included expressive therapies other than those based on visual arts.

Previous Art Therapy Outcome Reviews

Payne (1993) provided an early overview of research into arts-based therapies, with the stated aim of integrating process and outcome research in the future (p. 2), thereby highlighting two distinct strands of arts therapy research, namely qualitative (process) and quantitative (outcomes). This same publication included two chapters on art therapy research. Schaverien described the use of the "retrospective review of pictures [as] data review for research in art therapy" (1992, p. 91), whereas McClelland and her coresearchers (1993) investigated the use of collaborative inquiry into acute psychiatric states. Art therapist Andrea Gilroy and music therapist Colin Lee (1995) subsequently published a collection of articles that explored mainly qualitative (process-oriented) research methods.

Concerns that empirical evidence for the effectiveness of expressive therapies was lacking, despite claims of effectiveness in the expressive therapies literature, led Burleigh and Beutler (1997) to a critical analysis of art and drama therapy outcomes. The authors used the 1993 Task Force on Promotion and Dissemination of Psychological Procedures as their investigative framework. This task force required the existence of outcomes research from at least two randomized controlled trials (RCTs), treatment manuals, and established target patient groups to scientifically validate a particular procedure. According to these criteria, they concluded that while the best evidence was for the use of art therapy with children, this evidence "provided only suggestive support for the value of art therapy as a means of altering targeted problem behaviours" in children, in the studies they examined (Burleigh & Beutler, 1997, p. 377).

Reynolds, Nabors, and Quinlan (2000) conducted a systematic review of art therapy outcome studies, and identified 17 studies meeting their inclusion criteria. The authors included studies that "assessed the impact of art therapy on a measurable outcome" and "on a sample or treatment group" (p. 207). Of these, five were RCTs. The authors concluded that it was not possible to determine whether art therapy had specific benefits for a range of reasons. In some studies, for example, the control group improved as much as the art therapy group. In other studies, art therapy was combined with other interventions, making it inconclusive whether the specific factors of art therapy were responsible for the changes. Furthermore, the authors identified the absence of standardized treatment protocols and vast heterogeneity of participants as problematic.

Gilroy (2006) provided a broad and inclusive survey of published art therapy research, investigating a wide range of art therapy applications, and arguing that there is a large body of clinical evidence for art therapy, albeit using a range of qualitative and quantitative methodologies. There is still, however, some resistance to outcomes research using quantitative methodologies such as RCTs within the art therapy profession.

Metzl (2008) conducted a systematic analysis of art therapy research published in *Art Therapy: Journal of American Art Therapy Association* between 1987 and 2004. The aim of the review was to identify methodologies used in research rather than to investigate outcomes. The author identified eight methodologies commonly used in art therapy research, namely clinical case studies, self-studies, survey research, interviews, art therapy tests, historiography/anthropological research, behavioral observations, and exploration of clients' artworks (p. 60). Of the above, only clinical case studies could be considered as outcome studies, and many of these would not yield measurable data.

Interestingly, Metzl (2008) found that there was a significant difference between art therapists who published research and "the general demographic of art therapy" (p. 60) with a proportionally higher number of men publishing than are represented in the profession (19.3% compared to 6.2%). In addition, "male authors with doctoral level education without an art therapy specialisation" were overrepresented in the published group, as were "female authors with a masters level education registered as art therapists" (p. 66). Stuckey and Nobel (2010) published a comprehensive literature review of the health outcomes for creative therapies. They, like Burleigh and Beutler (1997) and Reynolds et al. (2000), found "clear indications that artistic engagement has significantly positive effects on health" (p. 261), but found limited high-quality empirical evidence (such as RCTs). They argued for more RCTs, using consistent measures, longitudinal follow-ups, combined qualitative and quantitative methods, standardized interventions, allowances for greater cross-cultural comparisons, and greater expansion into community treatment (nonhospital) settings.

A number of recent studies have attempted to review the effectiveness of art therapy (among other treatment methods) with specific populations. Eaton, Doherty, and Wildrick (2007) conducted a review of art therapy as a treatment for traumatized children and identified two experimental studies by Chapman, Morabito, Ladakokos, Schreier, and Knudson (2001) and Pifalo (2006). They found that, notwithstanding a number of limitations, "the published literature concerning the efficacy of art therapy for the treatment of children who have experienced trauma is quite compelling and should encourage further investigations" (Eaton et al., 2007, p. 260). However, a systematic review of the literature on trauma interventions by Wethington et al. (2008) reached the very different conclusion that "evidence was insufficient to determine the effectiveness of . . . art therapy . . . in reducing psychological harm" (p. 287). This conclusion was based on one controlled study (Appleton, 2001) of a single intervention with children immediately following physical trauma. Although the participants' symptoms were reduced by 21%, this improvement was not considered significant (Wethington et al., 2008, p. 295).

What Can We Conclude From Published Reviews of Art Therapy Outcome?

Published reviews of art therapy outcome studies have varied considerably, both with respect to their approach (especially inclusion criteria) and their conclusions. Those studies that had broad inclusion criteria tended to report positive outcomes, whereas those studies with more narrow inclusion criteria drew much more cautious conclusions. In other words, while the literature might be described as encouraging, published reviews were unable to identify sufficient high quality data to warrant confidence that art therapy yields the kinds of outcomes it is intended to produce.

Is There a Need for Another Review of Art Therapy Outcomes?

The overview of previously published reviews reveals several gaps or limitations that, in our view, justifies a further review. These may be summarized as follows:

- Recency. The most recent review was published in 2010. There is evidence of growth in formal outcome research in art therapy, which makes it likely that new studies (and possibly methodologically superior studies) have been published since this review.

- Review Methodology. Previous reviews have either been broad in scope, including quite diverse studies and having little regard to quality of evidence, or have been quite narrow and restrictive, including only studies of the highest quality. We think that, given the current state of art therapy outcome research, a middle course is preferable. We have therefore adopted a methodology that is more rigorous than a general narrative review but more inclusive than a formal meta-analysis.

STUDY AIMS

Our aim in this review was to obtain as clear a picture as possible of the impact of art therapy on health-related outcomes. Further, we wanted to quantify the outcomes so as to obtain an estimate of effect size that would enable us to make some preliminary comparisons between the impact of art therapy and the impact of other psychotherapy interventions.

OVERVIEW OF STUDY DESIGN

Our study is best described as a systematic review rather than a meta-analysis. We considered the published studies to be too disparate with respect to participants and interventions to enable a formal meta-analysis. However, we did informally use some meta-analytic strategies such as determining effect size on the basis of published data and estimating pooled effect size.

Inclusion Criteria

For the purposes of this review, we included studies that were designed to evaluate the impact of art therapy on health related outcomes. To be included, art therapy had to be the only or the primary intervention. Health-related outcomes included psychological symptoms (e.g., distress, anxiety, or depression), general well-being, and quality of life but excluded personality, cognitive functioning, and process scores such as alliance. We required that included studies used standardized tests and that means and standard deviations pre- and postintervention were available (either published or obtained from the authors). We included studies using single group repeated measures (SGRM) designs (i.e., no control group) and nonrandomized controlled (NRC) designs.

Exclusion Criteria

We excluded single-case studies, studies with only qualitative data, and studies in which art therapy was a component but not the primary component of the intervention.

Search Strategy

In order to locate the art therapy studies, we used the search terms *art therapy* plus either *outcome* or *research*. We searched the following databases: MEDLINE, PsychINFO, CINAHL, Cochrane Library, Embase, and AMED. We carried out an additional search of publications cited in two previous reviews (Gilroy, 2006; Ruddy & Milnes, 2005).

Data Analysis Strategy

Cohen's *d* was used as an estimate of effect size. Where reported data did not allow calculation of Cohen's *d* but another effect size (e.g., partial eta squared) was reported, this was converted to Cohen's *d*. Where multiple measures were used, separate effect sizes were calculated for each measure and then averaged to yield a study effect size. Because of the heterogeneity of studies included, we did not weight studies by sample size when calculating a pooled or mean effect size. We classified studies by quality (RCTs versus uncontrolled repeated measures studies) for purposes of subgroup analysis.

RESULTS

Using the search procedures and inclusion and exclusion criteria described above, we identified a total of 29 studies to include in the analysis. Of these, 12 were RCTs (Table 4.1), three were nonrandomized controlled studies (Table 4.2), and 14 were single group repeated measures studies (Table 4.3).

The combined total number of participants in all the studies included in this review was 1,442. The mean number of participants was 42.35 with a range of 7 to 158 participants. Study participants were broken down into the following age groups: 12 studies were with children and/or adolescents (Chemtob, Singer, Lyshak-Stelzer, & Patricia, 2007; Chin, Chin, Palombo, Palombo, Bannasch, & Cross, 1980; Dolgin, Somer, Zaidel, & Zaizov, 1997; Epp, 2008; Omizo & Omizo, 1989; Pifalo, 2006; Rosal, 1993; Rosal, McCulloch-Vislisel, & Neece, 1997;

(Text continued on page 42)

Table 4.1 Studies with a randomized control design.

Authors (Year)	Age, Population	Number	Sessions: Type and Number	Outcome Measures	Measurement Intervals	Average Relative Effect Size	Conclusion
Chemtob, Singer, Lyshak-Stelzer, & Patricia (2007)	Youth 13–17 PTSD Inpatient unit	29 14 treatment group and Treatment as Usual (TAU) 15 TAU	Group 16x1 hour	University of California, Los Angeles (UCLA) PTSD Reaction Index	Pre Post	1.0[a]	Decreased trauma symptoms
Beebe & Bender (2009)	Children with asthma	22 in total	Group 7 sessions	Formal Elements of Art Therapy Scale (FEATS) Health-Related Quality of Life (HRQOL) Pediatric Quality of Life (PedsQoL)	Pre Post 6 months	N/A	Decreased anxiety Increased self-concept Increased quality of life
Nainis et al. (2009)	Adults with HIV (Average age: 42)	79 39 (control) 40 (intervention)	Individual 1 hour art therapy session	Edmonton Symptom Assessment Scale (ESAS) Spielberger State-Trait Anxiety Index (STAI)	Pre Post	0.59	Improved physical and psychological symptoms
Svensk et al. (2009)	Adult women undergoing radiotherapy for breast cancer	41 20 (treatment) 21 (control)	Individual 5 x 1 hour sessions weekly	World Health Organization Quality of Life assessment – abbreviated version (WHOQOL-BREF) European Organization for Research and Treatment of Cancer instrument, EORTC Quality of Life Questionnaire (QLQ)-BR23, version 1.0 (EORTC QOL—BR23)	Pre 2 months 6 months	1.05	Increased quality of life, body image, future perspectives Decrease anxiety, depression, stress

(Continued)

33

Table 4.1 (Continued)

Authors (Year)	Age, Population	Number	Sessions: Type and Number	Outcome Measures	Measurement Intervals	Average Relative Effect Size	Conclusion
Richardson, Jones, Evans, Stevens, & Rowe (2007)	Chronic schizophrenia Standard Psychiatric Care (SPC): 42.6 years Art therapy: 39.6 years	90 43 (art therapy) 47 (SPC)	Group art therapy 12 weeks	Scale for the Assessment of Negative Symptoms (SANS) Health of the Nation Outcome Score (HoNOS) Brief Psychiatric Rating Scale (BPRS) Social Functioning Scale—32 Question version (SFS IIP-32)	Pre Post 6 months	0.39	Reduced negative symptoms
Thyme et al. (2007)	Women with depression	39 18 (art therapy) 21 (verbal therapy)		Impact of Event Scale (IES)— Intrusion subscale IES — Avoidance subscale The Symptom Checklist-90 (SCL90) Beck Depression Inventory (BDI)		0.33	Very similar outcomes between art therapy and verbal therapy
Rusted, Sheppard, & Waller (2006)	Adults with dementia 84.05 (women) 80.33 (men)	21	40 Group Interactive psychodynamic model	Mini Mental State Exam (MMSE) National Adult Reading Test (NART) Cornell Scale for Depression in Dementia Multi Observational Scale for the Elderly (MOSES)	0, 10, 20, 40 weeks and follow-up at 44, 56 weeks	−0.73[b]	Increase of depression in art therapy group Mental acuity increase in art therapy group

Authors (Year)	Age, Population	Number	Sessions: Type and Number	Outcome Measures	Measurement Intervals	Average Relative Effect Size	Conclusion
Puig, Lee, Goodwin, & Sherrard (2006)	51.4 Women with breast cancer	39	Individual 4	Profile of Mood States (POMS) Emotional Approach Coping Scales Early Screening Inventory – Revised (ESI-R)	Pre and post	0.66	Self-selected participants Not art therapists
Oster et al. (2006)	37–69 Women with breast cancer	41		Coping Resources Inventory (CRI)		0.49	
Monti et al. (2006)	53.6 Women with cancer	93	Group 8 Mindfulness-based art therapy (MBAT)	The Symptom Checklist-90 Revised (SCL90R) Short Form Health Survey (SF 36)	Pre Post (8 weeks)	0.8	
Kymissis, Christenson, Swanson, & Orlowski (1996)	13–17 Adolescent inpatients	37	Groups 3–4 per week	Children's Global Assessment Scale (CGAS) Inventory of Interpersonal Problems	Pre and post	N/A	Synallactic Collective Image Technique (SCIT) Significant increase in assertiveness, overall increased CGAS scores in both groups, greater for experimental group but not statistically significantly different

(Continued)

Table 4.1 (Continued)

Authors (Year)	Age, Population	Number	Sessions: Type and Number	Outcome Measures	Measurement Intervals	Average Relative Effect Size	Conclusion
Chapman, Morabito, Ladakokos, Schreier, & Knudson (2001)	7–17 Admissions to trauma center	31–27	Individual 1 session	Child PTSD Index PTSD Diagnostic Scale Family Environment Scale	Pre 1 week, 1 month, 6 months post discharge	N/A	Not statistically significant results. However, all avoidance symptoms reduced in art therapy group Used Chapman Art Therapy Treatment Intervention standardized single session based on retelling trauma narrative using art
Walsh & Hardin (1994)	Adolescents	158	One group	Self-Efficacy Scale	Pre and post	0.24	Decrease in mean self-efficacy in both groups, possibly due to outbreak of Gulf War in meantime
Rosal (1993)	10.2 Children with behavior problems	36	20 Group	Children's Nowicki and Strickland Internal-External Control Scale Teacher Rating Scale Parent–Child Dysfunctional Interaction	Pre and post (14 weeks)	0.33	Differences between two treatment (cognitive behavioral therapy and nondirective) conditions were nonsignificant

Authors (Year)	Age, Population	Number	Sessions: Type and Number	Outcome Measures	Measurement Intervals	Average Relative Effect Size	Conclusion
							Subjects in both treatment groups made greater gains than control group
							Antisocial and conduct disordered subjects made greater improvements than other children
Omizo & Omizo (1989)	8–11 years	50	Group 12 weekly	Self Esteem Inventory	Pre, Post	0.53	
Green, Wehling, & Talsky (1987)	40 Chronic psych patients	28	Group 10 weekly	Progress Evaluation Scales (PES) Rosenberg Self-Esteem Scale (RSES)	Pre, 5 months, 9 months	N/A	Promising changes noted in art therapy group; increased functioning in chronic patients PES better score than RSES
White & Allen (1971)	12.8 years Boys	30	Group Daily for 8 weeks	Trauma Symptom Checklist	Pre and post, 14 months follow-up	0.65	Significant increase in self-concept in experimental group

Note: N = 17 studies. Average relative effective size (*n* = 12) 0.59, range 0.24–1.05

a. Estimated from standard error

b. Excluded from average effect size calculations because authors claim effect is not due to intervention

Table 4.2 Studies with nonrandomized control design

Authors (Year)	Age, population	Number	Sessions: Number and Type	Outcome Measures	Measurement Intervals	Relative Effect Size	Conclusions
Hartz & Thick (2005)	13–18 Female juvenile offenders	31	10 × 1.5 hour Group	Self-Perception Profile for Adolescents	Pre/post	N/A	
Doric-Henry (1997)	83.5 Elderly nursing home residents	40	8 Individual sessions	Coopersmith Self-esteem Inventory Beck Depression Inventory Spielberger State-Trait Anxiety Index	Pre and post	0.53	Pottery, using wheel Significant reduction in anxiety and depression Significant increase in self-esteem Those who benefit most may be those with lower self-esteem and higher levels of depression and anxiety at the outset
Schut, de Keijser, van den Bout, & Stroebe (1996)	51.6 Bereaved inpatients	52	12 sessions bereavement therapy 8 sessions art therapy (groups)	GHQ	0, discharge (3 months, 6–7 months follow-up)	1.01	Changes medium to very large Greatest differences in daily functioning Least differences in depressions Combined behavior therapy and art therapy
Brooke (1995)	24–46, female sexual abuse survivors	11	8 weekly sessions	SEI	Pre and post	1.45	The gain score for experimental group approached significance Art therapy in group setting can improve self-esteem

Note: N = 4 studies. Average Effect Size (n = 3) 1.0, range 0.53–1.45

Table 4.3 Studies with a repeated measures design (no control)

Authors (Year)	Age, Population	Number	Sessions: Number and Type	Outcome Measures	Measurement Intervals	Average Effect Size	Conclusion
Hughes & da Silva (2011)	Adult Subfertile women	21	8 x 2 hr sessions	Beck Depression Inventory (BDI) Beck Anxiety Inventory (BAI) Beck Hopelessness Inventory (BHI)	Pre and post	.32	Decreases in all three measures with BDI and BHI significant and BAI nonsignificant
Visser & Op' t Hoog (2008)	Adults, mostly women 21–63 with cancer Two thirds had metastatic disease	35	Group 8 x 2.5 hours weekly	European Organisation for Research and Treatment of Cancer— C30 Profile of Mood States	Pre and post	.19	Improved quality of life, slowing the downhill trajectory of illness No change in mood
Epp (2008)	11–18 Autistic Spectrum Disorder school students	44	20 group sessions weekly	Social Skills Rating System	Pre and post	.09	Cognitive Behaviour Therapy + Art Therapy Decreases in internalization, hyperactivity, and increase in assertiveness
Franks & Whitaker (2007)	Adults with personality disorder	5	Group 1.75 hours weekly for 9 months	Clinical Outcome and Routine Evaluation Outcome Measure Group Styles Inventory Physical Symptoms Distress Inventory	Pre, post, follow-up (8 months)	3.18	Symptoms lower

(Continued)

Table 4.3 (Continued)

Authors (Year)	Age, Population	Number	Sessions: Number and Type	Outcome Measures	Measurement Intervals	Average Effect Size	Conclusion
Gantt & Tinnin (2007)	13–69 (mainly adults) Severe PTSD	72	1–2 weeks intensive group and individual	Dissociative Experiences Scale Symptom Check List–45 Toronto Alexithymia Scale Impact of Event Scale	Pre, 1 week, 3 months and 6 months post-treatment	0.90	Recovery or improvement across all groups Testing intensive treatment not just art therapy
Wallace-DiGarbo & Hill (2006)	13–16 At-risk youth	6	Group 10 sessions over 6 weeks	Adolescent Self-Assessment Profile Outcome inventory	Pre Post 6/12	0.16	
Pifalo (2006)	8–16 Children sexually abused	41	8 group	Trauma Symptom Checklist for Children	Pre and post	0.73	Art therapy and CBT Significant reduction in PTSD and other abuse-related symptoms
Walsh, Martin, & Schmidt (2004)	Over 18 Caregivers of patients with cancer	40	1 individual	Mini Profile of Mood States Beck Anxiety Index Derogatis Affects Balance Scale	Pre and post	0.63	Large effect for all variables, significant results related to stress reduction, anxiety, decreased negative emotion, and increased positive emotion Not done by art therapists
Gussak (2004)	21–63 Prison inmates	39	8 Group	Formal Elements Art Therapy Scale (FEATS)	Pre and post (4 weeks)	0.71	Significant change in 7 of 14 categories in FEATS

Authors (Year)	Age, Population	Number	Sessions: Number and Type	Outcome Measures	Measurement Intervals	Average Effect Size	Conclusion
Saunders & Saunders (2000)	2–16 Behavior problems	94	Unclear	Problem Behavior for Children Goals Therapeutic Relationship scale	Pre and post	0.69	Clients showed significant decrease in frequency and severity of problem behavior Number of sessions significantly correlated with higher scores on Therapeutic Relationship scale
Theorell et al. (1998)	22–58 Chronic somatic symptoms	24	Weekly over 2 years Individual	General Health Questionnaire	Pre, then every 3 months until end treatment, plus follow-up (no set time)	0.35	Significant reduction in anxiety, depression, and psychosomatic symptoms Global health improved but not to statistically significant level
Dolgin, Somer, Zaidel, & Zaizov (1997)	7–17 Siblings of children with cancer	23	Group 6 weekly sessions	Feelings and Attitudes Questionnaire Cancer Related Knowledge Questionnaire Mood Questionnaire	Pre and 6–8 weeks post	1.33	All measures except fears subscale showed significantly positive intervention effects
Rosal, McCulloch-Vislisel, & Neece (1997)	13–15 School students in grade 9	50	9 monthly group sessions	State Anxiety Scale Report cards School attendance	Pre and post	0.2	Significant changes in attitudes, no dropouts from school
Chin et al. (1980)	17–19 School students who fail to achieve	7	20 group sessions over 4 weeks	How I felt checklist and teacher checklist of behaviors	Daily	2.66	Increased self-esteem and interpersonal skills

Note: N = 14 studies. Average relative effect size = .87, range .09–3.18

(Text continued from page 32)

Saunders & Saunders, 2000; Wallace-Di Garbo & Hill, 2006; Walsh & Hardin, 1994; White & Allen, 1971), 16 with adults (Brooke, 1995; Franks & Whitaker, 2007; Gantt & Tinnin, 2007; Gussak, 2004; Hughes & da Silva, 2011; Monti et al., 2006; Nainis et al., 2009; Oster et al., 2006; Puig, Lee, Goodwin, & Sherrard, 2006; Richardson, Jones, Evans, Stevens, & Rowes, 2007; Schut, de Keijser, van den Bout, & Stroebe, 1996; Svensk et al., 2009; Theorell et al., 1998; Thyme et al., 2007; Visser & Op' t Hoog, 2008; Walsh, Martin, & Schmidt, 2004) and one was with the aged (Doric-Henry, 1997). The mean duration of treatment was 14.5 sessions (median = 8.5) with a range of 1 to 90 sessions.

The types of measures employed were as follows: current state (depression, anxiety, general well-being, self-esteem; $n = 24$); therapy process (mainly alliance; $n = 2$); social functioning ($n = 1$); creativity/artistic control ($n = 1$); and personality ($n = 1$). Of the 29 studies, 19 provided art therapy in groups, seven in individual sessions, one in both, and two did not specify. Nineteen studies were conducted in the United States, four in Sweden, two each in the Netherlands and the United Kingdom, and one each in Canada and Israel. Three studies were published before 1990, eight in the 1990s, and 18 since 2000. Peak years for publication were 2006 and 2007, with five studies being published in each year. One RCT with the aged was excluded because the authors attributed a negative effect to unusual events (Rusted, Sheppard, & Waller, 2006).

Overall Breakdown of Studies

Problem types represented were mental health ($n = 10$; Chemtob et al., 2007; Chin et al., 1980; Doric-Henry, 1997; Franks & Whitaker, 2007; Gantt & Tinnin, 2007; Omizo & Omizo, 1989; Richardson et al., 2007; Thyme et al., 2007; Walsh et al., 2004, White & Allen, 1971), social adjustment and behavioral problems ($n = 8$; Epp, 2008; Gussak, 2004; Rosal, 1993; Rosal et al., 1997; Saunders & Saunders, 2000; Schut et al., 1996; Wallace-DiGarbo & Hill, 2006; Walsh & Hardin, 1994), cancer ($n=6$; Dolgin et al., 1997; Monti et al., 2006; Oster et al., 2006; Puig et al., 2006; Svensk et al., 2009; Visser & Op' t Hoog, 2008), other physical health ($n = 3$; Hughes & da Silva, 2011; Nainis et al., 2009; Theorell et al., 1998), and sexual abuse ($n = 2$; Brooke, 1995; Pifalo, 2006).

The effect sizes of the outcome studies reviewed (n = 29) ranged from 0.09 to 3.18, with an average effect size of 0.82. This effect size is typically described as medium and is within the range commonly found for psychotherapy interventions (see, for example, Cuijpers, Smit, Bohlmeijer, Hollon, & Andersson, 2010). Our review therefore suggests that, overall, art therapy is broadly equivalent in effectiveness to other forms of psychotherapy. However it should be noted that effects were highly variable, suggesting that the impact of an art therapy intervention is likely to depend on variables such as client characteristics, duration of intervention, and outcomes measures.

DISCUSSION

Despite increasing workplace requirements for evidence-based research into art therapy outcomes in order to improve employment options for art therapists, this systematic review yielded a low number of eligible studies. The authors believe there may be a number of reasons for this.

First, art therapists are generally from a visual art background and are not usually trained in quantitative research methods. Moreover, it is likely that there is limited interest from art therapists in gaining skills in such methods.

Second, art therapists (like other creative arts therapists) are a minority profession within allied health, often competing for employment with other professions such as social workers, psychologists, and occupational therapists, who are perceived to have more general therapeutic skills, who often have training in quantitative research methods, and who have critical mass in terms of sheer numbers, which makes their professional associations more persuasive and powerful.

Art therapy positions are few and far between, and many art therapists take on other more generalist roles such as counselor or child therapist. This creates a scenario in which the focus for art therapists is on gaining and maintaining employment—and proving themselves as good as other health professionals—rather than conducting research into the more specialized skills they bring to the workplace, which would paradoxically improve their employment prospects in the longer term. Moreover, good quality research is resource intensive, requiring considerable support from the agency involved. Art therapists may be more likely to be employed in nongovernment agencies, which are less likely to have resources to do research than in the public sector.

Study Characteristics and Limitations

The interventions were typically not standardized, and there was little, if any, attempt to measure adherence. Art therapy was often combined with another intervention. Limited information was provided about the training of the art therapists who participated in the studies. Some studies were carried out by nonart therapists. In addition, studies were highly variable with respect to participant age, participant problem, study setting, duration of intervention, and whether art therapy was delivered individually or in groups.

Quality of Studies

A large group of studies ($n = 14$) used a repeated measures design with no control (Chin et al., 1980; Dolgin et al., 1997; Epp, 2008; Franks & Whitaker, 2007; Gantt & Tinnin, 2007; Gussak, 2004; Hughes & da Silva, 2011; Pifalo, 2006; Rosal et al., 1997; Saunders & Saunders, 2000; Theorell et al., 1998; Visser & Op' t Hoog, 2008; Wallace-DiGarbo & Hill, 2006; Walsh et al., 2004). These studies would be seen as yielding lower quality evidence than controlled studies. There was some evidence that higher quality studies were associated with recency and publication in a nonart therapy journal.

Those studies with control groups rarely utilized a balanced intervention for the control, and often used waitlist or treatment as usual. Allegiance effects were not managed. There was little evidence of measurement of possible art-therapy-related mediating variables such as creativity, expressive facility, or self-efficacy with art making.

Recommendations: Empirical Research in Art Therapy

There is need for clearer specification of art therapy interventions, although it is likely that specifications will be broad rather than narrow. Management of confounding factors is critical. Where the investigation is of a composite treatment (art therapy plus another therapy), the control must receive the nonart therapy intervention. The use of non-art-therapy-balanced interventions (e.g., exercise or other activity) in control groups is highly desirable. Investigation of art-therapy-specific mediators is important.

Where possible, art therapists need to collaborate with other disciplines with skills and training in quantitative research methods. This current study was the result of collaboration between an art therapist, a psychologist, and a consultant psychotherapist/social worker.

CONCLUSION

Although there may be disagreement about methodologies used, most art therapists understand the importance of being able to demonstrate the effectiveness of art therapy and would agree that more research into art therapy outcomes is needed. Due to the fact that it is becoming increasingly important to be able to provide evidence of efficacy, published art therapy outcomes research has been developing within the psychotherapy research paradigm. This reflects the demands of the health care environment within which art therapy is provided—and its links with other therapies—but has been a significant barrier to art therapy developing its evidence base since art therapists may avoid conducting research with which they do not identify professionally due to their primary identification as visual artists rather than social scientists (Metzl, 2008). As David Edwards (1996) suggests, it may be this inexperience and unfamiliarity that deters art therapists from engaging in outcomes research since using "traditional forms of research methodology may give rise to uncomfortable levels of anxiety" (p. 11).

The practical difficulties of conducting controlled trials on the one hand and the lack of quantitative research knowledge, skills, resources, interest, and experience of many art therapists—who have a background in the visual arts—on the other hand only serve to compound the barriers to art therapy outcomes research being fully embraced by the profession at this stage in its development. Despite this, there is increasing evidence for art therapy's effectiveness as art therapists develop collaborative relationships with other health care professionals who have broader research skills and experience. The growing number of published RCTs in recent years is an indication that increasingly robust empirical evidence for art therapy's effectiveness is likely to be established over time.

REFERENCES

An asterisk indicates the study was included in this systematic review of outcome studies.

Appleton, V. (2001). Avenues of hope: Art therapy and the resolution of trauma. *Journal of the American Art Therapy Association, 18*(1), 6–13. doi:10.1080/07421656.2001.10129454

*Beebe, A., & Bender, B. (2009). A randomized trial to test the effectiveness of art therapy for children with asthma. *The Journal of Allergy and Clinical Immunology, 123*(2), S64–S64. doi:10.1016/j.jaci.2008.12.213

*Brooke, S. (1995). Art therapy: An approach to working with sexual abuse survivors. *The Arts in Psychotherapy, 22*(5), 447–466. doi:10.1016/0197-4556(95)00036-4

Burleigh, L., & Beutler, L. (1997). A critical analysis of two creative arts therapies. *The Arts in Psychotherapy, 23*(5), 375–381. doi:10.1016/S0192-4556(96)00056-1

*Chemtob, C., Singer, P., Lyshak-Stelzer, F., & Patricia, S. J. (2007). Art therapy for adolescents with posttraumatic stress disorder symptoms: A pilot study. *Art Therapy, 24*(4), 163–169. doi:10.1080/07421656.2007.10129474

*Chin, R., Chin, M., Palombo, P., Palombo, C., Bannasch, G., & Cross, P. (1980). Project reachout: Building social skills through art and video. *The Arts in Psychotherapy, 7*(4), 281–284. doi:10.1016/0197-4556(80)90007-6

Cuijpers, P., Smit, F., Bohlmeijer, E., Hollon, S., & Andersson, G. (2010). Efficacy of cognitive-behavioural and other psychological treatments for adult depression: Meta-analytic study of publication bias. *The British Journal of Psychiatry, 196*(3), 173–178. doi:10.1192/bjp.bp.109.066001

*Dolgin, M., Somer, E., Zaidel, N., & Zaizov, R. (1997). A structured group intervention for siblings of children with cancer. *Journal of Child and Adolescent Group Therapy, 7*(1), 3–18. doi:10.1007/BF02548945

*Doric-Henry, L. (1997). Pottery as art therapy with elderly nursing home residents. *Art Therapy: Journal of the American Art Therapy Association, 14*(3), 163–171. doi:10.1080/07431656.1987.10759277

Eaton, L., Doherty, K., & Wildrick, R. (2007). A review of research and methods used to establish art therapy as an effective treatment method for traumatised children. *The Arts in Psychotherapy, 34*(3), 256–262. doi:10.1016/j.aip.2007.03.001

Edwards, D. (1996). Why don't art therapists do research. In H. Payne (Ed.), *One river, many currents: A handbook of inquiry in the arts therapies*. London, England: Jessica Kingsley.

*Epp, K. (2008). Outcome-based evaluation of a social skills program using art therapy and group therapy for children on the autism spectrum. *Children and Schools, 30*(1), 27–36. doi:10.1093/cs/30.1.27

*Franks, M., & Whitaker, R. (2007). The image, mentalisation and group art psychotherapy. *International Journal of Art Therapy, 12*(1), 3–16. doi:10.1080/17454830701265188

*Gantt, L., & Tinnin, L. (2007). Intensive trauma therapy of PTSD and dissociation: An outcome study. *The Arts in Psychotherapy, 34*(1), 69–80. doi:101.1016/j.aip.2006.09.007

Gilroy, A. (2006). *Art therapy, research and evidence-based practice*. London, England: Sage.

Gilroy, A., & Lee, C. (Eds.). (1995). *Art and music: Therapy and research*. London, England: Routledge.

*Gussak, D. (2004). Art therapy with prison inmates: A pilot study. *The Arts in Psychotherapy, 31*(4), 245–259. doi:10.1016/j.aip.2004.06/001

*Hartz, L., & Thick, L. (2005). Art therapy strategies to raise self-esteem in female juvenile offenders: A comparison of art psychotherapy and art as therapy approaches. *Art Therapy, 22*(2), 70–80. doi:10.1080/07421656.2005.10129440

*Hughes, E., & da Silva, A. (2011). A pilot study assessing art therapy as a mental health intervention for subfertile women. *Human Reproduction, 26*(3), 611–615. doi:10.1093/humrep/deq385

Kaplan, F. (2001). Areas of inquiry for art therapy research. *Art Therapy: Journal of American Art Therapy Association, 18*(3), 142–147. doi:10.1080/07421656.2001.10129734

Malchiodi, C. (Ed). (2003). *The handbook of art therapy*. New York, NY: Guilford Press.

McClelland, S., Pat & Ann. (1993). The art of science with clients: Beginning collaborative inquiry in process work, art therapy and acute states. In H. Payne (Ed.), *Handbook of inquiry in the arts therapies: One river, many currents*. London, England: Jessica Kingsley.

McNiff, S. (2004). *Art heals: How creativity cures the soul*. New York, NY: University of California Press.

Metzl, E. (2008). Systematic analysis of art therapy research. *The Arts in Psychotherapy, 35*(1), 60–73. doi:10.1016/j.aip.2007.09.003

*Monti, D., Peterson, C., Shakin Kunkel, E., Hauck, W., Pequignot, E., Rhodes, L., & Brainard, G. (2006). A randomized, controlled trial of mindfulness-based art therapy (MBAT) for women with cancer. *Psycho-Oncology, 15*(5), 363–373. doi:10.1002/pon.988

*Nainis, N., Paice, J., Eisin, A., Williams, L., Rao, D., & Langner, D. (2009). Art therapy for relief of symptoms associated with HIV/AIDS. *AIDS Care, 21*(1), 64–69. doi:10.1080/09540120802068795

*Omizo, M., & Omizo, S. (1989). Art activities to improve self-esteem among native Hawaiian children. *Journal of Humanistic Education, 27*(4), 167–176. doi:10.1002/j.2164-4683.1989.tb00173.x

*Oster, I., Svensk, A., Magnusson, E., Thyme, K., Sjodin, M., Astrom, S., & Lindh, J. (2006). Art therapy improves coping resources: A randomized, controlled study among women with breast cancer. *Palliative and Supportive Care, 4*(1), 57–64. doi:10.1017/S147895150606007X

Payne, H. (Ed.). (1993). *Handbook of inquiry in the arts therapies: One river, many currents.* London, England: Jessica Kingsley.

*Pifalo, T. (2006). Art therapy with sexually abused children and adolescents: Extended research study. *Art Therapy, 23*(4), 181–185. doi:10.1080/07421656.2006.10129337

*Puig, A., Lee, S., Goodwin, L., & Sherrard, P. (2006). The efficacy of creative arts therapies to enhance emotional expression, spirituality, and psychological well-being of newly diagnosed Stage I and Stage II breast cancer patients: A preliminary study. *The Arts in Psychotherapy, 33*(3), 218–228. doi:10.1016/j.aip.2006.02.004

Reynolds, M., Nabors, L., & Quinlan, A. (2000). The effectiveness of art therapy: Does it work? *Art Therapy, 17*(3), 207–213. doi:10.1080/07421656.2000.10129706

*Richardson, P., Jones, K., Evans, C., Stevens, P., & Rowe, A. (2007). Exploratory RCT of art therapy as an adjunctive treatment in schizophrenia. *Journal of Mental Health, 16*(4), 483–491. doi:10.1080/09638230701483111

Rosal, M. (1989). Co-perspective: Masters papers in art therapy: Narrative or research case studies? *The Arts in Psychotherapy, 16*(2), 71–75. doi:10.1016/0197-4556(89)90001-4

*Rosal, M. (1993). Comparative group art therapy research to evaluate changes in locus of control in behaviourally disordered children. *The Arts in Psychotherapy, 20*(3), 231–241. doi:10.1016/0197-4556(93)90018-W

*Rosal, M., McCulloch-Vislisel, S., & Neece, S. (1997). Keeping students in school: An art therapy program to benefit ninth-grade students. *Art Therapy, 14*(1), 30–36. doi:10.1080/07421656.1997.10759251

Ruddy, R., & Milnes, D. (2005). Art therapy for schizophrenia or schizophrenia-like illnesses. *Cochrane Database Systematic Review, 2005*(4), 1–27. doi:10.1002/14651858.CD003728.

*Saunders, E., & Saunders, J. (2000). Evaluating the effectiveness of art therapy through a quantitative, outcomes-focused study. *Arts in Psychotherapy, 27*(2), 99–106. doi:10.1016/S0197-4556(99)00041-6

Schaverien, J. (1992). *The revealing image.* London, England: Routledge.

*Schut, H., de Keijser, J., van den Bout, J., & Stroebe, M. (1996). Cross-modality grief therapy: Description and assessment of a new program. *Journal of Clinical Psychology, 52*(3), 357–365. doi:10.1002/(SICI)1097-4679(199605)52:3 < 357::AID-JCLP14 > 3.0.CO;2-H

Stuckey, H., & Nobel, J. (2010). The connection between art, healing, and public health: A review of current literature. *American Journal of Public Health, 100*(2), 254–263. doi:10.2105/AJPH.2008.156497

*Svensk, A., Thyme, K., Magnusson, E., Sjodin, M., Eisemann, M., Astrom, S., & Lindh, J. (2009). Art therapy improves experienced quality of life among women undergoing treatment for breast cancer: A randomised controlled study. *European Journal of Cancer Care, 18*(1), 69–77. doi:10.1111/j.1365-2354.2008.00952.x

*Theorell, T., Konarski, K., Westerlund, H., Burell, A., Engstrom, R., Lagercrantz, A., Terzary, J., & Thulin, K. (1998). Treatment of patients with chronic somatic symptoms by means of art psychotherapy: A process description. *Psychotherapy and Psychosomatics, 67*(1), 50–56. doi:10.1159/00012259

*Thyme, K., Sundin, E., Stahlberg, G., Lindstrom, B., Eklof, H., & Wiberg, B. (2007). The outcome of short-term psychodynamic art therapy compared to short term psychodynamic verbal therapy for depressed women. *Psychoanalytic Psychotherapy, 21*(3), 250–264.

*Visser, A., & Op' t Hoog, M. (2008). Education of creative art therapy to cancer patients: Evaluation and effects. *Journal of Cancer Education: The Official Journal of the American Association for Cancer Education, 23*(2), 80–84. doi:10.1080/08858190701821204

*Wallace-DiGarbo, A., & Hill, D. (2006). Art as agency: Exploring empowerment of at-risk youth. *Art Therapy, 23*(3), 119–125. doi:10.1080/07421656.2006.10129627

*Walsh, S., & Hardin, S. (1994). An art future image intervention to enhance identity and self-efficacy in adolescents. *Journal of Child and Adolescent Psychiatric Nursing, 7*(3), 24–34. doi:10.1111/j.1744-6171.1994.tb00201.x

*Walsh, S., Martin, S., & Schmidt, L. (2004). Testing the efficacy of a creative-arts intervention with family caregivers of patients with cancer. *Journal of Nursing Scholarship, 36*(3), 214–219. doi:10.1111/j.1547-5069.2004.04040.x

Wethington, H., Hahn, R., Fuqua-Whitley, D., Sipe, T., Crosby, A., Johnson, R., . . . Chattopadhyay, S. (2008). The effectiveness of interventions to reduce psychological harm from traumatic events among children and adolescents: A systematic review. *American Journal of Preventative Medicine, 35*(3), 287–313. doi:10.1016/j.amepre.2008.06.024

*White, K., & Allen, R. (1971). Art counselling in an educational setting: Self-concept change among pre-adolescent boys. *Journal of School Psychology, 9*(2), 218–225. doi:10.1016/0022-4405(71)90017-3

EXCLUDED STUDIES

Chapman, L., Morabito, D., Ladakakos, C., Schreier, H., & Knudson, M. (2001). The effectiveness of art therapy interventions in reducing post-traumatic stress disorder (PTSD) symptoms in pediatric trauma patients. *Art Therapy, 18*(2), 100–104. doi:10.1080/074256.2001.1012.9750

Green, B., Wehling, C., & Talsky, G. (1987). Group art therapy as an adjunct to treatment for chronic outpatient. *Hospital and Community Psychiatry, 38*(9), 988–991. Retrieved from http://www.ncbi .nlm.nih.gov/pubmed/3679106

Kymissis, P., Christenson, E., Swanson, A., & Orlowski, B. (1996). Group treatment of adolescent inpatients: A pilot study using a structured therapy approach. *Journal of Child and Adolescent Group Therapy, 6*(1), 45–52. doi:10.1007/BF02548513

Rusted, J., Sheppard, L., & Waller, D. (2006). A multi-centre randomized control group trial on the use of art therapy for older people with dementia. *Group Analysis, 39*(4), 517–536. doi:10.1177/0533316406071447

Visual Arts

Multidisciplinary Day Program in Practice for Young People With Severe Mental Health Problems

Sandra Drabant and Robert King

This chapter takes a close look at how art therapy is implemented in a multidisciplinary team providing services in a day program for children and adolescents with severe mental health problems. Four areas in which art therapy is utilized in the setting are examined. The first is the use of art therapy in the assessment phase. The second is the use of art therapy in individual therapy. The third is the use of art therapy within a multidisciplinary team, and finally, the fourth is the integration of art therapy at the treatment's end. The specific contribution and value of art therapy with this client group and in this treatment setting is discussed.

While the treatment setting (which is described below) is distinctive, it is likely that all four uses of art therapy will have relevance and application in other treatment settings—especially those involving multidisciplinary teamwork. Furthermore, while the client group for this setting has severe mental health problems, it is likely that the use of art therapy will be equally relevant to other client groups with significant health (but not necessarily mental health) problems.

Art therapy has been recognized as having particular value when working with clients who have difficulty expressing themselves verbally (Wadeson, 1980), but it can be equally beneficial for young people who tend to intellectualize or use words to distract or distance themselves from their concealed emotional world (Hinz, 2009). In a child and youth mental health setting, art making can contribute to engagement, assessment, intervention, and treatment as part of the recovery plan. Symbolic or visual language is often central to the way children and teens express themselves and they are often more at ease with this medium than with answering direct questions. Contemporary child and youth mental health services typically employ a multidisciplinary team and a case management model of service delivery. There are opportunities for the art therapist to contribute both as a case manager and as part of a therapy team.

THE MATER CHILD AND YOUTH MENTAL HEALTH SERVICE (CYMHS) DAY PROGRAM

Mater's CYMHS Day Program serves young people who are severely disabled by a mental illness, and their families. Typically, these young people, who are in the age range of 6 to 18 years, are unable to participate in ordinary school or work activities, have significant difficulties with peer relations, and have strained family relations. They have not responded to standard outpatient care or require ongoing care after brief inpatient treatment. They have a wide range of diagnoses that include but are not limited to various anxiety disorders, mood disorders, eating disorders, externalizing disorders, and sometimes psychosis. Suicidality and self-harm are common features.

The young people involved in treatment attend on a daily basis for two or more school terms (6–12 months) and participate in an intensive clinical program as well as in a school program. The entire environment and all interactions and events that occur in the space constitute the therapeutic milieu. Each young person is allocated a case manager who may be any member of the day program team, including the art therapist. The case manager builds a strong therapeutic relationship with the young person and also has the responsibility of coordinating treatment and coordinating further comprehensive assessments. Although each young person involved in the program has a designated case manager, typically she or he will work closely with several members of the multidisciplinary team and be involved in an extensive group therapy program as well as attending weekly individual and family therapy and case management sessions. The young person's caregivers or parents are asked to commit to family therapy sessions, weekly parenting groups, and case management.

Why Art Therapy at the Mater Day Program

Art therapy has a long history in Mater CYMHS programs. The reason for this is that art therapy and other expressive therapies are seen as an excellent means of engaging children and young people with mental health problems. Such people often find talking therapies difficult either because they are experienced as being intrusive or because they rely heavily on verbalizing challenging cognitions. Expressive therapies provide an alternative for young people who are resistant to talking therapies and may also provide a bridge into talking therapy.

In 1992, the Mater Hospital supported an art therapy position under the Department of Psychiatry so that an art therapist could work with children and their families in outpatient, day patient, and inpatient units. In 1995, the then newly structured day program began and art therapy was a part of the provided allied health services. In 2003, with the development of the then new Mater Children's Hospital, the full-time art therapy position was divided between day program and inpatient unit IPU. The Mater Hospital's holistic approach to care and overarching values align with and support the benefits that art therapy offers the young people who access the CYMHS service. Art therapy and the use of other expressive arts, including music therapy, continued to develop at Mater Hospital over time, and in 2009, a senior art therapist role was introduced. This senior role provided supervision for creative arts therapists working at Mater CYMHS, other clinicians and teams who work with creative mediums—including clinicians who are interested in utilizing creative therapies to explore their own clinical work—as well as other supporting programs that utilize the arts and creative therapies within Mater CYMHS.

First Encounter With Art Therapy at the Day Program

Each child and young person who attends the day program commences with a three-week assessment period where they are seen by a number of allied health team members for specialist assessments. These assessments include nursing, occupational therapy, family therapy assessment, speech and cognitive functioning (if appropriate), as well as art therapy.

The art therapist conducts two art therapy assessments with each young person. Some of the things that may be considered in an art therapist's observations and interactions during the art therapy assessments include

- the level of engagement the young person has with the creative process, the art materials, and the art therapist;

- the extent to which the young person is able to use art or a combination of art and speech to explain her or his understanding of the emotional difficulties;

- the extent to which the young person is able to use art or a combination of art and speech to communicate her or his experiences of the social/familial context;

- the young person's visual development and use of schematic language; and

- the young person's ability to explore her or his difficulties and internal world via artwork and symbolic/metaphoric thinking.

(Gilroy, Tipple, & Brown, 2012)

JACK'S STORY AND ART THERAPY ASSESSMENT

At the time I met Jack,[1] he was 9 years old and living with his mother, 10-year-old sister, and 3-year-old half sister, and having fortnightly access visits with his father. Jack had a long history of disruptive, defiant, and aggressive behavior both at home and school. He had difficulty with friendships and social interaction. At the time of referral, he had expressed thoughts of harm to himself and others and had acted on these thoughts. He had been excluded from at least one school and had been refused acceptance to several schools due to his level of emotional and behavioral disturbances. Jack's formal diagnosis (ICD-10) was oppositional defiant disorder (ODD; F91.3) and altered pattern of family relationships in childhood (Z61.2).

Jack had a number of significant background family and childhood factors that precipitated the referral and perpetuated his ongoing difficulties. Jack's mother separated from his father as a result of domestic violence when she was pregnant with Jack. Both parents had a history of drug use and possible mental health problems. His father died by suicide during the initial treatment year. Jack's mother repartnered when Jack was 2 years old. This partner was also a drug user and was abusive to her and the children. This relationship ended when Jack was 7 years old. At the time of the referral, Jack's mother was seeing another man. This relationship was reportedly nonabusive.

I began the first assessment session with a standard discussion about what the session would entail as well as establishing clear boundaries (time, use of materials, safety, etc.). Initial discussions also included finding out about Jack's previous art experience: materials he has used, what he enjoyed, disliked, and how he felt about making art. During this time Jack appeared attentive, cooperative, and animated. He reported he liked "making things" and drawing characters from a computer game he enjoyed playing. The first art activity was a scribble chase. This is a rapport-building activity where the therapist draws a line in one color and the client follows the therapist's line with his or her own color; then the client becomes the leader and the therapist follows the client's line. Jack was reactive and interactive in this process and appeared to enjoy the playful manner of the game and the kinesthetic and sensory components the activity offered. After we completed a number of cribble chases, I then invited Jack to create his own scribble drawing and develop an image from that scribble drawing. The scribble drawing is an art therapy technique that requires the child to create a scribble and then find shapes and forms within the scribble (Cane, 1951). From these drawn forms the child can then develop a story or express the meaning the image holds. Jack was immediately able to perceive several forms contained in his scribble. As he saw these forms, he defined them, quickly labeled them, and developed a story that connected them. After he created and completed the scribble drawing, it was pinned to the corkboard; this allowed Jack to have some reflective distance from his creation, encouraging Jack to tell a story about the forms in the scribble (Hinz, 2009).

The first object he identified within the scribble was a castle on an island. A figure appeared on the balcony of the castle; Jack stated it was "a dad." The dad was "distracting dangerous creatures" in the water below from a boy who was playing in the water. Jack stated, "One creature had already eaten the boy's brother." Jack told me that the "dangerous creatures sometimes were the dad's friend." In the image, the dad states in a speech bubble, "We're the biggest carnivores of all."

There were a number of other "dangerous" objects that Jack drew; however, as the narrative evolved some of these objects became "safe" objects. A shark became a boat that could take someone to safety. Jack drew "protection walls" in the water, "so dangerous creatures could not get to the boy." When I asked if he was in the drawing or, if not, where he would be, Jack immediately identified himself as the "most dangerous thing in the drawing." He identified himself as a rock near the safety wall. He said, "The rock looked small, but under the water it was huge." Jack asked me where I would be in the image, indicating he had skills and capacity to build a reciprocal relationship. Jack's question invited me into his process and into his artwork, so I responded by choosing a place near the safety wall and talked about how I imagined it might be to be in this safe place.

From this one assessment session, a number of themes became apparent. There appeared to be unresolved conflicted feelings about the dad figure in the drawing. I noted this in relation to Jack's own father and other father figures in his life thus far. Safety and protection was a repeated theme in this drawing, and his view of himself as "scary" was also a significant thing to note for Jack's future treatment plan.

I was encouraged by this initial assessment session and recommended Jack for continuing art therapy sessions for a number of reasons:

- Jack's level of engagement with the creative art process, materials, and therapist were very high.

- He could access information on a kinesthetic/sensory level as well as perceptually.

- He showed some affects during the process and within the content of the artwork.

- He demonstrated cognitive and symbolic processing in his story and the metaphors he used in his artwork.

- Jack's visual development and use of schematic language was aligned with his chronological age, and he was not hindered by self-doubt in his ability.

- He demonstrated capacity to explore difficulties via symbolic/metaphoric thinking and processing; a clear example of this was identifying himself as "scary."

From this single session, I was able to begin to formulate and hypothesize about some of the key problems in Jack's life. These were identified via the themes mentioned above that arose in the drawing. I was able to learn about and understand Jack's experiences as well as his perceptions about his social/familial context via the metaphors used in the story he developed. It was clear after Jack's first art therapy assessment that he was a good candidate for individual art therapy sessions. During a subsequent team case conference, I reported the key findings from this assessment and it was decided by the team that Jack would begin art therapy sessions with me.

Jack Starts Individual Art Therapy

Jack entered the day program with a diagnosis of ODD. The behaviors he displayed at home and at school appeared to support this diagnosis; however, as a team and as his individual therapist, it was important to pay attention the Z-code component to his diagnosis—altered pattern of family relationships in childhood. Given his family history, complex trauma also informs Jack's behavior and fits with his diagnostic formulation. Complex trauma (Malchiodi, 2011) describes a child's exposure to multiple traumatic events, often of an invasive, interpersonal nature such as abuse, domestic violence, or profound neglect. Jack's chronic exposure and experience of domestic violence, as well as other traumas, impacted him physiologically and psychologically. Complex trauma appeared to disrupt many aspects of his development such as self-formation and his ability to form a secure attachment bond. With this in mind, the overall goal for therapy was to provide a consistent, predicable, stable, and responsive environment in which Jack could begin to feel safe and to process some of his emotional experiences.

Jack's first session commenced two weeks after the art therapy assessment session. It was surprising to the therapist, especially since Jack had engaged so well in the assessment session, that the initial engagement with art therapy was difficult and unpredictable. For most of the first month he was irritable, saying, "I don't want to go to art therapy." When he did enter the room, he would often use avoidance strategies when the therapy seemed to approach topics that addressed any difficulties in his life. However, being cognizant of the traumas he experienced in his life, this hesitation to connect and engage in formal therapy would be congruent with his trauma history.

At times he would bring along character cards from one of his favorite computer games to share with me and then proceed to draw them by copying them. He would often take on the "teacher/expert" role, for example, showing the therapist how to fold paper boxes. This approach to art making engages clients on a perceptual level, allowing them to avoid being overwhelmed by affect (Hinz, 2009). It appeared to be important for Jack to feel he was in control and display expertise with his art making.

Sometimes, Jack engaged with me via interactive art processes such as the scribble chase and large versions of a join-the-dots game in which the therapist and client create as many large dot marks with dot paints all over a large piece of paper and, in a time limit, together they attempt to connect all the dots.

These processes were not only safe and fun but also engaged Jack on a kinesthetic/sensory level. This level of creativity often accesses the preverbal sensory motor stage of cognitive development (Piaget, 1969) where the focus is on the experience and connection rather than final image as an outcome. Generally, in the first month of his therapy, Jack's art process, products, and behaviors indicated ambivalence toward making an attachment to the therapeutic process and to me in particular. He struggled with trusting the therapeutic relationship and was extremely guarded in his art making. Often he was uncooperative, verbally hostile, angry, and he did not want his mother to leave him when he was dropped at the day program.

Jack's complex trauma had disrupted his basic abilities to trust and to attach. There were many times during and after the art therapy sessions when I was left feeling emotionally pushed and pulled. Safety, trust, and containment needed to be consciously and continually considered while interacting with Jack, and this was essential to progress any therapy. Not forgetting the impact that simply being with the client can have on the therapeutic alliance (Rothschild, 2000), the art process for Jack at this point focused on allowing him to experience success, draw images that he was confident with, experience a safe and fun connection with me by utilizing interactive art making, and encouraging him to engage his imagination and creativity via projective drawings.

Intimate connections can feel dangerous to children with complex trauma, yet often these children have an intense desire to attach. The child distrusts emotional connections but at the same time is preoccupied with unmet relational needs (Lanktree & Briere, 2008).

Jack's behavior during this period was an indicator of a difficult internal struggle that he needed to manage. Saakvitne, Gamble, Pearlman, and Lev (2000) emphasized the healing power of the relationship between the health professional and the survivor of trauma. While they view avoidance as an adaptive coping strategy, they note this avoidance can maintain symptoms. Art therapy with Jack was essentially about balancing the need to approach his traumatic issues while still allowing the space to maintain the need to protect himself.

An Interaction That Led to Jack's Engagement in Art Therapy

One day, Jack arrived at the day program to attend his weekly art therapy session. As with some previous sessions, he refused to go into therapy and sat on the waiting room couch, playing with his own toy car, repeatedly pushing it off the couch and letting it land on the floor. I sat with Jack noticing how far the car landed each time it launched off the couch. This became a game that Jack and I played, introducing more cars from the toy cupboard and tracking the distances by marking where they landed with masking tape. After doing this for some time, Jack asked me if we could go to the art room to play the squiggle game, which was a process he had enjoyed and engaged with periodically since the assessment session.

During this session, there appeared to be a shift with Jack's process. In a similar manner to his approach to the assessment session, Jack perceived shapes from his scribble and told a creative story about the symbols he formed. Jack drew two dinosaur creatures. One of these creatures appeared sad until he added lines to the mouth to represent teeth. He stated this was a "mean dinosaur just like me." He then drew a second dinosaur on the same piece of paper from another scribble he had created. This one had a downturned mouth that made it appear sad. He drew overlapping lines on the dinosaur's neck and said the dinosaur was "twisted inside." A curved line was drawn on the back of the dinosaur's body; Jack stated this was "his bum." He then drew an X on this area with a small circle near this. Jack said a "rock was thrown at him" and "he was hurt."

Through a familiar perceptual art process—scribble drawing—Jack was able to move to a more symbolic level of art making where meaning and a level of insight about his life's experiences were reached. Through the metaphor of the dinosaur in his artwork, Jack began to talk about his own life experiences; he created the safe, emotional distance he needed to explore this narrative.

At that point in time, one of Jack's acting-out behaviors was to throw rocks at people (as in the dinosaur story in his picture). Through this narrative, Jack was able to explore feelings and thoughts around being a victim and an antagonist. Once again, like in the assessment art piece, Jack communicated a negative perception of himself.

Jack utilized the art therapy sessions during this period of time to safely explore complex feelings via symbolism. Out of his ambiguous scribbles, lines, and forms came understanding about the symbols he created in his work. This process in art therapy encouraged Jack to tap into his own resourceful creativity. He was able to experience organizing an indefinable set of lines and marks into recognizable symbols, developed into an image that held personal meaning for him. He created these images with precision and confidence and now appeared to be attached to, and proud of, the artwork he produced, sometimes wanting to take them home or show them to his case manager or mother.

Jack continued to progress and positively use the art therapy sessions. Jack found creative and spontaneous ways to address a wide range of significant issues. Through the artwork, he was able to explore conflicted feelings about his relationship with his parents, specifically about his father and his father's death, as well as his ambivalent feelings toward his mother's current partner and specifically his relationship to his mother.

My Own Art Response to the Case

I experienced strong countertransference during this phase of therapy. A mother myself, I found myself feeling overprotective and connected to Jack. By contrast, I had strong feelings of irritation, anger, and annoyance toward Jack's mother, such as when she decided to go away on Mother's Day with her partner. I worried that this would hinder the progress that had been made thus far in treatment. Being fully aware that this was not conducive to productive therapy and to gain clarity about these strong feelings and reactions to Jack's mother, I created artwork in response to my countertransference. The image I created was a collage that combined representations of Jack as a small baby and his mother in her current relationship (see Figure 5.1).

I started by spontaneously ripping out images and text from magazines. The images were assembled in a composition that combined my perceptions of Jack's needs and his mother's needs. There were two key images that represented Jack. One was of a dismantled baby doll and the other, which I placed centrally in the collage, was an image of a small baby holding a large phone (see Figure 5.1). During the image collection from the magazines, I had some conscious awareness about what these symbols represented to me. However, the images connected to Jack's mother were more elusive in their meaning. The disassembled baby doll represented my thoughts about Jack's fragmented sense of self and the overwhelming task to try and piece this baby doll back together. The small baby holding an oversized phone symbolized Jack trying to connect and communicate with his mother. I was struck that both the images representing Jack were of small babies and this appeared to be connected to the attachment difficulties Jack experienced as an infant.

Figure 5.1   Judgment and blame—What is it good for? (Absolutely nothing!)

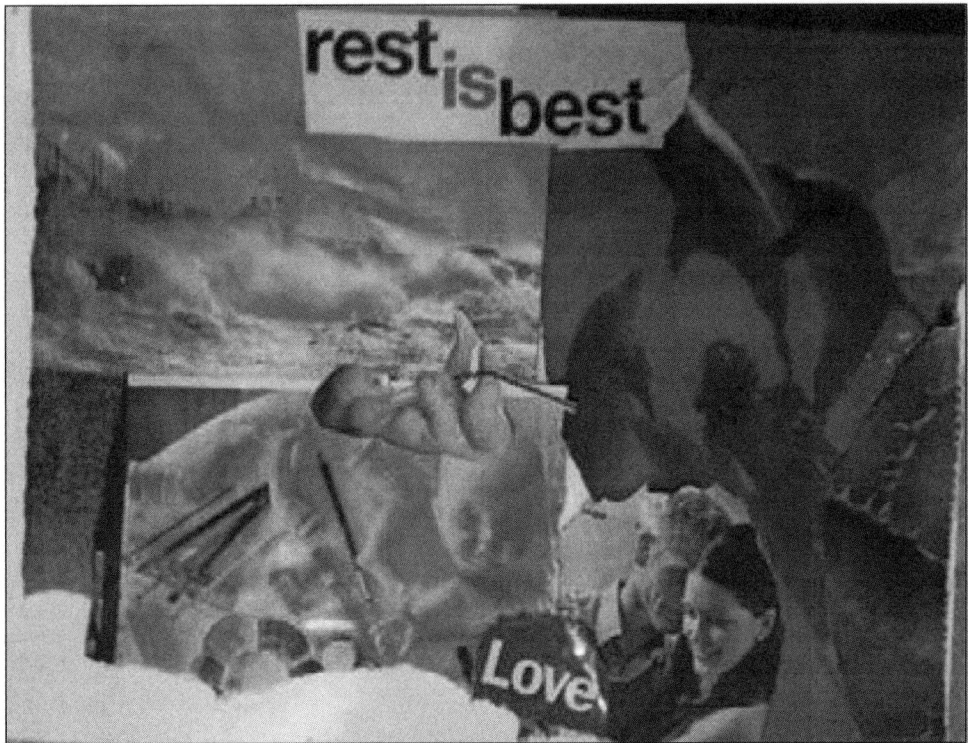

Source: Sandra Drabant.

The other images in the collage represented Jack's mother. An image of a woman swimming with dolphins evoked feelings of freedom and harmony; an image of a couple who appeared connected and affectionate represented a healthy relationship, and the word *love* was adhered near them. Finally, the text "rest is best" was glued at the top of the image. With these words, I came to the realization that Jack's mother was engaging in self-caring behavior. She was nurturing another important aspect of her life—her healthy relationship. Further, the baby in the middle of the image that holds the large phone does have a tool to connect with his mother, and that this experience of Jack's mother going away had potential to strengthen his attachment and address his separation anxiety while he had support around him. As I explored the symbolism and structure of images, I experienced more empathic feelings toward Jack's mother and her situation in life. A significant outcome from this art piece was that I developed a more balanced and hopeful outlook for the case.

Wendel, Gouze, and Lake (2005) discussed how multidisciplinary settings foster practitioners who have a strong commitment to the specific needs of their clients. The shared purpose of caring for the client as a collective but different group of clinicians helps identify the clinical issues that need to be focused on in treatment, which can lead to progress in treatment.

To ensure Jack's concerns about his mother's impending trip away were addressed systemically, I informed Jack's case manager about his "worried" feelings connected to his mother's trip. I also shared the insight I had developed after processing my own artwork. This helped the case manager to explore the trip away and its possible meaning for Jack in a curious, nonthreatening way with his mother.

One day, Jack entered the art therapy room after refusing to come to the session; this refusal had not occurred for some time. I was able to quickly engage him and he entered the room, albeit somewhat reluctantly. This quick engagement was a large shift in Jack's behavior and an indicator that Jack was able to now regulate his affect and better manage difficulties with his anxiety.

I had paper and his favorite medium—a black Sharpie permanent marker—already set up on the bench for him to use. Jack had consistently used this medium to create his artwork. This medium is considered more resistive and tends to elicit internal structure and boundaries during art making. The fact that it is not fluid in any way and eliminates color (which can quickly connect the person making art to affect) meant there was less chance that Jack would become overwhelmed by emotions (Kagin & Lusebrink, 1978). The artwork described below was created over a number of sessions, which in itself was an indicator of Jack's improved attention and concentration.

Jack usually took the initiative to begin his own creative process, not normally wanting me to direct the intervention in art therapy. However, in this session he allowed me to guide the intervention by making a suggestion that we draw an image together. Jack agreed with this and began the drawing by creating a road with a large incline that later became a bridge. Jack then passed the pen to me and I drew some houses near the declining side of the road. Jack took the pen and added fences all around the houses, referencing safety because it was a "suspicious" neighborhood. Jack drew the sun in one corner with a smiley face and then drew a cloud with some rain just above the houses. Jack then proceeded to draw a large umbrella over the houses, protecting the houses from becoming wet. At this point Jack drew another road underneath the incline of the bridge road, and off this road he drew a smaller road with a roundabout that led off the page.

Just before the edge of the page, Jack drew a man with a gun. He then asked me for another piece of paper that he taped to the previous piece and began drawing a complex scene that he described as a shopping center. He went on to say there were "bad guys/robbers" who had guns and were stealing things as well as hurting people. In the drawing he included police who tried to catch the "bad guys," but they were ineffective and got hurt as well. Jack said the people were scared, and he described the scene itself as "scary." At this point, Jack developed a character that he called "The Assassin." It was this character that took charge and put all the robbers in jail.

The next time Jack came to art therapy, he wanted to continue the image, asking me for yet another piece of paper that he taped to the previous one. Jack began his drawing by continuing the road through the image, and then alongside this road he created a jail scene, in which to put the "bad people."

As the session progressed, part of the jail became a place where "young kids" who did "bad things" went to be punished. As the image and the narrative developed further, the kids that were in the jail were given a chance to be "rehabilitated." He created a drawing of a "coach" who would help the kids with this rehabilitation. In his drawing, he drew a young boy with a speech bubble saying, "I miss Mum." I asked Jack what that must be like for the young boy. Jack said that he would feel "worried" if he were in this picture. As the session progressed, Jack stated that once the kids came out of jail they got to go to an orphanage and he nominated me to run the orphanage. Jack worked on this one image for the entire time of the session and tolerated conversations with me that directly addressed his feelings connected to the narrative he was developing.

In the next session, Jack once again wanted to continue adding sheets to the images he previously created. He added a final two sheets to complete the story. Once again, Jack linked the image via the metaphor of the road and then created a scene centered on a large roundabout depicting what he called "Friend Town," where people are safe and The Assassin protects all. In large words he wrote "Friend Town," and he also wrote my full name with the title "Mayor" of the town. He placed speed limit signs with "50" written on them so that there would not be any speeding on the roads around the town. As he continued, he encapsulated the entire town with an overarching line where The Assassin stood looking down. I noted that, in this image, The Assassin character that he associated as himself was no longer holding a gun.

As he worked on the image, he verbally described it, saying he added a skateboard park and a graffiti wall so the kids had things to do. He added a school for the kids as well as a tree in the center of the roundabout. I noted that the houses he drew did not have any fences around them. He drew a small child with a speech bubble saying, "I like this place," and told me that he would be "happy" here.

Jack created a final scene where he drew on another piece of paper and attached it below the Friend Town image. The road that had been the visual link through all the images ended at the far boundary of Friend Town and turned into sand with a sandcastle shape at the end of it. The image that was taped below depicted a beach scene.

Jack drew a number of smiling "Protectors"; he no longer called them "Assassins." He drew people enjoying themselves in the ocean, with one figure riding on top of a jellyfish and others on surfboards. He drew similar creatures to those he had drawn in his initial art therapy assessment session but described them as harmless. He drew himself (as Protector) and myself on the beach. The speech bubble above his head said, "Go on in, it won't hurt you," referring to the creatures in the water. Jack identified the place he drew as one where everyone could "relax."

At the end of the session, Jack chose the emotion card "Proud" to describe how he felt about his entire taped-together art piece. He wanted to share the final product with the other staff at the day program and another group member in the program. He took the art piece outside of the art room and it stretched the expanse of the hallway.

Ending Art Therapy and Treatment at the Day Program

Saying farewell is an important part of the therapeutic process. It is essential that this phase of therapy be addressed with sensitivity and a whole team approach to ensure the developments made in therapy thus far are not jeopardized.

When a client finishes at the day program, there are a number of goodbye processes that are put in place as part of their discharge experience. At a small goodbye gathering with the client and family, staff members have a chance to wish them well, say goodbye, give feedback about their achievements and challenges they have overcome, all while sharing a cake that is often prepared by the case manager. The client is also given a goodbye card that many of the staff sign.

The rituals that the day program team has in place for farewells allowed Jack to feel celebrated and held in mind. By personalizing and adapting the traditional rituals that were in place at the day program (making and signing a goodbye card), in Jack's case, creating a large paper plane (inspired by an object Jack created and used to communicate in one of his family therapy sessions) as the goodbye card ensured Jack felt his therapeutic process was acknowledged. This farewell became not only a reflection of the work Jack had done, but also became a time where his and his mother's efforts were celebrated.

As a part of the goodbye rituals at the day program, the client can choose to participate in an art therapy session where they are invited to create a "farewell tile." This tile is left at the day program and, with consent, displayed collectively on the entry wall. When the client enters the day program, these tiles are referenced and the concept is explained to the whole family. Jack was very willing to engage in this process and came to the session with a preconceived, planned-out image that he wanted to create on his farewell tile. This session offered an opportunity to reflect on Jack's time at the day program, reminiscing about his experiences, accomplishments, and challenges, as well as addressing feelings about leaving the program. Jack chose to create a symbol that he created in therapy, a symbol that was a representation of himself. It was important to let Jack know that the tile would be displayed with all the other tiles clients had created and that he would always be held in mind and remembered.

At the end of his therapy, Jack chose to take many of his art pieces home. These tangible reminders of the art therapy and his progress would serve as a transitional object, or bridge, between the day program's therapeutic work and his home environment.

DISCUSSION

When Jack began therapy, he exhibited physical, cognitive, emotional, and behavioral impacts from complex trauma, and his behavior was severe enough to warrant a diagnosis of ODD. By the end of therapy, it was clear that many of these impacts had lessened, and in particular his poor self-image and esteem had improved dramatically.

Working with Jack through his artwork helped me to experience him as a whole person, not just the problem he came to therapy with. Together we utilized art therapy as a focus of the treatment to assist Jack to externalize and remain at a safe distance from overwhelming feelings so that he was able to process them. It was important to assess how much distance from the metaphor Jack would tolerate, and this distance altered over the time of therapy as I tried to find the right emotional distance that would be containing without being intrusive and would allow Jack to experience a sense of control and choice in therapy.

Jack was able to give visual form to his fears through imaginary characters, gaining a sense of mastery and confidence to face both external fears and negative perceptions of self. There were numerous times where Jack drew his story and talked about the characters and events in his picture rather than talking about himself directly, creating the safe, emotional distance he needed to explore the complexities of his internal state (Klorer, 2008).

Once safety was established and Jack was able to regulate his affect, he began to develop an attachment to me as therapist. The art therapy process helped Jack reframe and integrate feelings and thoughts connected to many of his traumatic experiences. As the therapy progressed, Jack's executive functioning was enhanced, his attention was engaged, and he developed good visual problem solving skills (Malchiodi, 2011). Jack experienced a sense of mastery by creating his own art, while his improved self-esteem and self-efficacy were observed as exponentially improved by family members, teachers, and other clinicians in the day program.

The end of art therapy and the therapeutic relationship can be a difficult phase of therapy, especially for a client like Jack whose challenges centered on fragile attachments and object relations with his family members. As separations can be difficult and challenging, the farewell tile along with other significant farewell processes in place at the day program helped Jack experience a supportive farewell and a positive goodbye.

NOTES

1. Sandra Drabant has provided all accounts of working with Jack.

2. All names have been changed and some details altered to ensure the confidentiality of the client.

REFERENCES

Cane, F. (1951). *The artist in each of us*. New York, NY: Pantheon Books.

Gilroy, A., Tipple, R., & Brown, C. (Eds.). (2012). *Assessment in art therapy*. New York, NY; London: Routledge Taylor and Francis Group.

Hinz, L. (2009). *Expressive therapies continuum: A framework of using art in therapy.* New York, NY; London: Routledge Taylor and Francis Group.

Kagin, S., & Lusebrink, V. (1978). The expressive therapies continuum. *Art Psychotherapy, 5*(4), 171–180. doi:10.1016/0090-9092(78)90031-5

Klorer, P. (2008). Expressive therapy for severe maltreatment and attachment disorders: A neuroscience framework. In C. Malchiodi (Ed). *Creative interventions with traumatised children* (pp. 43–61). New York, NY: Guilford.

Lanktree, C., & Briere, J. (2008). *Integrative treatment of complex trauma for children (ITCT-C): A guide for the treatment of multiply-traumatized children aged eight to twelve years.* Retrieved from John Briere Website: http://www.johnbriere.com/child%20trauma%20tx%20manual%20%28lc%20 pdf%29.pdf

Malchiodi, C. (2011). Trauma informed art therapy with sexually abused children. In P. Goodyear-Brown (Ed.), *Handbook of child sexual abuse: Prevention, assessment, and treatment.* New York, NY: Wiley.

Piaget, J. (1969). *The psychology of the child.* New York, NY: Basic Books.

Rothschild, B. (2000). *The body remembers: The psychophysiology of trauma and trauma treatment.* New York, NY: W.W. Norton & Company.

Saakvitne, K., Gamble, S., Pearlman, L., & Lev, B. (2000). *Risking connection: A training curriculum for work with survivors of childhood abuse.* Baltimore, MD: Sidran Institute Press.

Wadeson, H. (1980). *Art psycho-therapy.* New York, NY: John Wiley & Sons.

Wendel, R., Gouze, K., & Lake, M. (2005). Integrative module-based family therapy: A model for training and treatment in a multidisciplinary mental health setting. *Journal of Marital and Family Therapy, 31*(4), 357–370. doi:10.1111/j.1752-0606.2005.tb01576.x

CHAPTER 6

Visual Arts

The Place of the Art Exhibition in Mental Health Recovery

Patricia Fenner and Margot J. Schofield

The painting will move the soul of the beholder when the people painted there each clearly shows the movement of his own soul . . . we weep with the weeping, laugh with the laughing, and grieve with the grieving. These movements of the soul are known from the movements of the body.

(Alberti, 1972, p. 80)

INTRODUCTION

The annual art show is a regular feature on the events calendar of many mental health recovery services both in Australia and internationally. Staging these art shows consumes substantial human and material resources and provides a valued social interface between consumers, staff, family, friends, and the general public. While these celebratory public events have been discussed in literature (Johnson, 2013; Lundin & Rashid, 1998; Spaniol, 1990; Vick, 2000), their functions in relation to the goals of recovery have received little scholarly attention. In this chapter, we investigate the layered levels of purpose, function, and meaning addressed by the art exhibition in mental health recovery contexts at both the individual and service level. The terms *art show* and *art exhibition* have been used interchangeably throughout.

We argue that the art show provides consumers with opportunities above and beyond that of exhibiting their artwork. We assert that, for those in recovery contexts, the public display of their artwork provides an opportunity to explore, refine, and affirm expressions of identity. We similarly argue that the art exhibition supports consumers to locate themselves within a purposeful and meaningful social context that serves the function of reinforcing recovery values including belonging, empowerment, social contribution, and the exercising of citizenship. We also explore the function of the art show as a ritual undertaken within recovery services that benefits not only the individuals who participate but also the wider human network that supports the recovery of people living with mental illness.

In preparing this chapter, the first author met with consumer/artists and staff from two leading recovery services in Melbourne, Australia: Prahran Mission and Neami National. Consultation was also undertaken with staff at the Dax Centre, a unique educational and gallery setting dedicated to education about mental illness through art exhibitions and learning activities. Like many similar, these organizations dedicate significant resources to providing art-making activities and regular exhibitions. While these consultations were conducted on an informal basis, the views and experiences expressed have informed the writing of this chapter to ensure consumer and service-based perspectives are incorporated into the authorial lens.

THE ART EXHIBITION: WHAT ARE WE TALKING ABOUT?

Service-sponsored consumer art exhibitions are usually modeled on the conventions of art exhibitions more broadly in terms of decisions related to theme selection, curatorship, marketing, the opening night and speech, managing sales, and the exhibition catalogue. This model serves as the primary focus for this chapter. It should be acknowledged, however, that consumers may also participate in broader community art exhibitions. For instance, they may submit their artwork to collections, competitions, and selective shows beyond the service domain where the mental health history of the artist is not explicitly acknowledged.

There are also specific theme-focused events or permanent collections, which have a specific agenda of destigmatizing mental illness through education and art display or artwork by those who have experienced mental illness. One notable example of this is the Dax Centre in Melbourne, which stages sophisticated professional exhibitions to which consumers have become increasingly attracted. The Dax Centre—named after the psychiatrist Dr. E. Cunningham Dax, who supported the incorporation of art making in psychiatric care in the 1950s and 1960s—houses an internationally acclaimed collection of artwork made by people who have experienced mental illness. The collection and exhibition programs today differ significantly from their original forms and are not directly consumer driven or managed. Nevertheless, consumer voice and participation are addressed in a variety of ways, such as through the use of personal narrative texts to accompany the artists' works. While a recovery focus is not primary to the function of the Dax Centre, its practices are aimed at being empowering for the consumers who donate to the collection (Jones, Koh, Veis, & White, 2010). The collection currently houses 15,000 works of art and many of the consumers who make an initial donation of their art to the Dax Centre return to donate again, demonstrating their endorsement of the acquisition and exhibition practices.

Art exhibitions are also offered by art-specific services for mental health consumers, such as that offered by Neami National through its Splash Art Studio program (www .neaminational.org.au). Here the art making and art show become the primary focus of the recovery program and thus support the artist identity of participants. This distinguishes such programs from recovery services in which art making and art shows are offered but are not the primary focus of the service. The Splash Art Studio shows are held at the service studio setting and take place four times a year, providing consumers the opportunity to reveal themselves artistically and personally over time.

Much of what follows in this chapter concerns the Splash Art Studio art show. However, in addition to this, artists practicing at the Splash Art Studio are encouraged to exhibit elsewhere in the mainstream art circuit. This is understood as congruent with a recovery focus, most particularly in the development of an evolving artist identity.

Where and to whom a consumer elects to submit artwork reflects that emerging identity. All exhibition venues have specific audiences. Consumers are able to ask, "What audience would I like to access? How can I be strategic and where might I gain recognition?" It is in this showing, revealing, and risk taking that issues of identity and identity differentiation are addressed as consumers negotiate where and how to exhibit, beyond the more familiar recovery service system. Finding the right venue can facilitate recovery values of contribution, communication development, purposefulness, belonging, and meaningful relationships.

It should be acknowledged early on that not all artwork created in the recovery service setting is made for exhibition. One fundamental quality of images is that they do not inherently communicate whether they should be exhibited or not. In our visually saturated world, we run a certain risk of becoming desensitized to issues related to the conditions of making and the intentions of expression. Images made within an art psychotherapeutic context, for example, may be inappropriate for exhibition, as doing so may leave the maker feeling exposed and vulnerable and viewers potentially confronted and possibly even traumatized. Exhibiting artwork made in some mental health services remains a debate among some art therapists. Authority for decision making in this domain needs to lie firmly with the art maker himself or herself, within the context of service system support and mentorship.

THE REALIZATION OF THE ART SHOW

Different types of art shows involve similar phases in their realization. Burton (2001) outlined these as conceptualization of a theme according to a specific audience; development of the timeframe, design of the physical space, mounting and installing the art; the running of the show, including opening night, sales, and dismantling; and review of the course of the event. The consumer art show set within a recovery context places similar emphasis on how these phases progress but with the additional consideration that recovery values are foundational to the event. For instance, the annual art shows of recovery services such as the Prahran Mission are generally consumer organized and led. This means consumers play a central role in decision making on the look and design of the catalogue, choice of marketing materials, coordination of artists, and decisions regarding artwork to be hung. Consumers set their own sales prices within a context of mentoring by more experienced artist consumers. Prestigious community gallery settings are sought for the show, and opening night is largely organized by the consumer artists. Thus the involvement, autonomy, and well-being of the consumer artists has priority over the commercial motive that may be more dominant in the realization of more mainstream art shows.

The Prahran Mission art show typifies those service-sponsored strategies, which utilize regular cultural forms and norms to facilitate recovery experiences. The perceived benefits for consumers of participating in the art show include social, psychological, and vocational aspects involving empowerment, enhanced self-esteem, social connection, contribution, reduction of social isolation, sense of belonging, destigmatization, and—for some—development of vocational skills as an artist. The art show thus involves a more complex developmental experience for mental health consumers and may provide a pathway to greater integration into wider society.

THE SOCIAL NATURE OF THE ART SHOW: BEING PART OF A COLLABORATIVE EVENT

Self-Expression

The art show is, in part at least, about aesthetics and self-expression. As the art maker represents objects and subjects from the world beyond herself or himself, art is a medium for expressing subjectivity and emotionally rich responses (Williams, 2004). Thus the artwork is more than a product; it is a communication of human experience and emotion wherein the ordinary is made special and extraordinary (Dissanayake, 1988). The context of the recovery service art exhibition allows for a fuller and more dedicated explanatory framework within which the subjective expressions can be valued and appreciated by the audience.

Social Participation

Equally, the art exhibition can be viewed as a participatory and social event. Both the processes of making and viewing art can be understood as collaborative and culturally located, coconstructed affairs (Gilroy, 2008; Wolff, 1981). Art makers engage not only with the materials required for the practical production of their art but are also immersed in social, cultural, and ideological discourses about issues such as the nature of mental illness and recovery, the role of creativity and the arts, empowerment, autonomy, and hope. Similarly, viewing of the artwork is a socially and culturally located act. Images can be understood to speak to particular viewing groups and carry meanings that reinforce the identities of those groups. In this sense, just as viewers construct meanings in artwork, the images can be understood as constructing audiences (Sturken & Cartwright, 2001).

Coconstructed Meaning

The art show invites its participants into an exchange of responses and meanings attached to the artwork and the wider context of the recovery setting. The interaction between artist and audience is understood to involve an "interactive, hermeneutic circle of projection and modification between the object and its viewer that allows a mediated meaning to be produced" (Gilroy, 2008, p. 258). Within the recovery service milieu, this interactive construction of meaning is influenced by the recovery values and ethos of the service agency and the wider mental health system and community contexts (Gilroy, 2008). This provides a supportive context in which the symbolic meaning of the artwork has a better chance of being mutually understood, valued, and enhanced. Gilroy argued that art works viewed in settings other than where they were created can become "blurred by the surroundings" and thus be misunderstood (2008, p. 252).

Affirmation

Artwork made within organizational settings, in this case the recovery sector, are shaped not only by the individual artist's subjective experience but also by the socially affirming discourses that exist within that sector. Exhibited within this context, they communicate in a manner that is congruent with the audiences' expectations. The validity of this contextual loop was endorsed through consultations with artists from both Neami National and Prahran Mission, who said they were already thinking of the exhibition when making their artwork, anticipating the empowering positive feedback they expected to receive. Affirming experiences such as these stand in stark contrast to feelings of disenfranchisement and stigma often felt by people with mental illnesses. The context of the art show extends the discussion to a level beyond mental health issues and into a framework of social acceptability (Van Lith, Fenner, & Schofield, 2011). Furthermore, in the context of the art show, the consumer artist becomes the competent or expert party in their relationship with staff and visitors to the art show and thus experiences a reversal in the usual role of less expert mental health consumer.

Empathic Resonance

The social benefits of communicating inner experience and symbolic meanings to others through the art show has received support through recent neuroscience studies of neurological responses to the viewing of art works (Gallese, 2005; Iacoboni et al., 2005; Ishizu & Zeki, 2011; Urgesi, Moro, Candidi, & Aglioti, 2006). For instance, mirror neuron research suggests that the viewer looking at the details of an artist's gestures in a painting or sculpture can experience an empathic response to the emotions contained in its visual elements (Gallese, 2005; Iacoboni et al., 2005). In other words, marks made on the canvas are traces of directed movements that can induce activation of the same motor area in the brain of the observer. Freedberg and Gallese (2007) asserted that these automatic empathic responses constitute part of an embodied experiential understanding of the emotional content of artwork of others. Thus, the opportunity for mental health consumers to exhibit artistic expressions of their human experience offers the potential to be better understood by others on a range of neurological, psychological, and empathic levels. While this research may be in its infancy, it holds intriguing promise to develop understanding of people who often live marginalized lives. Expressed differently, viewing the art of those with different mental health issues has the potential not only to expose viewers to the lived experiences of artists with mental health issues but to provide a gateway to knowing oneself differently (Chalkley, 2005).

Broadening and Deepening Social Recovery

In a critical review of the benefits of art-based practices for mental health recovery, social recovery was identified as the second most important dimension of impact (Van Lith, Schofield, & Fenner, 2013). Art making in group contexts is known to reduce isolation and loneliness through engagement with others, induce a sense of belonging and universality, and reduce a sense of stigma. Participation in the recovery-oriented art exhibition seems to provide additional social benefits beyond the art making experience. It can be seen as a broadening and deepening experience in which oneself and one's artwork become a center point of attention and facilitates a different level of interaction with others. When managed well, this has the potential to provide a more integrative social experience in which one moves from the periphery to the center of the social context. It thus makes a stronger contribution to the artist's developing identity as well as facilitating the experience of holding a central place within a meaningful community.

THE RELATIONSHIP BETWEEN EXHIBITING ART AND IDENTITY DEVELOPMENT IN MENTAL HEALTH CONTEXT

Defining the Self

The practices of creating and exhibiting art make issues of identity figural for the art maker. Where and how one exhibits can impact a differentiated sense of self and identity development. Stacey and Stickley (2010) proposed a model for thinking about identity in relation to the art exhibition in the mental health context. They saw identity as referring to a person's self-perception and the role of art in their lives. Through the process of exhibiting, this identity is subjected to a complex and cyclic process incorporating self-statement in the art work, feedback from others (including possibly influential others), and the value placed on level of prestige associated with the show setting.

Redefining the Self

Having the opportunity to both make and exhibit art generates a sensibility that Thompson (2011) defined as "an awareness of the self as an artist through the integration of artistic and aesthetic attributes toward self and other" (p.160). This artistic sensibility facilitates navigation of the internal psychological world as well as the experience of being in the world. Within a respectful and culturally congruent setting, such as the art show, a nonjudgmental, nonpathologizing, and empowering critique is made possible, supporting the recovery goals of identity redefinition, agency, and empowerment (Thompson, 2011). In this sense, the gallery setting becomes a site for the demonstration of capacity, and the honor of exhibiting in a prestigious setting can result in a huge boost in self-confidence and potentially self-belief.

Pathway of Identity Development

The pathway of recovery from mental illness is not a smooth linear journey. With the ups and downs of recovery, identity is both transformed and continues to be challenged as relapses or setbacks occur. This is not, of course, an experience restricted to those experiencing mental illness. Artists have previously tracked their experiences of other health conditions such as cancer, heart disease, and Parkinson's disease (Atkin, 2011; Lapum, Church, Yau, David, & Ruttonsha, 2012; Niran, 2013). However, making art as an expression of identity when one has a mental illness holds a particular place in art history (MacGregor, 1989) and in the history of the development of the practice of art therapy as a health care discipline (Vick, 2003). The notion that images have a link to the state of mind and sense of meaning of the maker emerged with seriousness through the work of collectors such as psychiatrists Hans Prinzhorn in Germany and E. Cunningham Dax in Australia during the 20th century. These collections placed the artwork of those experiencing mental illness on the international stage and impelled what has become an enduring interest in the place and role of art in the lives of those experiencing mental illness.

Outsider Identity

Artists with mental health issues have been labeled *outsiders* in the mainstream art world, and this identity can hold both appeal and create ambivalence (Gwinner, Know, & Hacking, 2009; Williams, 2004). The term *outsider art* was first coined in 1972 to denote artwork made outside the conventions of the mainstream art world (MacGregor, 1989). Outsider art has over time established its own *insider* status with popular appeal within the art market drawn to expressions of raw human emotion. Gwinner et al. (2009) studied the experiences of eight artists with mental illness. These artists described being attracted to the good sales that can accompany the exhibiting of works related to mental illness. These sales then served to support the artists financially and reinforce their artist identities. Consumers within recovery contexts have expressed that selling their works leads to enhanced self-esteem, a sense of validation, acceptability, and prestige. The label *outsider artist*, while limiting in some respects, holds appeal to some consumers as an established convenient and recognized identity with a broadly understood and accepted historic artist narrative (Gwinner et al., 2009). In addition, this outsider artist identity serves to combine the artist and illness aspects of identity and is experienced by some as loosening public expectations on aesthetic capacity (Gwinner et al., 2009).

Insider Identity: Developing as an Artist

Showing one's artwork in a public art show provides an additional opportunity for developing one's identity as a professional artist distinct from self-identity. This identity is developed through choosing where to exhibit, how to present the artwork and artist identity, and through taking risks and expanding the circle of social connections. The emerging identity provides a pathway beyond recovery toward having a meaningful vocation in life and feeling part of the wider group of artists in the community. It also provides the opportunity to step back further from the work and engage in more critical appraisal. Such actions may further contribute to recovery.

Developing Discipline and Motivation

Consumers have noted that preparing for an exhibition has a number of positive benefits for them. The deadline for preparing material for the show can promote greater discipline and motivation to complete works. Support workers can assist the artist to feel more in control by developing a timeline and working toward that. A sense of control is also enhanced by involvement in decisions such as who to invite, what to show, where to place the works, and what information to provide with them. However, the artist is also called on to surrender control once opening night arrives, and they have to stand back and observe the responses to their artwork. One person described her delight in secretly observing and listening to responses of others to her work.

Identity Development Over Time

When artists participate in consecutive art shows, they can come to see a pattern of self expressed in and through art over time. The art show provides the means of recording this development and seeing how one's expression of self is changing. This artist identity can also be visible, known, and appreciated by others who have the potential to reinforce and support these emergent expressions of self.

Such issues of identity are intrinsic to the experience of the art show in recovery and nonrecovery contexts to varying degrees. We return again to the factor of the setting, context, and the intentions within which the art show is held and the degree to which authority can be exercised by the artist exhibitors.

THE PURPOSE OF THE ART SHOW FOR THE RECOVERY COMMUNITY NETWORK

The art show is as dependent upon its viewing community as it is upon its artist exhibitors. It is also evident that the meaning and role of the art show goes well beyond the aesthetic. In the life of recovery services, the art show can be seen to function as a unifying service ritual, which benefits not only individual artists but also the collective network that dedicates itself to the recovery of people with mental illnesses. It provides a motivational and unifying focus over time as well as a highly significant ritual event that provides added meaning to the life of the recovery community.

The art show provides an opportunity for symbolic communication to the wider participating community about the nature of mental illness and recovery and the values underpinning the provision of services within the recovery framework. The art show allows an opportunity for individuals to act as members of a group, participating not only for individual gain but in service of the group or like-minded community as a whole. Furthermore, it provides the opportunity for them to be seen as both individuals and members of a group. Brown and Dissanayake (2009) identified art making as one mechanism that links ritual practices with belief systems. They suggested that one of the strongest drivers of the arts is social affiliation, something they identified as

> an emotion of strong reward value. This is tied in with our view that one of the most important functions of the arts is to create and reinforce a sense of social unity so as to promote cooperation and cohesion within social groups. In fact, affiliative interactions are the very basis for group formation. (p. 52)

Working in the interests of people with mental illnesses with a commitment to recovery, the group in this context can be conceptualized as incorporating consumers, staff, families, friends, funding bodies, and so on. Brown and Dissanayake (2009) asserted that small-scale cultures (such as the recovery community) utilize the arts as a way to affirm a sense of common cause that energizes and propels the group to sustain itself. In this sense, the art show can be conceptualized as a unifying, activating, and celebratory behavior necessary in the recovery service life cycle. The gallery that hosts the art exhibition for artists with mental illnesses becomes a site for affirmation, appreciation, and renewal.

Potential Risks of Exhibiting in Art Shows

While there are clear benefits of art making and art exhibition within the mental health context (Gwinner et al., 2009; Van Lith et al., 2009, 2011, 2013), it must also be acknowledged that exhibiting is not free of risks. These risks pertain in large part to the manner in which an exhibition is organized and how the individual and collective authority of the exhibiting consumers is acknowledged and incorporated into the show design and execution. It should also be stated that many artworks made in the individual art therapy setting are made for the purposes of personal psychotherapy and rightfully should remain in that private domain. Many mental health consumers have significant trauma histories and may feel highly sensitive to comments from others. There may also be a subtle peer pressure to exhibit before the participant is ready to do that. Art show organizers should thus ensure that the consumer is fully consulted and is an active participant in decision regarding exhibition. Thus the first risk management strategy is to ensure that the consumer is fully informed, supported, and actively involved in decision making at all stages of the art show.

A further aspect of risk is management of the exhibition environment itself. It is essential that recovery values and principles underpin every aspect of the preparation and staging of the art show. This includes firmly establishing the culture and environment of the show so that viewers are supported and educated while being led on a path of empathic engagement and affirmative responding. This can be demonstrated through direct engagement by artists in discussion of the works and their meanings with service providers, family, friends, and other members of the public.

Some artwork that reflect personal experience and autobiographical stories may pose challenges for family and friends when displayed publicly. Without careful consideration of the art to be exhibited and its potential impact on others, there is potential for harm to the artist's relationships and for others to feel negatively challenged by the content. Of course, it may be important to the consumer to present such work even though it may be challenging. Then, it may be useful to provide some context for the work. The Dax Centre must grapple with this issue for each exhibition as the artwork are acquisitions and thus the context of their showing can vary over time. Artists usually provide a personal narrative to support the collection of their artwork being exhibited, but this may be changed depending on the purpose of the exhibition or changes in the artists' lives or experiences. Prior to each show, careful negotiation is carried out with the consumer, as well as their family or others involved, to ensure their support for the aesthetics and purpose of the exhibition. Other means by which risks are reduced are to have the option of exhibiting anonymously or under a pseudonym.

RECOMMENDATIONS FOR STAGING AN ART SHOW IN THE MENTAL HEALTH RECOVERY CONTEXT

Based on the literature as well as consultations with staff and consumers involved in staging art shows in the mental health recovery context, we offer some recommendations to enhance the positive outcomes associated with staging an art show by mental health consumers. The aims are to optimize the value of such activities for both consumers and audience and reduce the potential risks involved.

Organization

- The recovery framework should guide all stages of development and management of the art show. The recovery framework is based on values of respect, integrity, hope, collaboration, fostering creativity, individualized plans, and empowerment of consumers.

- Strategies should be developed to ensure that consumer participation is fully informed, voluntary, and undertaken in consultation with staff, where relevant.

- Care should be taken to ensure that social pressure from other participants does not override the needs of an individual.

- Consumers should be involved in each stage of the organizational process including selecting and hanging the art work and approving any written description of the work.

- Consumers should have the right to withdraw if they change their mind or become uncomfortable about any aspect of the show.

Environment

- The setting for the art show should be compatible with the aims of the art show and support the recovery values such as empowerment, autonomy, and respect.

- The choice of a recovery setting or public exhibition space for the art show will depend on the needs and preferences of consumers.

- Attention should be paid to strategies to lead the viewers on a journey of empathic engagement, understanding and appreciation, and suspension of judgment. This can be achieved through the way the exhibition is displayed, educational input provided, and the availability of guides to discuss the work in an appreciative manner. Figure 6.1 was taken at the opening night of a Splash art show. These events typically involve many of the customs and trappings of art shows in general including a guest address, which may be delivered by one of the exhibiting artists about his or her work. Such addresses aim to illuminate the role of both art making and exhibiting processes from a personal perspective. In addition to this, artists are available to speak to family, friends, and members of the public about specific artwork. Typically, this is an interactive and celebratory affair.

Figure 6.1   Opening night Splash Art Show, winter 2013.

Source: Author.

Artist

- Artists should be given the opportunity to reflect on the meaning and process of exhibition and possible impacts on their recovery.

- Artists exhibiting for the first time could be mentored through the process by a more experienced exhibitor.

- Recovery workers could assist the consumer artist to develop an individual plan in relation to exhibiting their work and identify the skills to be developed and a plan for achieving this.

- Consumer artists should have access to appropriate support workers throughout the exhibition and be facilitated to reflect on the experience after the show ends, and lessons learned.

CONCLUSION

The place, function, and role of the art show in the recovery context is multifaceted, fluid, and individually specific. This chapter describes benefits of the art show in the process of mental health recovery as well as some of the risks. It also describes the value of the art show as a ritual event that contributes to the well-being and sustainability of the service context and its people as a whole. These factors are real within the present state of art exhibitions in the recovery sector and potentially enhance our understanding of how the art exhibition is conceptualized.

ACKNOWLEDGMENTS

Valuable perspectives for this chapter were gained in conversation with staff and consumers from Neami National Splash Art Studios, Prahran Mission, and the Dax Centre. Appreciation and thanks are extended to Guler, Trish, Katrina, Gila, Tania, Robert, Sally, Charlotte, Chris, Quinn, and Bobbie for their insights and contributions based on personal experience.

REFERENCES

Alberti, L. (1972). *On painting and on sculpture: The Latin texts of De Pictura and De Statua* (C. Grayson, Transl.). London, England: Phaidon Press.

Atkin, A. (2011). *Living and laughing with Parkinson's*. Burwood East, Australia: Memoirs Foundation.

Brown, S., & Dissanayake, E. (2009). The arts are more than aesthetics: Neuroaesthetics as narrow aesthetics. In M. Skov O. Vartanian (Eds.), *Neuroaesthetics*. Amityville, NY: Baywood.

Burton, D. (2001). Social dynamics in exhibiting art: Rethinking the practices of art education. *Art Education, 54*(1), 41–46.

Chalkley, L. (2005). Me first and other quite possible dreams. *A Life in the Day, 9*(2), 3–6. doi:10.1108/13666282200500012

Dissanayake, E. (1988). *What is art for?* Seattle: University of Washington Press.

Freedberg, D., & Gallese, V. (2007). Motion, emotion and empathy in aesthetic experience. *TRENDS in Cognitive Sciences, 11*(5), 197–203. doi:10.1016/j.tics.2007.02.003

Gallese, V. (2005). Embodied simulation: From neurons to phenomenal experience. *Phenomenology & Cognitive Science, 4*(1), 23–48. doi:10.1007/s11097-005-4737-z

Gilroy, A. (2008). Taking a long look at art: Reflections on the production and consumption of art in art therapy and allied organisational settings. *International Journal of Art and Design Education, 27*(3), 251–262. doi:10.1111/j.1476-8070.2008.00584.x

Gwinner, K., Know, M., & Hacking, S. (2009). The place for a contemporary artist with a mental illness. *Journal of Public Mental Health, 8*(4), 29–37. doi:10.1108/17465729200900025

Iacoboni, M., Molnar-Szakacs, I., Gallese, V., Buccino, G., Mazziotta, J., & Rizzolatti, G. (2005). Grasping the intentions of others with one's own mirror neuron system. *PLoS Biology, 3*(3), 529–535. doi:10.1371.journal.pbio.0030079

Ishizu, T., & Zeki, S. (2011). Toward a brain-based theory of beauty. *PLoS ONE, 6*(7), e21852. doi:10.1371/journal.pone.0021852

Johnson, E. (2013). Patient art exhibitions in health care settings. In C. Malchiodi (Ed.), *Art therapy in health care*. New York, NY: Guildford.

Jones, K., Koh, E., Veis, N., & White, A. (2010). *Framing marginalised art*. Parkville, Australia: Cunningham Dax Collection.

Lapum, J., Church, K., Yau, T., David, A., & Ruttonsha, P. (2012). Arts-informed research dissemination: Patients' perioperative experiences of open-heart surgery. *Heart & Lung*, *41*(5), e4–e14. doi:10.1016/j.hrtlng.2012.04.012.

Lundin, R., & Rahsid, F. (1998). Issues relevant to a consumer art show. *Psychiatric Rehabilitation Skills*, *2*(2), 158–170. doi:10.1080/10973435.1998.10387560

MacGregor, J. M. (1989). *The discovery of the art of the insane*. Princeton, NJ: Princeton University Press.

Niran, R. (2013). The body's betrayal: Works by Rosa Niran. Retrieved from http://www.daxcentre.org/whats-on/past%20exhibitions/

Spaniol, S. (1990). Exhibiting art by people with mental illness: Issues, process and principles. *Art Therapy*, *7*(2), 70–78. doi:10.1080/07421656.1990.10758896

Stacey, G., & Stickley, T. (2010). The meaning of art to people who use mental health services. *Perspectives in Public Health*, *130*(2), 70–77. doi:10.1177/1466424008094811

Sturken, M., & Cartwright, L. (2001). *The practices of looking: An introduction to visual culture*. Oxford, England: Oxford University Press.

Thompson, G. (2011). Artistic sensibility in the studio and gallery model: Revisiting process and product. *Art Therapy*, *26*(4), 159–166. doi:10.1080/07421656.2009.10129609

Urgesi, C., Moro, V., Candidi, M., & Aglioti, S. M. (2006). Mapping implied body actions in the human motor system. *Journal of Neuroscience*, *26*(30), 7942–7949. doi:10.1523.JNEUROSCI.1289-06.2006

Van Lith, T., Fenner, P., & Schofield, M. J. (2009). Toward an understanding of how art making can facilitate mental health recovery. *Australian e-Journal for the Advancement of Mental Health (AeJAMH)*, *8*(2), 1–11. Retrieved from http://search.informit.com.au/documentSummary;dn=266042545238600;res=IELHEA

Van Lith, T., Fenner, P., & Schofield, M. J. (2011). The lived experience of art making as a companion to the mental health recovery process. *Disability & Rehabilitation*, *33*(8), 652–660. doi:10.3109/09638288.2010.505998

Van Lith, T., Schofield, M. J., & Fenner, P. (2013). Identifying the evidence-base for art-based practices and their potential benefit for mental health recovery: A critical review. *Disability & Rehabilitation*, *35*(16), 1309–1323. doi:10.3109/0938288.2012.732188

Vick, R. (2000). Creative dialogue: A shared will to create. *Art therapy: Journal of the American Art Therapy Association*, *17*(3), 216–219. doi:10.1080/07421656.2000.10129707

Vick, R. (2003). A brief history of art therapy. In C. Malchiodi (Ed.), *Handbook of art therapy*. New York, NY: Guilford.

Williams, C. (2004). Reclaiming the expressive subject: Deviance and the art of non-normativity. *Deviant Behaviour*, *25*(3), 233–254. doi:10.1080/01639620490431192

Wolff, J. (1981). *The social production of art*. London, England: Macmillan.

RESOURCES

General Resources

Mental Spaghetti: http://mentalspaghetti.org/
Neami National: http://www.neaminational.org.au
The Other Side Gallery: http://www.theothersidegallery.org/
Prahran Mission: http://prahranmission.org.au

Australia

Mental Illness Fellowship of Queensland: http://www.mifq.org.au

Mind Australia: http://www.mindaustralia.org.au/

Reflections Art Studio (Western Australia): http://www.health.wa.gov.au/arttherapy/reflections/gallery
.cfm

The Dax Centre: http://www.daxcentre.org/

United Kingdom

Core Arts UK: http://www.corearts.co.uk/

Start in Manchester—arts based mental health service for adults: http://www.startmc.org.uk/index.php

Scottish Mental Health Arts and Film Festival: http://www.mhfestival.com/index.php

Sane UK online gallery: http://www.sane.org.uk/what_we_do/art_and_awards1/

North America

The Brain & Mental Health Art Show (Society for Neuroscience Ottawa): http://sfn-ottawa.ca/events/
artshow/

Fresh A.I.R. (Artists in Recovery Gallery—Ohio): http://www.southeastinc.com/fresh_air.php

Creative Writing

Literature Review and Evidence-Based Research

Philip Neilsen

INTRODUCTION

There is growing evidence, especially in the United States and United Kingdom, that creative writing can form an important part of the recovery experience of people affected by severe mental illness. In this chapter, I consider theoretical models that explain how creative writing might contribute to recovery and discuss the potential for creative writing in psychosocial rehabilitation. It is argued that the rehabilitation benefits of creative writing might be optimized through focus on process and technique in writing, rather than expression or content alone, and that consequently the involvement of professional writers might be important.

I will explore the recent history of theoretical frameworks and explanatory models that link creative writing and recovery and examine such empirical evidence as is available on the contribution of creative writing to recovery from severe mental illness. (In the next chapter, I discuss a pilot study conducted to investigate the feasibility of providing workshops in creative writing for people engaged in a community-based psychosocial rehabilitation program.)

CREATIVE WRITING: DEFINITION

For the purposes of this book, *creative writing* is defined as the use of crafted writing for purposes of personal expression in communication with an actual or potential readership. Creative writing might take the form of prose or poetry and might be fictional or nonfictional, as in life writing—particularly memoir. The focus is on creative writing that is substantially independent of psychotherapy, although I acknowledge that people who engage in creative writing will often also be engaged in some form of concurrent therapy.

THEORETICAL FRAMEWORKS AND EXPLANATORY MODELS

In this section, I consider three distinct theoretical frameworks that have proposed logical links between creative writing and recovery from severe mental illness. The first and most developed model, to which I will devote primary attention, describes the relationship between the development of a narrative and the emergence or consolidation of personal identity. The second explains how writing can reconstitute what was previously a void in the internal symbolic order of the person and is especially associated with the work of French psychoanalyst and psychiatrist Jacques Lacan. The third, only recently articulated as a formal model, proposes creative writing as a form of cognitive remediation (King, Neilsen, & White, 2012).

Narrative and Identity

There are several strands of theory in this area, but overall a strong area of agreement, that language, narrative, and storytelling are essential elements in the construction of a coherent identity, sense of self, and connectedness to others and therefore are powerful tools in creative therapy (Smyth, 1998; Wright & Chung, 2001). Narrative theory and narrative therapeutic approaches provide useful explanatory models that emphasize the importance of storytelling in the creation and recreation of the self (Bruner, 2004).

Historically, the United States has led this field; psychotherapists advocated poetry therapy as early as the 1960s, and today the use of creative writing in therapy is professionally organized and advanced. In the United States, the National Association for Poetry Therapy (NAPT) has published the *Journal of Poetry Therapy* since 1987. Poetry therapy has the practical virtue of brevity and the creative virtue of encouraging imaginative play with imagery. Lapidus (literary arts in personal development) was founded by the English Arts Council in 1996. Like the NAPT, it promotes fiction and storytelling as well as poetry for health and well-being.

Personal disclosure was initially a key factor for those investigating writing therapy (Pennebaker, 1995); a link was established between writing and boosted autonomic nervous system activity and immune function. Important pioneering work was done by Pennebaker, who argued that disclosure alone was not as effective as creating a narrative with language (Pennebaker, 2000; Pennebaker & Seagal, 1999).

There was also an escalating interest in life writing (especially memoir) as a mediated, reflexive, creative process of narrative and identity construction. McAdams (2003) observed that in a contemporary context, "the self is a reflexive project that a person is expected to . . . develop, improve" (p. 202). Paul Eakin (1999) stressed the link between narrative and identity in both internal life story and autobiography: "Narrative is not merely a literary form but a mode of phenomenological and cognitive self-experience, while self—the self of autobiographical discourse—does not necessarily precede its constitution in narrative" (p. 100). In other words, narrative may make the self just as much as self makes narrative. So a self-in-time and socially viable identity perhaps depend on such narrative. The term *dysnarrativia* has been coined to describe the documented inability to construct self-narrative by those suffering amnesia, autism, severe child abuse, or brain damage. The lack of ability to achieve narrative construction seems to be correlated with identity disorders (Eakin, 1985, p. 124).

Roe and Davidson (2005) argue that "processes of re-authoring one's life story are actually integral components of the recovery process itself" (p. 89). They found in interviews with people recovering from schizophrenia that a four-stage process of identity reconstruction could be described: discovery of an alternative sense of self to that in the previous, dominant, illness narrative; a reflection upon this self and the potential to change; acting to revise and enhance integration of that new sense of self; and using this more integrated self that has been salvaged in order to make progress toward recovery (Davidson & Strauss, 1992). For people with schizophrenia, "narrative is one of the few tools available that enable the person" (Roe & Davidson, 2005, p. 93) to regain agency with an emerging, reconstituted self that can recognize both the severe challenges of the illness and a more promising future. Narrative grants the individual a sense of authoring their story as the protagonist or principal character of the story.

These findings are consistent with the earlier work of Lysaker, Wickett, Wilke, and Lysaker (2003), who suggest that among people with a diagnosis of schizophrenia, personal narratives are compromised such that it is difficult to locate the self as the agent–protagonist in the teller's story. In their study, transcripts, case notes, and supervision notes were examined to explore the strengths and weaknesses of narrative construction in three individuals with schizophrenia. They found that while narratives about other people were coherent and well-constructed, narratives about the self were frequently lacking coherence. They argue that people with incoherent personal narratives benefit from the development of greater flexibility of narrative, which grants the individual a sense of authoring and owning their story as the protagonist of the story.

Central to narrative therapy is the proposition that language provides the means by which people make sense of and tell their stories (Polkinghorne, 2004). Drawing from social constructivist theory, White and Epston (1990) argue that language and meaning are socially constructed through discourses. Social and power relations are inherently linked to discourses, and these govern whose voice becomes heard and what gets said (Foucault, 1984). Influenced by the work of Foucault on the inseparability of power and knowledge, White and Epston (1990) theorize that dominant discourses are privileged by society as "truths." They believe that the problem story a person brings to therapy is but one story exerting a powerful influence over the person because it is a dominant story that society has deemed the status quo. The process of narrative therapy involves creating an alternative story by searching for exceptions to the dominant story, which then open up possibilities for the person in therapy to reauthor their life.

More recently, in a commentary on the psychoanalytic work of Schafer (1983) and Spence (1982) drawing on the anthropological work of Levi-Strauss (1966), King (2012) offers a rethinking of the nature of the reauthoring that occurs during psychotherapy. He suggests that objectively evaluated narrative coherence might be less important than the ability to cobble together a subjectively workable narrative from ideas and memories available to the person. This mental capacity, which Levi-Strauss (1966) termed *bricolage*, might be eroded by mental illness. The process of writing, which requires the writer to draw on experience, memory, and imagination, might actively develop the capacity for bricolage. That is, the construction of narrative might be central to the value of writing in recovery of identity, but this might be substantially independent of the coherence of the narrative as externally judged.

Writing as a Means of Repairing a Fundamental Flaw in Symbolic Functioning

Lacan's position is that psychosis involves a structural deficit in the symbolic functioning of the psyche (Lacan, 1977, 1993). In seminar three (Lacan, 1993), he refers to a missing signifier, which he terms *nom-du-pere*, conveying at the one time a failure at the level of the Oedipus complex and a corresponding failure at the cultural level that might be termed a failure of exogamy. As a result of this structural deficit, the person lacks full access to the domain of culture in the broadest sense of the term. The person is not fully inscribed into the social order, and this has implications for interpersonal relations and any other kind of functioning that requires symbolic exchange as it occurs as a part of ordinary social-cultural activity (King, 2012). As Robert King (2012) has pointed out:

> For Lacan, failure at the level of personal identity is a secondary effect of psychosis. The primary effect is in what he terms the "register of the symbolic," which is that part of the psyche organized by language that governs social relations. In contrast, personal identity is primarily registered in the imaginary. Failure in the symbolic destabilizes the imaginary, thereby disrupting personal identity. Any repair at the level of identity is contingent on repair of the rupture in the symbolic. (p. 446)

According to Lacan, Daniel Paul Schreber and James Joyce demonstrated evidence of this structural deficit but were able to function reasonably effectively in society. Schreber was a federal court judge in Germany and Joyce a renowned writer, especially of highly sophisticated and linguistically experimental fiction (e.g., *Ulysses* and *Finnegan's Wake*). Both produced works that simultaneously testified to the effect of the structural deficit and stabilized the effect of this deficit. In the case of Schreber, the deficit manifested in the form of frank paranoid delusions and bizarre experiences. In the case of Joyce, the deficit manifested in the form of idiosyncratic language, which in *Finnegan's Wake* approximated thought disorder. As Ragland-Sullivan (1990) puts it, "Lacan's reading of Joyce's prose is the idea that *Finnegan's Wake* is not intended to mystify readers but is Joyce's desperate effort to keep a link to the symbolic order intact" so as not to "fall into the abyss of psychotic *jouissance*" (p. 77).

Lacan argues that writing serves the function of what he terms a *suppleance*—an artificial, but nonetheless stabilizing, replacement for the missing signifier. He proposes that while writing does not fully repair the symbolic, it can be sufficient to stabilize the imaginary (and therefore, personal identity) and thus permit adequate social functioning. That is, while writing does not eliminate psychosis, it might protect the writer from its more catastrophic effects (King, 2012).

Finnegan's Wake has been the subject of many contested interpretative studies; but importantly, Lacan's reading of the novel does make a credible case for writing as mechanism for repair of a rupture in symbolic functioning. In this context, Joyce provided Lacan with focus for his 1975–1976 seminar and enabled him to develop and illustrate a theory that had its origins two decades earlier.

Writing as a Form of Cognitive Remediation

Cognitive remediation (CR) refers to systematic training in basic cognitive processes, such as attention, concentration, memory, and response to stimuli, as well as some more complex processes, such as problem solving. It was introduced into rehabilitation programs for people recovering from schizophrenia because of evidence that cognitive deficits are a major source of impairment for this group of people (Medalia & Thysen, 2008). There is now a substantial body of research, including several meta-analyses, showing that CR consistently improves cognitive functioning for people with a diagnosis of schizophrenia with at least a medium effect size (Wykes, Huddy, Cellard, McGurk, & Czobor, 2011). Furthermore, there is evidence that these gains flow through to functional improvements and that there are also beneficial effects on symptoms (Bell, Zito, Greig, & Wexler, 2008). Emma White (King et al., 2012) has put this succinctly:

> One of the interesting findings from the CR research is that cognitive gains are not dependent on the form of CR. A wide variety of CR interventions, including computerized drill exercises, pencil-and-paper activities, and even mentally-stimulating games, have been found to be equally effective (Wykes et al., 2011). It is therefore possible that any kind of focused, cognitively-demanding activity will have equal beneficial effect on cognitive deficits of people with severe mental illness. (p. 447)

These discoveries provide the basis for a different pathway for the beneficial effect of creative writing in recovery from severe mental illness. It is possible that the act or process of writing and editing itself makes cognitive demands that are broadly equivalent to those made by the various CR programs that have been evaluated and found to be effective. The beneficial effects on cognition then flow through to functional advantages, which in turn yield benefits with respect to self-esteem and an enhanced sense of personal agency.

COMMENTARY ON THEORETICAL FRAMEWORKS

The theoretical frameworks discussed here provide coherent explanations for why creative writing might assist in recovery from mental illness, particularly for those people disposed toward creative writing. Narrative theory explains how writing can promote the development of a stronger identity; Lacanian theory explains how writing can compensate for, even if not fully repair, a rupture in symbolic functioning; and CR provides a framework for understanding how writing might help overcome cognitive deficits. While these frameworks might be understood to be competing models in that they offer alternative explanations, they are not mutually exclusive. It is possible that, for some people at least, writing can contribute to recovery at multiple levels.

Furthermore, there is no reason to suppose that these different explanations are equally relevant in any specific case. The benefits of writing are likely to depend on the characteristics of the individual engaged in writing. For example, not all people affected by severe mental illness have marked cognitive deficits. For such people, the benefits associated with creative writing are more likely to flow from either the development of narrative coherence and personal identity or the reduction of acute episodes. However, for a person struggling with problems of concentration, focus, and memory, the most important gains from writing might derive from its capacity to develop and enhance these basic cognitive functions.

How Can Creative Writing Be Most Effectively Used to Optimize Recovery in the Light of These Theoretical Frameworks?

As a consequence of studies by Eakin (1985, 1999, 2008), Alschuler (1997), and others, the process of writing narrative has assumed greater importance than content in contemporary understandings of writing therapy. Pennebaker (2000) argues that "catharsis or the venting of emotions" without cognitive processing has little therapeutic value, and individuals need to "build a coherent narrative that explains some past experience in order to benefit from writing" (pp. 10–11). Writing necessitates organizing events coherently and has the effect of providing a "sense of predictability and control" over a person's life; the life-writing process

> allows one to organise and remember events in a coherent fashion while integrating thoughts and feelings . . . [T]his gives individuals a sense of predictability and control over their lives. Once an experience has structure and meaning, it would follow that the emotional effects of that experience are more manageable. Constructing stories facilitates a sense of resolution, which results in less rumination and eventually allows disturbing experiences to subside gradually from conscious thought. Painful events that are not structured into a narrative format may contribute to the continued experience of negative thoughts and feelings. (Pennebaker & Seagal, 1999, p. 1243)

Underlying these arguments is a belief in the textuality of the self, and prominent novelists and poets, such as Celia Hunt and Fiona Sampson, researching the therapeutic effects of writing workshops have drawn on the work of Bollas (1993), Damasio (2000), and Milner (1952), among others, to argue that writing therapy in health-care settings assists in constructing a space in which more positive and less fragmented self-narratives can be achieved by clients (Hunt, 2000; Sampson, 2004).

Creative writing therapists informed by psychoanalytic theory have reported on the benefits of quite complex and sophisticated forms of writing, such as fictionalized autobiography (Hunt, 2000) and poetry (Hunt & Sampson, 1998; Lerner, 1978, 1981; Lester & Terry, 1992; Mazza, 1993, 1999, 2003; Penn & Frankfurt, 1994; Wright, 2004). Moreover, a growing number of researchers have argued that the greatest efficacy of writing therapy can be attained through the client being facilitated and guided toward crafted, disciplined, even reflexive writing. There is evidence that writing of stories that contain more "positive emotion words," increased "causal and insight words," and increased coherence are "strongly associated with improved health" (Pennebaker, 1997). However, the appropriate first step with clients might be to encourage brief, spontaneous, and unguided freewriting. Freewriting aids in overcoming the initial obstacle of a person paying too much attention to their inner critic or censor. The first unguided writing, therefore, can begin to achieve a sense of control over inner chaos, but such writing—which is not structured according to formal creative requirements—tends to be repetitive, unengaged, or emotionless and lacks deeper metaphorical resonance (Herman, 1992; Lindner, 2004). The next step, to rewrite and edit in a more formal and reflexive manner according to a few fundamental craft or technical conventions—such as structure, avoidance of cliché, use of concrete detail rather than abstraction, and observing the dictum to "demonstrate not state"—is a more assertive action that builds self-esteem (Hunt, 2000) and prepares work to a standard that is a product that can be seen by an audience (via newsletter, website, etc.), allowing the writer to connect with the external social world in a symbolic way.

A more crafted product requires more discipline and concentration on the part of the writer, and so agency is required (Chandler, 1990; Hunt, 2000; Jensen & Blair, 1997; Pollard, 1993). Crafted writing has the capacity for more layering of the work and strengthening of self-understanding (Penn & Frankfurt, 1994), and the shaping that goes into the work such as a beginning, middle, and end also provides shape and therefore coherence for the self.

> If we have at our disposal the techniques of poetry or prose fiction, we may find that crafting our words deepens their impact on us, or provides is with a metaphor or image of ourselves that is new . . . Through crafting, of course, we may shift the writing into a more structured form in which it can demand the attention of an audience, so that we are simultaneously using our writing as "art" and "therapy." (Hunt, 2000, p. 188)

There is emerging consensus in the United States and United Kingdom that there might be advantages if writing therapy is received from a facilitator who is herself or himself a trained writer who can work in collaboration with health-care professionals (Hunt & Sampson, 1998; McLoughlin, 2004). The trained creative writer represents literary rather than clinical authority and might be less constricting for the client. This is consistent with the findings from our pilot work described in the following chapter.

The distinguished UK poet Fiona Sampson has written about conducting writing workshops in a hospital setting. One of the participants, Sam Moran, gives a valuable account of his experience as a participant:

> Perhaps when I started going to the Kingfisher writing group I used my writing skills to express my personal feelings about my life and my mental health problems but it soon became quite obvious that this was not what it was all about: that I had other things to say, other stories to tell, because I am part of society not just part of my mental-health problems. It was like this for the other group members too . . . This wasn't just about therapy; the therapeutic aspect of creative writing is a by-product. This was about creativity itself. About knowing that . . . the work we were producing could stand on its own merits: worth being read, inescapably accessible to everyone. (Sampson, 2004, p. 105)

Sam describes previous occupational therapy writing groups as "fun but not very serious"; they did not sufficiently stress writing as a useful tool he could continue to pursue in his life. He contrasts this with the group led by the professional writer:

So what made this group different? Two things: first, all the members had a genuine interest in writing and, second, Fiona Sampson who led this group took us seriously. I can't emphasis this enough: straightaway she saw that we could write, that we were interested in writing for writing's sake, and that it wasn't beyond our capabilities to actually achieve something for ourselves from within the group. This was a creative writing group, not an exercise in psychobabble . . . with guidance I was beginning to find my own distinctive voice, we all were. (Sampson, 2004, pp. 106–109)

Sampson sums up the importance of this focus: "Like Sam, I would argue that writing in health and social care, as in all writings, must be about *writing* itself—about the transformative power of language—before it can enable any other kind of benefit" (p. 111). The Kingfisher Project was evaluated by peer-practitioner Graham Hartill, who concluded that

Any creative writing workshop demands a wide range of experience from its facilitator; never more so than in health-care contexts. He or she needs to be not only a good writer who knows the tricks of the trade of each writing genre, but also a good "presence," capable of holding a group (often comprised of seriously troubled individuals) together, of reading the situation for its possibilities and potential, and of enthusing people about what is going on. [The need to recognize] when language work is taking place, even when nothing is, or even can be, actually written down. (Hartill, 2001)

In a similar vein, Celia Hunt argues:

the facilitator has to suspend her own needs and tendencies (for example, the desire to please others or have power over them) and to sense intuitively when to distance herself and be quietly observant and when to intervene and be assertively active. Moving smoothly back and forth between these two states . . . she will create a framework within which people can feel not only free enough to engage with their own feelings . . . but safe enough to do so. (Sampson, 2004, p. 167)

DISCUSSION

I have identified three theoretical frameworks that explain why creative writing might play an important role in recovery from mental illness: development of personal identity, repair of symbolic functioning, and cognitive remediation. These theories propose that writing can contribute to the development of personal identity and a more coherent self, can contribute to the repair of symbolic functioning, and can remediate cognitive functioning.

When considered in the light of a possible genetic link between schizotypy and creativity, these theories help us to understand why writing is an important and valued form of self-expression for many people recovering from severe mental health problems, such as schizophrenia.

The first two theories focus on what might be termed *intrapsychic functioning*. They emphasize that writing contributes to the creation of intrapsychic coherence and the development of a more structured and stable personal identity. The first framework (the most developed at this stage) emphasizes the importance of narrative in this process and is commonly linked to narrative psychology and poststructuralist linguistic theory. The second emphasizes the capacity of writing to construct a replacement for a specific critical signifier that is thought to be absent in psychosis. The third theory, like the first, accepts the concept of the narrative construction of self but argues further that creative writing might operate as a form of cognitive remediation and mitigate some of the cognitive deficits characteristic of the negative symptoms of schizophrenia.

Clearly, then, these frameworks overlap and are not mutually exclusive, and it is not a priority to determine which has greater explanatory power. However, I have noted that while there is some suggestive evidence, especially with respect to narrative theories and cognitive remediation, there is no direct evidentiary link between writing and recovery processes for people affected by severe mental illness. I believe that this indicates a direction for future research.

I have argued that the therapeutic value of creative writing might be most effectively achieved when there is a focus on the process and techniques or craft of writing and not just on self-expression. When a person develops skill in writing process and technique builds, it is likely to enhance the capacity to develop and sustain a coherent and lively narrative. Equally importantly, these skills expand capacity for what could be termed *bricolage*. Bricolage requires the ability to make use of locally or informally available resources, and I believe that writing technique is, in part, concerned precisely with the development of this ability. Finally, I believe that a focus on process and technique—which itself imposes the discipline required by creative writing for problem solving, selection of material, and making meaningful patterns—might also optimize the cognitive remediation benefits associated with creative writing. The development of writing technique requires the development of cognitive procedures starting with basic processes, such as concentration, and then learning rules and more complex decision making concerning style and form.

It seems that creative writing has been underutilized in psychosocial rehabilitation. Yet of all the creative arts, writing is the least dependent on equipment and/or special environments. It therefore lends itself to deployment in a wide range of settings. Writing workshops are probably better provided by professional writers than by mental health professionals, especially when the focus is on process and technique, as I have argued is preferable in terms of effective outcomes. Most communities have a pool of professional or semiprofessional writers—for example, those who have achieved the level of expertise required to have their own creative work published—and who, with some training in provision of workshops and possibly in mental health first aid, could make a valuable contribution to psychosocial rehabilitation services.

ACKNOWLEDGMENT

An earlier version of some parts of this chapter appeared in articles by King, Neilsen, and White (2012) and Neilsen and Murphy (2008).

REFERENCES

Alschuler, M. (1997). Lifestories: Biography and autobiography as healing tools for adults with mental illness. *Journal of Poetry Therapy, 11*(2), 113–117. doi:10.1012/B:JOPT.0000010862.52199.b2

Bell, M., Zito, W., Greig, T., & Wexler, B. (2008). Neurocognitive enhancement therapy with vocational services: Work outcomes at two-year follow-up. *Schizophrenia Research, 105*(1–3), 18–29. doi:10.1016/j.schres.2008.06.026

Bollas, C. (1993). *Being a character: Psychoanalysis and self-experience.* London, England: Routledge.

Bruner, J. (2004). The narrative creation of self. In L. E. Angus & J. McLeod (Eds.), *The handbook of narrative and psychotherapy: Practice, theory and research* (pp. 3–14). London, England: Sage Publications.

Chandler, M. (1990). *A healing art: Regeneration through autobiography.* New York, NY: Garland.

Damasio, A. (2000). *The feeling of what happens: Body, emotions and the making of consciousness.* London, England: Vintage.

Davidson, L., & Strauss, J. (1992). Sense of self in recovery from severe mental illness. *British Journal of Medical Psychology, 65*(2), 131–145. doi:10.1111/j.2044-8341.1992.tb01693

Eakin, P. (1985). *Fictions in autobiography: Studies in the art of self-invention.* Princeton, NJ: Princeton University Press.

Eakin, P. (1999). *How our lives become stories: Making selves.* Ithaca, NY: Cornell University Press.

Eakin, P. (2008). *Living autobiographically: How we create identity in narrative.* Ithaca, NY: Cornell University Press.

Foucault, M. (1984). Space, knowledge and power. In H. Dreyfus & P. Rainbow (Eds.), *The Foucault reader* (pp. 239–256). New York, NY: Pantheon Books.

Hartill, G. (2001). *The Kingfisher Project: Evaluation.* Unpublished report.

Herman, J. (1992). *Trauma and recovery: The aftermath of violence—From domestic abuse to political terror.* New York, NY: Basic Books.

Hunt, C. (2000). *Therapeutic dimensions of autobiography in creative writing.* London, England: Jessica Kingsley.

Hunt, C., & Sampson, F. (Eds.). (1998). *The self on the page: Theory and practice of creative writing in personal development.* London, England: Jessica Kingsley.

Jensen, C., & Blair, S. (1997). Rhyme and reason: The relationship between creative writing and mental well-being. *British Journal of Occupational Therapy, 60*(12), 525–530. Retrieved from http://psycnet.apa.org/psycinfo/1999-13882-001

King, R. (2012). A bricoleur or two in the consulting room. *American Imago, 69*(4), 543–558. doi:10.1353/aim.2012.0024

King, R., Neilsen, P., & White, E. (2012). Creative writing in recovery from severe mental illness. *International Journal of Mental Health Nursing, 22*(5), 444–452. doi:10.1111/j.1447-0349.2012.00891.x

Lacan, J. (1977). On a question preliminary to any possible treatment of psychosis. In *Ecrits: A Selection* (pp. 198–249). London, England: Tavistock.

Lacan, J. (1993). *Seminar 3: The psychoses.* London, England: Routledge.

Lerner, A. (Ed.). (1978). *Poetry in the therapeutic experience.* Elmsford, NY: Pergamon Press.

Lerner, A. (1981). Poetry therapy. In R. Corsini (Ed.), *Handbook of innovative psychotherapies* (pp. 472–479). New York, NY: Wiley & Sons.

Lester, D., & Terry, R. (1992). The use of poetry therapy: Lessons from the life of Anne Sexton. *The Arts in Psychotherapy, 19*(1), 47–52. doi:10.1016/0197-4556(92)90063-T

Levi-Strauss, C. (1966). *The savage mind.* London, England: George Weidenfeld and Nicholson Ltd.

Lindner, V. (2004). The tale of two Bethanies: Trauma in the creative writing classroom. *New Writing: The International Journal for the Practice and Theory of Creative Writing, 1*(1), 6–14. doi:10.1080/14790720408668186

Lysaker, P., Wickett, A., Wilke, N., & Lysaker, J. (2003). Narrative incoherence in schizophrenia: The absent agent-protagonist and the collapse of internal dialogue. *American Journal of Psychotherapy, 57*(2), 153–166. Retrieved from http://www.ncbi.nlm.nih.gov/pubmed/12817547

McLoughlin, D. (2004). Any-angled light: Diversity and inclusion through teaching poetry in health and social care. In F. Sampson (Ed.). *Creative writing in health and social care* (pp. 170–188). London, England: Jessica Kingsley.

Mazza, N. (1993). Poetry therapy: Toward a research agenda for the 1990s. *Arts in Psychotherapy, 20*(1), 51–59. doi:10.1016/0197-4556(93)90031-V

Mazza, N. (1999). *Poetry therapy: Interface of the arts and psychology.* Boca Raton, FL: CRC Press.

Mazza, N. (2003). Editor's note. *Journal of Poetry Therapy, 16*(1), 1–4. doi:10.1080/08893670310001600792

McAdams, D. P. (2003). Identity and the life story. In R. Fivush & C. Haden (Eds.), *Autobiographical memory and the construction of a narrative self: Developmental and cultural perspectives.* Mahwah, NJ: L. Erlbaum.

Medalia, A., & Thysen, J. (2008). Insight into neurocognitive dysfunction in schizophrenia. *Schizophrenia Bulletin, 34*(6), 1221–1230. doi:10.1093/schbul/sbm144

Milner, M. (1952). *A life of one's own.* Harmondsworth, England: Penguin.

Neilsen, P., & Murphy, F. (2008). The potential role of life-writing therapy in facilitating "recovery" for those with mental illness. *Journal of Media and Culture, 11*(6). Retrieved from http://journal.media-culture.org.au/index.php/mcjournal/article/viewArticle/110

Penn, P., & Frankfurt, M. (1994). Creating a participant text: Writing, multiple voices, narrative multiplicity. *Family Process, 33*(3), 217–231. doi:10.1111/j.1545-5300.1994.00217.x

Pennebaker, J. W. (Ed.). (1995). *Emotion, disclosure and health.* Washington, DC: American Psychological Association.

Pennebaker, J. (1997). Writing about emotional experience as a therapeutic process. *Psychological Science, 8*(3), 162–166. doi:10.1111/j.1467-9280.1997.tb00403.x

Pennebaker, J. (2000). Telling stories: The health benefits of narrative. *Literature and Medicine, 19*(1), 3–18. doi:10.1353/lm.2000.0011

Pennebaker, J., & Seagal, J. (1999). Forming a story: The health benefits of narrative. *Journal of Clinical Psychology, 55*(10), 1243–1254. doi:10.1002/(SICI)1097-4679(199910)55:10 < 1243::AID-JCLP6 > 3.0.CO;2-N

Polkinghorne, D. (2004). Narrative therapy and postmodernism. In L. Angus & J. McLeod (Eds.), *The handbook of narrative and psychotherapy: Practice, theory and research* (pp. 53–70). London, England: Sage Publications.

Pollard, N. (1993). On doing the write thing. *Reading Therapy Newsletter, 5*(2), 8–9.

Ragland-Sullivan, E. (1990). Lacan's seminars on James Joyce: Writing as symptom and "singular solution." In R. Feldstein & H. Sussman (Eds.), *Psychoanalysis and . . .* (pp. 67–86). New York, NY: Routledge.

Roe, D., & Davidson, L. (2005). Self and narrative in schizophrenia: Time to author a new story. *Medical Humanities, 31*(2), 89–94. doi:10.1136/jmh.2005.000214

Sampson, F. (Ed.). (2004). *Creative writing in health and social care*. London, England: Jessica Kingsley.

Schafer, R. (1983). *The analytic attitude*. New York, NY: Basic Books.

Smyth, J. (1998). Written emotional expression: Effect size, outcome types, and moderating variables. *Journal of Consulting and Clinical Psychology, 66*(1), 174–184. doi:10.1037/0022-006X.66.1.174

Spence, D. (1982). *Narrative truth and historical truth*. New York, NY: Norton.

White, M., & Epston, D. (1990). *Narrative means to therapeutic ends*. New York, NY: W. W. Norton.

Wright, J., & Chung, M. (2001). Mastery or mystery? Therapeutic writing: A review of the literature. *British Journal of Guidance and Counselling, 29*(3), 277–291. doi:10.1080/03069880120073003

Wright, J. K. (2004). The passion of science, the precision of poetry: Therapeutic writing—A review of the literature. In G. Bolton, S. Howlett, C. Lago, & J. Wright (Eds.). *Writing cures: An introductory handbook of writing in counselling and therapy* (pp. 7–17). Hove, England: Brunner-Routledge.

Wykes, T., Huddy, V., Cellard, C., McGurk, S., & Czobor, P. (2011). A meta-analysis of cognitive remediation for schizophrenia: Methodology and effect sizes. *American Journal of Psychiatry, 168*(5), 472–485. doi:10.1176/appi.ajp.2010.10060855

Creative Writing

A Practice-Based Account of Designing and Facilitating Life-Writing Workshops for a Group With Severe Mental Illness

Philip Neilsen and Robert King

INTRODUCTION

This chapter is based on the experience and findings of a pilot project developed to investigate the feasibility of conducting writing workshops for people participating in psychosocial rehabilitation programs provided by a nongovernment agency in Brisbane, Australia. It was a qualitative study making use of observational data, interviews with participants, and informal reports. We did not seek to test theoretical models concerning the link between creative writing and recovery through the pilot project but rather to evaluate the immediate impact of a writing workshop.

The theory and empirical literature pertaining to writing therapy for psychosis or other kinds of severe mental illness can be summed up as proposing three theoretical frameworks. The first and most prominent model describes the relationship between the individual who develops a written narrative and the consolidation and strengthening of a coherent sense of self and personal identity. The second, drawing on Lacan, argues that a void in the internal symbolic order of an individual can be reconstituted or repaired by language in the form of engagement in creative writing. The third suggests that the practice of creative writing can be an effective form of cognitive remediation. As explained in the previous chapter, the three models overlap and are not mutually exclusive. Recent literature also suggests that enhancing the quality of craft and technique in such creative writing can produce the strongest benefits in terms of well-being and recovery, and that there is a useful role for the creative writing practitioner in working collaboratively with health professionals to guide this attention to craft.

MATERIALS AND METHODS, PARTICIPANTS, AND SETTING

The participants were 11 people who were engaged in one of two psychosocial rehabilitation programs provided by Richmond Fellowship Queensland, a major nongovernment provider of psychosocial rehabilitation for people with severe mental illness. Participants were predominantly female and ranged in age from young adults to older adults with most participants being middle aged. We did not collect diagnostic information, but advice provided by agency staff suggested that participants had diagnoses of schizophreniform disorders, major mood disorders, and/or personality disorders. The psychosocial rehabilitation program was designed for people with a high or moderately high level of impairment as a result of mental illness.

INTERVENTION

The workshops' content was based on principles and procedures I[1] had used in workshops for aspiring writers in both community and tertiary education settings. Robert King provided advice and suggestions regarding modifications for people affected by severe mental illness with particular emphasis on cognitive problems and personal vulnerabilities. I was able to play a major role in the design and implementation of the workshops as both an academic in the field of creative writing and a well-published author of poetry and fiction. I also had a long-standing interest in life writing and writing therapy.

The workshops consisted of three sessions over a period of three weeks. Each session lasted at least two hours. The focus was on writing technique rather than content. While the focus was on technique, participants were asked to engage in *life writing* (as I explained, this meant "telling a story from your life, and perhaps musing or commenting on it at the same time"). Participants were also encouraged to write on positive themes consistent with White and Epston's (1990) emphasis on the value of constructing or developing alternatives to the dominant (illness) narrative and in the expectation that such themes would contribute to a more enjoyable and recovery-promoting experience. The workshops were in part didactic with the writer using worksheets and examples to explain sentence structure, descriptive language, sequencing, and other technical issues affecting the quality of writing. All participants were provided with a writing kit—a pamphlet that provided written support for the didactic component. There was also a substantial interactive component of the workshops with participants encouraged to read their work, receive feedback from the writer and other participants, and give feedback to others. Between and after workshops, participants were encouraged to send work to the writer conducting the workshops for review and comment. The workshops were conducted in an informal manner with the writer reading some of his own work and sharing some anecdotes about his experience writing.

PREPARATION FOR AND DELIVERY OF THE WORKSHOPS

I was acutely aware that I had no formal training in delivering a program to clients with mental illness. I was counseled during several meetings with experienced psychologists and a social worker that the participants in the three workshops would largely be people who had degrees of difficulty in living independently and could well have perceptual problems, could misjudge signals from outside and inside the group, and could be taking medication that could affect their degree of engagement. Some clients could have impaired concentration and cognition and a deficit in volition. Participants needed to be free to leave and rejoin the workshops during the afternoon sessions. Attendance might well fall as the workshops progressed. Full ethical clearance was attained through the University of Queensland medical faculty (after providing detailed description of the content and conduct of the proposed workshops) and consent forms prepared for participants. I also consulted a valuable handbook that dealt with facilitation (King, Lloyd, & Meehan, 2007).

I was encouraged by accounts of therapeutic creative writing workshops conducted by writers in various mental health settings in the United Kingdom: Fiona Sampson and Celia Hunt especially have reported extensively in academic publications on the effectiveness of professional writers working collaboratively with health professionals (Hunt & Sampson, 1998; Hunt, 2000; Freely, 2004). Writer and translator Maureen Freely (2004) has observed perceptively that

> it's essential to take every piece of writing seriously, even if you have reservations about it. You can show that respect by giving your honest response to it, and then urging the writer to do more, to the degree that seems right and appropriate . . . Most important, you can make it clear to them that their accounts of what they've been through matter just as much or more than what the experts say about them. Working honestly with the written word means conducting a dialogue, so that . . . the therapist and the client, the doctor and the patient, become equal and cooperating partners, with shared values and agreed goals. When this happens, the patient-student-writer is no longer passive, no longer just a case for treatment, but recognised as fully human. (pp. 86–87)

My original workshop kit to be distributed to participants underwent some significant changes as I was counseled and prepared for the workshops. The major adjustment to my usual choice of material and approach was made in view of advice and references in the literature that the recounting of traumatic events can have a negative effect on some participants, at least in the short term. For the sake of both the individuals and the group as a whole, this was to be avoided. Accordingly, I changed my initial emphasis on encouraging participants to recount their traumatic experiences in a cathartic way (as suggested by the narrative psychology literature) to an emphasis on encouraging them to recount positive narratives from their lives—narratives of "recovery."

I was also counseled that clients with mental health problems might dwell on retelling their story—their case history—rather than reflecting upon it or using their creative and imaginative ability to shape a life story that was not a catalogue of their medical history. Subsequently, some participants did demonstrate a desire to retell their medical history or narrative—including a recurring theme of the difficulty in gaining continuity with one trusted medical professional. When this occurred, I gently guided these participants back to fashioning a different and more creative narrative with elements of scene creation, description, and so on. I did this by first listening intently to and acknowledging their medical narrative for a few minutes and then suggesting we try to move beyond that.

This simple strategy was largely successful; several participants commented explicitly that they were tired of having to retell their medical history to each new health professional they encountered in the hospital system, for example.

My principal uncertainty was whether I should conduct the workshops at the same level of complexity that I had in the past with groups of university students or community groups. While in both of those cohorts there will often be some participants with mental health issues, for the most part this possibility does not affect the level or kind of content of material discussed in workshops. But this pilot group all had been diagnosed with moderate to severe mental illness.

The fact that my credentials were as a published author and professor of creative writing, not as a health professional, was also a strong concern to me initially, as I have written elsewhere (Neilsen, 2008b). But the clients readily accepted me as someone who knew the difficulty of writing well and getting published. I stressed to them that my primary aim was to teach effective creative writing as an end in itself. That it might also be beneficial in health terms was stated to be a secondary consideration. An experienced health professional, Robert King, introduced me and briefly outlined the research aims of the workshops—including some attempt to measure qualitatively any possible benefits. It was my impression that the participants did not have a diminished sense of my usefulness because I was not a health professional. Their focus was on having the opportunity to practice creative writing and/or participate in a creative group activity.

As mentioned above, I had prepared a workshop kit of 15 pages for the participants. It contained the usual guidelines for effective writing—extracts from professional writers' published work (including an extract from my own published work—a matter of equity, since the participants were allowing me to read *their* work)—and a number of writing exercises. These exercises were chosen to illustrate fundamental but important creative writing techniques or strategies such as the use of description; the use of concrete rather than abstract words; keeping a unified narrative point of view in either first or third person; writing in scenes; showing the reader rather than telling them; and employing the overall narrative structure of a beginning, middle, and end. The kit contained some extracts from popular writers, including Bill Bryson's memoir *The Life and Times of the Thunderbolt Kid* and a descriptive passage from the first chapter of Charles Dickens's *Bleak House*. An extract from Inga Clendinnen's account in *Agamemnon's Kiss: Selected Essays* (2006) of her positive interaction with fellow cancer patients (a narrative with the underlying theme of recovery) was also valuable for the participants. I drew on principles of creating effective life writing that I have analyzed at length in a chapter of a creative writing text published more recently (Morley & Neilsen, 2012).

I stressed to the group that this material was very similar to that used with beginning writers among university students. I described the importance of life writing as follows:

> Life writing is simply telling a story from your life and perhaps musing or commenting on it at the same time. When your write a short account of something chosen from your life, you are making a pattern, using your memory, using your powers of description—you are being creative. You are being a storyteller. And story-telling is one very important thing that makes us humans different from all other animals—and it is a way we find a lot of meaning in our lives. (Neilsen, 2008a)

My central advice in the introduction to the kit was "just try to be as honest as you can—and to remember as well as you can . . . being honest and direct is both the best and the easiest way to write memoir" (Neilsen, 2008a). The only major difference between my approach with these clients and that with a university class was in the selection of possible topics offered. In keeping with the advice of the psychologists with whom I collaborated, the topics were predominantly positive, though one or two topics gave the opportunity to recount and/or explore a negative experience if the participant wanted to do so:

- A time when I was able to help another person

- A time when I realized what really mattered in life

- A time when I overcame a major difficulty

- A time when I felt part of a group or team

- A time when I knew what I wanted to do with my life

- A time when someone recognized a talent or quality of mine

- A time I did something that I was proud of

- A time when I learned something important to me

- A memorable time when I lived in a certain house or suburb

- A story that begins, "Looking back, I now understand that . . ."

The group expressed satisfaction with these topics, though they had the usual writing students' difficulty in choosing the one that best suited them. In the first two workshops, we worked our way through the kit; in the third workshop, two weeks later, each participant read their own work to the group and received feedback from their peers and from me. The feedback was encouraged to be constructive, and the group spontaneously adopted a positive reinforcement approach, applauding each piece of writing and finding aspects of each piece that they considered effective or easy to relate to.

WORKSHOP DYNAMICS

The venue for the workshops was a suburban house in the Logan area of Brisbane, Australia, used as a drop-in center for those with mental illness and with which the majority of the participants would be familiar. It had a large, breezy deck on which a roundtable configuration of seating was arranged. This veranda-type setting was sheltered enough to enable all to be heard easily and formal enough to emphasize this was a learning event taking place, yet it was also open enough to encourage a relaxed atmosphere.

The week before the first workshop, I visited the house to have lunch with a number of the participants. This gave me a sense of some of the participants' personalities, degree of engagement, and the way in which they related to each other; in turn, it enabled them to begin to have some familiarity with me and ask questions. As a relative novice at working with this kind of client, I found this experience extremely valuable, especially as it suggested that a reasonably high degree of communication and cognition would be possible and so reduced the anxiety I had about pitching the workshops at an appropriate level.

In the course of the first workshop, the most initially skeptical participant ended up being the most engaged contributor. A highly intelligent woman, she felt it would be too upsetting to write about negative events but ultimately wrote a very effective piece about the empowerment she gained from caring for a stray cat and locating the owner. Her narrative also expressed her realization that the pet was partly a replacement for spending time with her son, who lived in another state. Another strong participant previously had written a book-length narrative of her years of misdiagnoses and trauma in the hospital system before coming under the care of her current health professionals. The participant who had the least literacy skills was accepted by the group as an equal and after a while contributed enthusiastically. Though he refused to sign the consent form at the outset, he asked to do so at the close of the first afternoon.

The workshops were comprised of clients from two health provider organizations; at first, the two groups tended to speak primarily with those people they already knew (as in any such situation in the broader community), but by the third workshop, a sense of larger group identity was being manifested in their comments as they discussed what "the group" would like in the future—such as their work being published in some form.

It was clear that, as in a university setting, part of the beneficial effect of the workshops came from group and face-to-face interaction. It would be more difficult to have this dimension of benefit achieved via a web-based version of the workshops, though a chat room scenario would presumably go some way toward establishing a group feeling. Computer-mediated delivery would certainly suit participants who lacked mobility or who lived in the regions outside major cities. It is now well accepted that the Internet is a vital social networking tool, and an Internet-based version of the workshops could well be attempted in the future.

My own previous experience of community digital storytelling workshops (Neilsen, 2005) suggests that a high degree of technical proficiency cannot be expected throughout such a cohort, but with adequate technical support, a program (the usual short, self-written script, recorded voice-over, and still images scanned from the participants' photo albums, etc.) could make digital storytelling a further dimension of therapeutic life writing for clients with mental illness.

One of the most useful teaching techniques in a classroom setting is the judicious use of humor—in order to relax the group, to create a sense of sharing a perspective, and simply to make material more entertaining. I tested the waters at the outset by referring to the mental health worker sitting in the background and declaring—with some comic exaggeration—my concern that if I didn't run the workshops well, he would report adversely on me. There was general laughter and this expression of my vulnerability and self-deprecation seemed to defuse anxiety on the part of some participants. As the workshops progressed, I found I could use both humorous extracts of life writing and ad hoc comic comments (never at the expense of a participant) just as freely as in a university class. Participants themselves made some droll comments in the overall context of encouraging one other in their contributions, both oral and written.

Only one participant exhibited some temporary distress during one of the workshops. I was allowing another participant the freedom to digress from the main topic, and the participant beside me displayed agitation and sharply demanded we get back to the point.

I apologized and acknowledged I had not stayed as focused as I should have and returned the group's attention to the topic. I suspect I had a fortunate first experience of such arts therapy workshops and that this was largely due to the voluntary nature of the study, the fact that most of the participants brought a prior positive experience of the workshop scenario, and that they all had a prior interest in creative writing.

A positive outcome that I appreciated as a facilitator was that no participants left during the workshops. Though I had been prepared to curtail each session if interest flagged, workshops proceeded longer than the two hours allotted on each occasion.

DATA COLLECTION

Robert King used three kinds of data collection methods to evaluate the workshops: systematic observation of workshop process and activity, post-workshop telephone interviews with participants, and feedback from staff employed at the rehabilitation center. He observed that participants appeared to understand the writing tasks set during the group activity and engaged in tasks as requested. All the participants produced some writing, though the productivity was variable. His participant interviews yielded valuable insights.

The key themes to emerge from this analysis were: it was especially valuable working with a real writer rather than a mental health professional; the informal, friendly style of the workshops was helpful; it was good to hear examples of the writer's own work; it was useful focusing on technique, and this helped improve writing; it was good to hear other participants reading their work; the writer was respectful and encouraging; the workshops were a positive and helpful experience; it was good getting personal feedback on writing; and it would be valuable to have additional workshops. Participants made several suggestions for minor modifications or improvements, but none of the participants had a generally negative experience and most were very enthusiastic. Several asked if a way could be found to show their work more widely, such as via a newsletter.

Overall, the evaluation revealed that the workshops promoted a high level of engagement and participation and were rated highly by both participants and staff. The findings suggest that a key component of the success of the workshops were that they were conducted by a person whose expertise was in creative writing rather than in mental health. This enabled participants to identify as writers rather than people affected by mental illness. It also retained a focus on technique rather than content. Participants had a genuine desire to improve their writing style and were not for the most part seeking help with content (King, Neilsen, & White, 2012).

CONCLUSION

The pilot study had a limited ambition, which was to demonstrate the feasibility of this kind of writing workshop. We felt it was broadly successful in doing this, though the sample was small and drawn from just two rehabilitation services. Our conclusion that the involvement of a professional writer was important suggests that recovery involves the development of an identity separate from that of being a person with an illness.

When health professionals or disability support workers provide activities, such as a writing workshop, there is a risk that identification with the illness is reinforced. When a professional writer provides a similar activity, it is the person's identify as a writer that is reinforced rather than his or her identity as a person with an illness.

The next step is research leading to the development of an evidence base for the effectiveness of such workshops. Well-designed studies should make use of an active control group so that it is possible to identify effects that are specific to the creative writing activity rather than a nonspecific response to a group rehabilitation program. Measurement of cognitive change, as well as the use of measures of functioning and personal recovery, would enable testing of a model that proposes cognitive gains as a mediator for functional recovery.

ACKNOWLEDGMENT

The authors would like to thank Seiji Humphries from the Richmond Fellowship Queensland, which hosted the workshops described in this chapter.

NOTE

1. Philip Neilsen is the author of this chapter except as otherwise noted.

REFERENCES

Clendinnen, I. (2006). *Agamemnon's kiss: Selected essays.* Melbourne, Australia: Text Publishing Company.

Freely, M. (2004) Writing as therapeutic practice. In F. Sampson (Ed.), *Creative writing in health and social care.* London, England: Jessica Kingsley.

Hunt, C. (2000). *Therapeutic dimensions of autobiography in creative writing.* London, England: Jessica Kingsley.

Hunt, C., & Sampson, F. (Eds.). (1998). *The self on the page: Theory and practice of creative writing in personal development.* London, England: Jessica Kingsley.

King, R., Lloyd, C., & Meehan, T. (2007) *Handbook of psychosocial rehabilitation.* Oxford, England: Blackwell Publishing.

King, R., Neilsen, P., & White, E. (2012). Creative writing in recovery from severe mental illness. *International Journal of Mental Health Nursing, 22*(5), 444–452. doi:10.1111/j.1447-0349.2012.00891.x

Morley, D., & Neilsen, P. (Eds.). (2012). *The Cambridge companion to creative writing.* Cambridge, England: Cambridge University Press.

Neilsen, P. (2005). Digital storytelling as life writing: Self-construction, therapeutic effect, textual analysis leading to an enabling "aesthetic" for the community voice. *Proceedings from the Speculation and Innovation (SPIN).*

Neilsen, P. (2008a). *Workshop kit.* Unpublished.

Neilsen, P. (2008b). The potential role of life writing therapy in facilitating "recovery" for those with mental illness. *Journal of Media and Culture, 11*(6). Retrieved from http://journal.media-culture.org.au/index.php/mcjournal/article/viewArticle/110

White, M., & Epston, D. (1990). *Narrative means to therapeutic ends.* New York, NY: W. W. Norton.

CHAPTER 9

Music Therapy and Mental Health Recovery

What Is the Evidence?

Claire Stephensen and Felicity Baker

WHAT IS MUSIC THERAPY?

Music therapy is "a research-based practice and profession in which music is used to actively support people as they strive to improve their health and wellbeing" (Australian Music Therapy Association, 2013). Music is used intentionally to establish a therapeutic relationship with individuals or groups of people to improve or maintain the physical, emotional, cognitive, psychosocial, communicative, cultural, aesthetic, and spiritual well-being of people across the lifespan. People with autism and developmental disabilities, mental health disorders, substance use disorders, dementia, cancer and degenerative diseases, and neurological injury or diseases may benefit from participation in a music therapy program.

Evidence of the effectiveness of music therapy in the recovery of people with mental health disorders is increasing. Neuroimaging studies indicate that neural networks responsible for music processing are widely distributed throughout the brain (e.g., Platel, Baron, Desgranges, Bernard, & Eustache, 2003), suggesting music can stimulate brain activity in people affected by dysfunction from varying neural networks. For example, music stimulates the neural networks responsible for pleasure and reward (the mesolimbic system) and emotions (Blood & Zatorre, 2001) and is therefore beneficial in addressing avoidance of emotions associated with substance use disorder, anxiety, and depression (Baker, Gleadhill, & Dingle, 2007; Dingle, Gleadhill, & Baker, 2008). Brain imaging studies show that depression can present with lower activity in the left side of the brain, reducing capacity to express and process emotions (Fachner, Gold, & Erkkila, 2013). There is emerging evidence that music therapy significantly improves symmetry in the brain (Fachner et al., 2013).

MUSIC THERAPY METHODS IN RECOVERY

Music therapists practice according to various theoretical and psychological orientations. At the most fundamental level, approaches to practice are categorized according to how music is understood within the therapy context. Some clinicians use music as a catalyst, a primer for stimulating the emotions, to bring what is unconscious to the preconscious for further processing (Baker, 2013a). These emotional responses are then transformed into verbal reflections that offer participants[1] opportunities to gain insight into their feelings, experiences, and life contexts and focus on problem solving, improved mood, and coping skills. Such music plus verbal reflection approach has been given the label of music *in* therapy (Bruscia, 1998).

In contrast, music *as* therapy subscribes to the notion that it is the transformative power of music itself and the musical interactions between a therapist and participant that facilitate changes in the well-being of the therapy participants (Bruscia, 1998). While some dialogue may follow the music interventions, it is through music itself that the participant experiences the direct effects of music and musical interactions.

Active Music Therapy Methods

Through active music therapy interventions, the participant and therapist enter into an active relationship with music—and thereby create music independently or collaboratively. Clinical improvisation is inarguably the most researched intervention in music therapy. An improvisation is a creative musical activity where music is created spontaneously with no predetermined musical outcome and without expectation of reproducing it at a later moment. An improvisation becomes clinical when the spontaneous music creation between therapist and participant(s) has specific therapeutic intentions underpinning it. The process is systematic, it is "purposeful, temporally organized, methodical, knowledge-based, and regulated" (Bruscia, 1998, p. 26). Clinical improvisations are designed to engage participants in a musical interaction with the therapist or others that leads to the exploration of ways of relating to others, of experiencing positive and/or challenging experiences, stimulating emotional responses, or gaining insight into the self or others (Bruscia, 1987). During clinical improvisation, the therapist purposefully responds to the participants by imitating, reflecting, grounding, or extending their musical contributions to create empathy or a musical space for safe exploration (Bruscia, 1987).

Therapeutic songwriting is a music therapy method whereby the therapist and participant(s) cocreate lyrics and music to address a range of needs (Baker & Wigram, 2005). Songwriting is typically used to promote feelings of mastery, self-confidence, self-esteem, and a sense of self; to externalize thoughts, fantasies, and emotions; to tell their story; and gain personal insights (Baker, Wigram, Stott, & McFerran, 2008). Through rewriting the words to precomposed songs or creating new lyrics and music (Baker, Wigram, Stott, & McFerran, 2009), participants can "find their song." The music created during the process can intensify the emotional expression embedded in the lyrics, help overcome blocks, express (musical) identity, heighten climax and resolution of issues, and communicate the inner world for the participant (Baker, 2013a). Further, the song products can have additional therapeutic benefits beyond their initial creation, including providing opportunities to share their song with significant others, and function as a transitional object when reintegrating into the community following inpatient discharge (Baker, 2013b).

Receptive Music Therapy Methods

During receptive music therapy, the participants are recipients of live or recorded music (Grocke & Wigram, 2007). Bruscia (1998) suggests that "the client listens to music and responds to the experience silently, verbally or in another modality" such as drawing, music improvisation, journaling/writing, lyric writing, painting, movement, or dancing (pp. 120–121). While music is considered the focus in therapy, these other processing modalities offer opportunities for the participant to have insight into the meaning of the experience and its relevance to their past, present, or future.

Lyric analysis or song lyric discussion are music therapy methods whereby the therapist or participant purposefully selects a song for participant(s) to listen to and then engages the participants in a discussion about the lyric's meaning—the narrative, feelings, or message of the song—and relevance to their lives and context (Silverman, 2009). For example, "Under the Bridge" (Red Hot Chili Peppers, 1991) stimulates discussion about depression and loneliness and "The Drugs Don't Hurt" (The Verve, 1997) facilitates reflections on drug addiction (Baker & Tamplin, 2006).

Imaginal listening involves "the use of music listening to evoke and support imaginal processes or inner experiences" (Bruscia, 1998, p. 125). It facilitates increased self-awareness, psychological and/or physical relaxation, or autobiographical recall. The therapist will select music to suit the therapeutic intention and then facilitate a relaxation induction so that the participant(s) listens to the music in a highly relaxed state. At the end of the music, the therapist engages participant(s) in a discussion or creative activity, such as mandala drawing, so they can connect their imagery with their own life experiences (Grocke & Wigram, 2007). In directed imagery, the therapist incorporates verbal prompts or a guided script to support the participant(s) imagery experiences. Experiences include visual or autobiographical imagery, emotions and feelings, body sensations, or somatic sensations (Grocke & Wigram, 2007).

MUSIC THERAPY APPROACHES IN RESEARCH AND PRACTICE

Music therapists practice across all levels of treatment and recovery in mental health and are employed in acute psychiatric wards, outpatient psychiatric units, specialized psychiatric units, community centers, and private practice settings. Within these settings, music therapists identify with single or multiple philosophical orientations, including but not limited to behavioral, cognitive, psychodynamic, humanistic, biomedical, or ecological paradigms (Wigram, Nygaard Pedersen, & Bonde, 2002).

Cognitive behavioral music therapy (CBMT) combines theories of cognitive, behavioral, and music therapies to affect a change in cognition and behavior. The CBMT framework is based on the assumption that music elicits physiological, emotional, cognitive, and behavioral responses, and the premise of CBMT is to challenge or restructure maladaptive thinking and establish healthy behaviors and coping strategies.

Within mental health recovery, CBMT sessions embed psychoeducation principles within music therapy interventions. Songwriting, lyric analysis, clinical improvisation, and music games are paired with verbal processing and CBT oriented counseling (Silverman, 2009). CBMT sessions aim to explore and manage emotions, enhance communication styles and strategies, improve planning and scheduling skills, address cognitive distortions, promote change, and enhance self-esteem and self-identity (Baker et al., 2007).

Thaut (1999) defined neurologic music therapy (NMT) as the "therapeutic application of music to cognitive, sensory, and motor dysfunctions due to neurologic disease of the human nervous system" (p. 7). NMT is based on a neuroscience model of music perception, music production, and the "influence of music on functional changes in the nonmusical brain and behavior functions" (p. 8). Due to music's shared neural networks, Thaut (2008) reports that music optimizes neuroplasticity and drives retraining in critical brain networks. Neurologic music therapists draw from nine evidence-based NMT cognitive training techniques to enhance attention, sensory modulation, memory, executive function, and psychosocial behavior. Techniques integrate music therapy techniques with evidence from neuropsychological practice and research (Thaut, 2008).

Guided imagery and music (GIM—The Bonny Model) is a receptive approach in which specifically sequenced classical music programs are used to stimulate imagery, memories, and feelings so they can be made conscious and then explored with an expanded awareness (Bruscia & Grocke, 2002). The guided music experiences enable participants to discover their own answers through recognizing, feeling, reflecting, and processing emotions in a constructive way. GIM assists with resolving relationship issues and addressing depression, anxiety, grief and loss, and stress-related problems. It is important to note that GIM is not recommended for participants with severe mental illness because of its capacity to bring unconscious distressing thoughts, feelings, and memories into conscious awareness.

Creative music therapy (CMT) is an active music therapy approach in which music is used *as* therapy within a humanistic philosophy (Wigram et al., 2002). During CMT, creative improvisation facilitated by the therapist(s) engages participants in a music experience to foster verbal, nonverbal, or musical communication; enhance emotional expression and spontaneity; support change; and allow an individual to engage more creatively and resourcefully in life.

Two other improvisational models of music therapy include analytically oriented music therapy (AMT—The Priestly Model) and free improvisation therapy (FIT—Alvin model). Both are grounded in psychoanalytical and analytical theories but have unique histories and development. AMT has more recently incorporated communication and developmental theories, particularly around psychosocial and personality development (Wigram et al., 2002). It is based on therapeutic improvisation and has been specifically developed for people with a range of mental health diagnoses. AMT belongs to the music *in* therapy cluster and therefore is only suitable for participants who are able to engage in a therapeutic dialogue before and after music interactions (Wigram et al., 2002). FIT has remained grounded in Freud's psychoanalytical theories on the unconscious and may be appropriate for those who are nonverbal since verbal processing is not required. Clinical improvisation within the FIT approach is used without rules, restrictions, directions, or guidelines by the therapist.

The concept of community music therapy (CoMT) is one of the new forces in music therapy theory and practice that has evolved from traditional and cultural applications of music for health outcomes within a community context (Stige & Aarø, 2012). Stige (2003) proposed that community music therapy involves a planned process of collaboration between participant and therapist with a specific focus on sociocultural, communal, and ecological change. CoMT practice is guided by seven principles: Participatory, Resource-oriented, Ecological, Performative, Activist, Reflective, and Ethics-driven, which form the acronym PREPARE (Stige & Aarø, 2012). CoMT encourages active music making (or *musiking*) whereby usually unheard individual and collective voices maybe expressed and heard beyond the boundaries of therapy (Stige & Aarø, 2012).

The resource-oriented music therapy approach researched and practiced by Rolvsjord (2010) is based on philosophies of empowerment and positive psychology and oriented toward participant strengths and potentials as opposed to focusing on problems or deficits. Four principles characterize Rolvsjord's resource-oriented music therapy approach: music therapy nurtures strengths, resources, and potentials; music therapy involves collaboration rather than interventions; music therapy views the individual within his or her context; and music is seen as a resource (p. 74). In resource-oriented music therapy, specific techniques are not defined, as the emphasis is on collaboration and mutuality within the therapeutic relationship and process of change.

CURRENT EVIDENCE

Classification and diagnosis of mental illness is currently under debate among mental health professionals. Similarly, there are contrasting views about what orientation is most suitable for practice in mental health. To accommodate for varying views, we have synthesized the literature according to symptoms and clinical presentation rather than by diagnosis or orientation.[2] Our literature synthesis was undertaken systematically and cross-checked by both authors to ensure all evidence supporting or refuting the benefits of music therapy was identified and reported in this chapter.

Feeling, Expressing, and Managing Emotions

Over the last decade, studies have concluded that music has the capacity to elicit and modulate emotions by stimulating neurobiological change. Studies have demonstrated that music listening increases levels of dopamine (Menon & Levitin, 2005) and serotonin (Evers & Suhr, 2000) and reduces levels of peripheral beta-endorphin (McKinney, Tims, Kumar, & Kumar, 1997), cortisol (Kreutz, Bongard, Rohrmann, Hodapp, & Grebe 2004), and epinephrine and norepinephrine—all of which are key functions in psychiatric medications to decrease stress and improve mood.

People with mental health difficulties experience a myriad of emotional symptoms including low or repressed mood, mania, anxiety, depression, extreme feelings of guilt and shame, and excessive anger (American Psychiatric Association, 1994). Some therapies may focus on immediate mood modulation or suppression while others target longer-term adjustment to mood and enhanced coping skills. Thaut (2005) notes that music-based "emotional and mood experiences can be guided to help an individual a) experience, b) identify, c) express different emotions verbally or non-verbally, d) perceive emotional communications of others, and e) modulate (i.e. freely control, adjust or adapt appropriately) one's emotional behavior" (p. 98).

Emotional expression naturally occurs when engaging in creative activities; however, through the therapeutic relationship, music therapy allows one to experience emotional expression within a limited environment and explore and overcome barriers to self-expression, such as conflicting core beliefs and values or negative past experiences. Iliya (2011) explored the experiences of music therapy with men diagnosed with alcohol misuse, a forensic history, or psychotic episodes through seven case studies. Following voice-centered music psychotherapy, the men laughed more and presented with greater emotional expression, allowing them to access and express a greater range and depth of feelings.

Studies show that music therapy interventions promote experiences of being in the present (Ansdell, Davidson, Magee, Meehan, & Procter, 2010; Grocke, Bloch, & Castle, 2009), improve relaxation (Chou & Lin, 2006; Lipe et al., 2012), and reduce anxiety (Fachner et al., 2013). Music therapy directly affects changes in stabilization (McCaffrey, Edwards, & Fannon, 2011) and regulation (Degmečić, Požgain, & Filaković, 2005) of mood and emotions and offers participants opportunities to experience the full spectrum of positive and negative emotions (Baker et al., 2007).

Cognitive Function

When in an acute phase of illness, participants may present with hypo- or hyperaroused states with limited capacity to engage in cognitive tasks inside or outside of therapy (Maxmen & Ward, 1995). Music directly affects physiological functions involved in arousal, which enables music therapists to use live or recorded music to engage the participant and move with them toward optimal engagement in therapy (Thaut, 2008). From this optimal state, music therapy interventions may engage higher cognitive functions such as learning, memory, attention, problem solving, organization, and decision making (Thaut, 2008). Music therapy can address cognitive skills that have been compromised as a consequence of trauma or stress, psychosis, or medication side effects.

Degmečić et al. (2005) proposed that music therapy interventions provide opportunities for people to explore cognitive patterns related to self-esteem, self-awareness and insight, concentration and attention, support healthy thinking, reality testing, and problem-solving skills. Clinical studies of music therapy with people with mental illness support their propositions and indicate notable increases in self-confidence and self-esteem (Baker et al., 2008; Iliya, 2011) and motivation for change (McCaffrey et al., 2011). Similarly, studies conclude that music therapy interventions support improvements in insight and rational thinking (Baker et al., 2008; Silverman, 2003) and changing thought patterns (Loue, Mendez, & Sajatovic, 2008).

Meaning and Purpose

Meaning and purpose are recognized as integral factors for those seeking happiness and quality of life (Seligman, 2011). While meaning and purpose are subjective, therapies commonly use terms such as *values*, *spirituality*, *identity*, *meditation*, and *mindfulness* to describe the concept. Cultivating meaning and purpose requires one to develop a sense of self-identity, self-awareness, a positive self-image, a culture of hope, and a spiritual connection. Several studies illustrate how music therapy significantly facilitates the development or restoration of self-awareness and identity (Baker & MacDonald, 2013a, 2013b; Baker et al.,

2008; McCaffrey et al., 2011; Vander Kooij, 2009). Through a lyric analysis of songs written in therapy by participants experiencing severe and enduring mental illness, Grocke et al. (2009) revealed that participants perceived religion and spirituality as sources of support. Though not explored thoroughly in the mental health literature, there is growing evidence to support that music therapy significantly improves spiritual connection for those in palliative care and oncology settings (Cook & Silverman, 2013).

Social Engagement

Human beings are wired for social connection. The connection that human beings experience during interactions can regulate (or dysregulate) physiological systems, emotions, immunity, and thinking patterns (Goleman, 2006). Therapeutic interactions offer an opportunity for physiological and emotional regulation to occur while allowing one to develop a stronger understanding of themselves, others, and their environment.

Festivals, rituals, and traditions practiced across the world bring people together and connect them through the power of music (Packer & Ballantyne, 2010). Porges, the psychiatrist and researcher behind the Polyvagal Theory (Ridder, 2011), refers to the capacity of music and specifically music therapy to influence and regulate physiological responses to stress or trauma. Such regulation allows participants to engage in social interactions in situations where they may not have been able to otherwise.

Ansdell et al. (2010) noted the importance of the relational aspects of music therapy: "The music within a therapeutic musical relationship seems to be able to take the dysregulated person from somewhere to somewhere better" (p. 23). Current research shows that music therapy allowed participants to experience a more active and improved social life (Cathro & Devine, 2012; Dingle, Brander, Ballantyne, & Baker, 2013; Iliya, 2011; Ulrich, Houtmans, & Gold, 2007), to (re)establish stronger family and peer relationships (Degmečić et al., 2005), and significantly increase support from friends (Grocke et al., 2009). Consequently there was a decrease in feelings of isolation (Iliya, 2011) and enhanced sense of belonging (Lipe et al., 2012; Dingle et al., 2008; Dingle et al., 2013), and significant improvements in social functioning (Mössler, Chen, Heldal, & Gold, 2011).

These studies show promising evidence for the use of music therapy to promote social relationships, build stronger support networks, and provide opportunities for social inclusion. Through the culturally and socially appropriate medium of music, the interventions can also be extended into community participation and existing resources within communities.

Promoting Independence

Living with a mental health condition often leads to feelings of disempowerment and a fractured sense of self. When working toward recovery, music therapy programs often target independent living rather than dependence on a service. For example, music therapy can offer opportunities for autonomy and informed decision making, build existing strengths, empower, and enable participants to self-actualize (Rolvsjord, 2010). This can be achieved through offering psychoeducation (Silverman, 2009) or through a collaborative therapeutic relationship fostered during the therapy process (Rolvsjord, 2010). Music therapists often report that music therapy builds on participants' existing strengths and capacities. Baker et al. (2008) surveyed

477 music therapists across the globe (103 worked in psychiatry) about their use of songwriting in therapy. Clinicians frequently reported that songwriting aimed to assist participants to experience mastery and to empower them through opportunities for decision making.

Qualitative studies of participants' perceptions have revealed that music therapy assists in participants regaining a healthy identity, as well as having the opportunity to have enough choice, develop independence, and make decisions (Cathro & Devine, 2012; Degmečić et al., 2005; McCaffrey et al., 2011). Other studies found engagement in music therapy leads to participants feeling more active outside of music therapy (Cathro & Devine, 2012), owning responsibility and taking charge of recovery (McCaffrey et al., 2011), and actively journeying from "illness" to "health" (Vander Kooij, 2009). Ulrich et al. (2007) reported that music therapy increased participants' abilities to adapt to the social environment in the community after discharge from hospital. Quantitative self-reports show significant improvement in awareness and use of internal resources (Korlin & Wrangsjo, 2002).

Adaptive and Maladaptive Behaviors

When people experience psychological, emotional, social, or cognitive disturbances, they may present with behaviors outside of social norms. The behaviors (whether conscious or not) can be a natural response to, compensation for, or a way to cope with the experience of the illness. Some people present with acts of self-harm or suicide, addictive or obsessive behaviors, dissociation, or avoiding or escaping certain experiences (American Psychiatric Association, 1994).

The strategic use of music can bring awareness to participants' behaviors, inhibit undesired behaviors, and initiate and/or sustain appropriate behaviors. Within the mental health framework, music therapists usually examine and explore the root of the behavior alongside other elements of mental health recovery (i.e., social, emotional, cognitive, etc.). Some examples of behavioral change evident in the literature include developing and using new coping strategies inside and outside of treatment (Degmečić et al., 2005; Lipe et al., 2012); increased ability to manage self-care (Lipe et al., 2012); improved attendance, motivation, or engagement in therapy (Baker et al., 2007; McCaffrey et al., 2011; Silverman, 2011); and adopting positive forms of behavior (Degmečić et al., 2005; Mössler et al., 2011). In a study of participants with dual diagnosis of mental illness and substance use disorder, participants recognized that music therapy assisted them in exploring emotions without the use of substances (Baker et al., 2007).

Psychosis

Evidence suggests that most participants experience relief from psychotic symptoms when prescribed antipsychotic medications. However, some people experience an increase in negative symptoms while on medication while others report recovering without medications at all (Maxmen & Ward, 1995). A recent neuroimaging study may explain why music decreases negative symptoms of schizophrenia. Menon and Levitin (2005) found that music listening stimulates the affective and motivational neural systems of the brain that are dysfunctional in people with schizophrenia. Therefore, stimulating these neural systems through engagement in music may reverse some of the neural deficits responsible for schizophrenia.

Systematic reviews and meta-analyses by Gold, Solli, Kruger, and Lie (2009) and Mössler et al. (2011) conclude that music therapy added to standard care has strong and significant effects on global state, general symptoms and negative symptoms (e.g., affective flattening, poor social relationships, and loss of interest and motivation). Another self-report study of people experiencing acute schizophrenia found negative symptoms were reduced in those participating in music therapy (Ulrich et al., 2007).

Silverman and Marcionetti (2005) explored the impact of music listening and active music making on managing auditory hallucinations in participants diagnosed with a range of psychotic disorders. Participants engaged in a single music therapy session all reported a reduction in auditory hallucinations and motivation to strategically use music to reduce auditory hallucinations in the future. Further, Silverman (2003) conducted a meta-analysis to determine how music influences psychotic symptoms and concluded that both live and recorded music reduced symptoms of and were effective in managing psychosis. While there were no significant differences between live and recorded music, Silverman argued that live music employs multiple senses and is therefore more likely to ground participants in reality. Further research is required to understand the workings and effects of music on the experience of psychosis.

Physical and Somatic Symptoms

Those experiencing mental health challenges may present with low or high energy, fatigue, pain, discomfort, sleeping difficulties, and many other physical or psychosomatic disturbances (American Psychiatric Association, 1994). Music listening is effective in decreasing pain, blood pressure, breathing, and heart rates (Lin et al., 2011) and some researchers have explored music therapy's impact on the relief of physical symptoms specific to mental health.

Studies have found that music regulates hormone levels associated with sleep quality while also inducing relaxation and distraction from anxious thoughts (e.g., Stefano, Zhu, Cadet, Salamon, & Mantione, 2004). However, at present, there are no music therapy sleep studies associated specifically with mental health difficulties.

Despite extensive investigations into music's effect on pain across multiple medical contexts (Mitchell & MacDonald, 2012), the full potential for music therapy to assist with psychosomatic pain management is not yet known. Some studies have highlighted its impact on the qualitative experience of pain. For example, Chou and Lin (2006) explored the effects of GIM programs on head, neck, and shoulder pain and found participants experienced less pain. Grocke et al. (2009) found statistically significant effects on self-rated physical pain after participants with severe and enduring mental illness engaged in a community based music therapy program.

Changes to somatic symptoms such as cardiovascular, gastrointestinal, respiratory, neurological, and headache have been measured in a small number of studies. A study by Korlin and Wrangsjo (2002) found statistically significant effects of weekly GIM on somatization with participants who experienced depression, anxiety, and phobias. Further research is needed to determine the full potential of music therapy to address the physical and somatic symptoms of people with mental illness.

Dose Response

Gold et al. (2009) conducted a meta-analysis of music therapy trials to explore the dose–response relationship of participants with a mental health diagnosis. Results demonstrated that music therapy had strong and significant dose–effect relationships for general, negative, and depressive symptoms as well as functioning. The findings indicated that a small effect occurs after 3 to 10 sessions, while large clinical effects emerge when participants attend 16 to 51 sessions of group and/or individual music therapy.

CONCLUSION

According to current evidence, music therapy is an effective therapy in the treatment of people with mental illness. Some reviews and trials have explored the impact of music therapy with standard care against standard care alone. Among these studies, there have been nonsignificant differences between groups but with higher effects noted in global state, negative symptoms, general mental state, depression, and social functioning for those in the music therapy condition (Maratos, Gold, Wang, & Crawford, 2008; Mössler et al., 2011). Further, Silverman (2011) conducted a registered music therapist comparing psychoeducational group music therapy to standard psychoeducation groups with a significant effect noted for working alliance and nonsignificant effect for attendance rates, knowledge of psychoeducation topic, enjoyment, and verbal engagement in those attending the music therapy program.

The current evidence is indeed promising, but further empirical research is needed to understand the full potential of music therapy in mental health recovery.

NOTES

1. Several terms have been used in the literature to refer to the people participating in a therapeutic context—participant, client, patient, and resident. In this chapter, we have chosen to refer to them as participants unless we are quoting an author directly.

2. Please note that the evidence presented does not include key literature from psychological trauma, addiction, or dementia and has a specific focus on adult mental health (rather than infant, child, or youth).

REFERENCES

American Psychiatric Association. (1994). *Diagnostic and statistical manual of mental disorders: DSM-IV*. Washington, DC: Author.

Ansdell, G., Davidson, J., Magee, W., Meehan, J., & Procter, S. (2010). From "this f***ing life" to "that's better" . . . in four minutes: An interdisciplinary study of music therapy's "present moments" and their potential for affect modulation. *Nordic Journal of Music Therapy, 19*(1), 3–28. doi:10.1080/08098130903407774

Australian Music Therapy Association. (2013). Defining music therapy. *What is music therapy?* Melbourne, Australia: Author. Retrieved from http://www.austmta.org.au/content/what-music-therapy

Baker, F. (2013a). What about the music? Music therapists' perspectives of the role of music in the therapeutic songwriting process. *Psychology of Music.* doi:10.1177/0305735613498919

Baker, F. (2013b). The ongoing life of participant-composed songs within and beyond the clinical setting. *Musicae Scientiae, 17*(1), 40–56. doi: 10.1177/1029864912471674

Baker, F., Gleadhill, L., & Dingle, G. (2007). Music therapy and emotional exploration: Exposing substance abuse clients to the experiences of non-drug induced emotions. *Arts in Psychotherapy, 34*(4), 321–330. doi:10.1016/j.aip.2007.04.005

Baker, F., & MacDonald, R. (2013a). Flow, identity, achievement, satisfaction and ownership during therapeutic songwriting experiences with university students and retirees. *Musicae Scientiae, 17*(2), 129–144. doi:10.1177/1029864913476287

Baker, F., & MacDonald, R. (2013b). Students' and retirees' experiences of creating personally meaningful songs within a therapeutic context. *Arts & Health, 35*(1), 67–82. doi:10.1080/17533015.2013.808254

Baker, F., & Tamplin, J. (2006). *Music therapy in neurorehabilitation: A clinician's manual.* London, England: Jessica Kingsley.

Baker, F., & Wigram, T. (Eds.). (2005). *Song writing methods, techniques and clinical applications for music therapy clinicians, educators and students.* London, England: Jessica Kingsley.

Baker, F., Wigram, T., Stott, D., & McFerran, K. (2008). Therapeutic songwriting in music therapy: Part 1. Who are the therapists, who are the clients, and why is songwriting used? *Nordic Journal of Music Therapy, 17*(2), 105–123. doi:10.1080/08098130809478203

Baker, F., Wigram, T., Stott, D., & McFerran, K. (2009). Therapeutic songwriting in music therapy: Comparing the literature with practice across diverse populations. *Nordic Journal of Music Therapy, 18*(1), 32–56. doi:10.1080/08098130802496373

Blood, A., & Zatorre, R. (2001). Intensely pleasurable responses to music correlate with activity in brain regions implicated in reward and emotion. *Proceedings of the National Academy of Sciences of the United States of America, 98*(20), 11818–11823. doi:10.1073/pnas.191355898

Bruscia, K. (1987). *Improvisational models of music therapy.* Springfield, IL: Charles C. Thomas.

Bruscia, K. (1998). *Defining music therapy* (2nd ed.). Gilsum, NH: Barcelona.

Bruscia, K., & Grocke, D. (Eds.). (2002). *Guided imagery and music: The Bonny method and beyond.* Gilsum, NH: Barcelona.

Cathro, M., & Devine, A. (2012). Music therapy and social inclusion. *Mental Health Practice, 16*(1), 33–36. doi;10.7748/mhp2012.09.16.1.33.c9282

Chou, M., & Lin, M. (2006). Exploring the listening experiences during guided imagery and music therapy of outpatients with depression. *The Journal of Nursing Research, 14*(2), 93–102. doi:10.1097/01.JNR.0000387567.41941.14

Cook, E., & Silverman, M. (2013). Effects of music therapy on spirituality with patients on a medical oncology/hematology unit: A mixed-methods approach. *The Arts in Psychotherapy, 40*(2), 239–244. doi:10.1016/j.aip.2013.02.004

Degmečić, D., Požgain, I., & Filaković, P. (2005). Music as therapy. *Glazba Kao Terapija, 36*(2), 287–300. Retrieved from http://www.jstor.org/stable/30032173

Dingle, G., Brander, C., Ballantyne, J., & Baker, F. (2013). "To Be Heard"—the social and mental health benefits of choir singing for disadvantaged adults. *Psychology of Music, 41*(4), 405–421. doi:10.1177/0305735611439981

Dingle, G., Gleadhill, L., & Baker, F. (2008). Can music therapy engage patients in group cognitive behaviour therapy for substance abuse treatment? *Drug and Alcohol Review, 27*(2), 190–196. doi:10.1080/09595230701829371

Evers, S., & Suhr, B. (2000). Changes of the neurotransmitter serotonin but not of hormones during short time music perception. *European Archives of Psychiatry and Clinical Neuroscience, 250*(3), 144–147. doi:10.1007/s004060070031

Fachner, J., Gold, C., & Erkkila, J. (2013). Music therapy modulates fronto-temporal activity in rest-EEG in depressed clients. *Brain Topography, 26*(2), 338–354. doi:10.1007/s10548-012-0254-x

Gold, C., Solli, H., Krüger, V., & Lie, S. (2009). Dose–response relationship in music therapy for people with serious mental disorders: Systematic review and meta-analysis. *Clinical Psychology Review, 29*(3), 193–207. doi:10.1016/j.cpr.2009.01.001

Goleman, D. (2006). *Social intelligence: The new science of human relationships.* New York, NY: Bantam Dell.

Grocke, D., Bloch, S., & Castle, D. (2009). The effect of group music therapy on quality of life for participants living with a severe and enduring mental illness. *Journal of Music Therapy, 46*(2), 90–104. doi:10.1093/jmt/46.2.90

Grocke, D., & Wigram, T. (2007). *Receptive methods in music therapy: Techniques and clinical applications for music therapy clinicians, educators and students.* London, England: Jessica Kingsley.

Iliya, Y. (2011). Singing for healing and hope: Music therapy methods that use the voice with individuals who are homeless and mentally ill. *Music Therapy Perspectives, 29*(1), 14–22. doi:10.1093/mtp/29.1.14

Korlin, D., & Wrangsjo, B. (2002). Treatment effects of guided imagery and music (GIM) therapy. *Nordic Journal of Music Therapy, 10*(2): 133–143.

Kreutz, G., Bongard, S., Rohrmann, S., Hodapp, V., & Grebe, D. (2004). Effects of choir singing or listening on secretory immunoglobulin A, cortisol, and emotional state. *Journal of Behavioral Medicine, 27*(6), 623–635. doi:10.1007/s10865-004-0006-9

Lin, S., Yang, P., Lai, C., Su, Y., Yeh, Y., Huang, M., & Chen, C. (2011). Mental health implications of music: Insight from neuroscientific and clinical studies. *Harvard Review of Psychiatry, 19*(1), 34–46. doi:10.3109/10673229.2011.5497.69

Lipe, A., Ward, K., Watson, A., Manley, K., Keen, R., Kelly, J., & Clemmer, J. (2012). The effects of an arts intervention program in a community mental health setting: A collaborative approach. *Arts in Psychotherapy, 39*(1), 25–30. doi:10.1016/j.aip.2011.11.002

Loue, S., Mendez, N., & Sajatovic, M. (2008). Preliminary evidence for the integration of music into HIV prevention for severely mentally ill Latinas. *Journal of Immigrant and Minority Health, 10*(6), 489–495. doi:10.1007/s10903-008-9142-6

Maratos, A., Gold, C., Wang, X., & Crawford, M. (2008). Music therapy for depression. *Cochrane Database of Systematic Reviews, 2008*(1): CD004517. doi:10.1002/14651858.CD004517.pub2

Maxmen, J., & Ward, N. (1995). *Essential psychopathology and its treatment, second edition, revised for DSM-IV.* New York, NY: W. W. Norton.

McCaffrey, T., Edwards, J., & Fannon, D. (2011). Is there a role for music therapy in the recovery approach in mental health? *Arts in Psychotherapy, 38*(3), 185–189. doi:10.1016/j.aip.2011.04.006

McKinney, C., Tims, F., Kumar, A., & Kumar, M. (1997). The effect of selected classical music and spontaneous imagery on plasma beta-endorphin. *Journal of Behavioral Medicine, 20*(1), 85–99. Retrieved from http://www.ncbi.nlm.nih.gov/pubmed/9058181

Menon, V., & Levitin, D. (2005). The rewards of music listening: Response and physiological connectivity of the mesolimbic system. *NeuroImage, 28*(1), 175–184. doi:10.1016/j.neuroimage.2005.05.053

Mitchell, L., & MacDonald, R. (2012). Music and pain: Evidence from experimental perspectives. In R. MacDonald, G. Kreutz, & L. Mitchell (Eds.), *Music, health and wellbeing* (pp. 230–238). Oxford, England: Oxford University Press.

Mössler, K., Chen, X., Heldal, T., & Gold, C. (2011). Music therapy for people with schizophrenia and schizophrenia-like disorders. *Cochrane Database of Systematic Reviews, 2011*(12): CD004025. doi:10.1002/14651858.CD004025.pub3

Packer, J., & Ballantyne, J. (2010). The impact of music festival attendance on young people's psychological and social wellbeing. *Psychology of Music, 39*(2), 164–181. doi:10.1177/0305735610372611

Platel, H., Baron, J., Desgranges, B., Bernard, F., & Eustache, F. (2003). Semantic and episodic memory of music are subserved by distinct neural networks. *NeuroImage, 20*(1), 244–256. doi:10.1016/S1053-8119(03)00287-8

Red Hot Chili Peppers. (1991). Under the bridge. On *Blood Sugar Sex Magik* [CD]. Burbank, CA: Warner Brothers.

Ridder, H. (2011). How can singing in music therapy influence social engagement for people with dementia? Insights from the Polyvagal theory. In F. Baker & S. Uhlig (Eds.), *Voicework in music therapy: Research and practice* (pp. 131–147). London, England: Jessica Kingsley.

Rolvsjord, R. (2010). *Resource-oriented music therapy in mental health care.* Gilsum, NH: Barcelona.

Seligman, M. (2011). *Flourish.* New York, NY: Free Press.

Silverman, M. (2003). The influence of music on the symptoms of psychosis: A meta-analysis. *Journal of Music Therapy, 40*(1), 27–40. doi:10.1093/jmt.40.1.27

Silverman, M. (2009). The effect of single-session psychoeducational music therapy on verbalizations and perceptions in psychiatric patients. *Journal of Music Therapy, 46*(2), 105–131. doi:10.1093/jmt.46.2.105

Silverman, M. (2011). The effect of songwriting on knowledge of coping skills and working alliance in psychiatric patients: A randomized clinical effectiveness study. *Journal of Music Therapy, 48*(1), 103–122. doi:10.1093/jmt.48.1.103

Silverman, M., & Marcionetti, M. (2005). The effects of reading, interactive live music making, and recorded music on auditory hallucinations: A pilot study. *Music Therapy Perspectives, 23*(2), 106–110. doi:10.1093/mtp.23.2.106

Stefano, G., Zhu, W., Cadet, P., Salamon, E., & Mantione, K. (2004). Music alters constitutively expressed opiate and cytokine processes in listeners. *Medical Science Monitor, 10*(6), 18–27. Retrieved from http://www.ncbi.nlm.nih.gov/pubmed/15173680

Stige, B. (2003). *Elaborations toward a notion of community music therapy.* Oslo, Norway: UniPub.

Stige, B., & Aarø, L. (2012). *Invitation to community music therapy.* New York, NY: Routledge.

Thaut, M. (1999). *Training manual for Neurologic Music Therapy Training Institute.* Fort Collins: Colorado State University.

Thaut, M. (2005). Toward a cognition-affect model in neuropsychiatric music therapy. In R. F. Unkefer & M. H. Thaut (Eds.), *Music therapy in the treatment of adults with mental disorders: Theoretical bases and clinical interventions* (pp. 86–103). Gilsum, NH: Barcelona Publishers.

Thaut, M. (2008). *Rhythm, music, and the brain: Scientific foundations and clinical applications.* New York, NY: Routledge.

The Verve. (1997). The drugs don't work. On *Urban Hymns* [CD]. Oxfordshire, England: Virgin Records.

Ulrich, G., Houtmans, T., & Gold, C. (2007). The additional therapeutic effect of group music therapy for schizophrenic patients: A randomized study. *Acta Psychiatrica Scandinavica, 116*(5), 362–370. Retrieved from http://www.ncbi.nlm.nih.gov/pubmed/17919155

Vander Kooij, C. (2009). Recovery themes in songs written by adults living with serious mental illnesses. *Canadian Journal of Music Therapy, 15*(1), 37–58. Retrieved from https://www.questia.com/library/journal/1P3-1654035381/recovery-themes-in-songs-written-by-adults-living

Wigram, T., Nygaard Pedersen, I., & Bonde, L. O. (2002). *A comprehensive guide to music therapy.* London, England: Jessica Kingsley.

CHAPTER 10

Music

The Interface of Music Therapy and Psychotherapy With Adolescents in a Hospital-Based Consultation-Liaison Mental Health Service—Eclecticism in Action

Kate Aitchison

This chapter explores the interface of music and verbal psychotherapy with adolescents in a hospital-based consultation-liaison (CL) mental health service. The chapter commences with a description of the CL service with reference to the role of music therapy. Second, theoretical orientation in psychiatric music therapy practice is discussed. Third, the current evidence base for the efficacy of music therapy in child and youth mental health is highlighted and an argument for the application of an eclectic or blended approach put forward. Last, three case studies outlining the use of songwriting with adolescents to address varied goals are provided. McFerran's "map of the relationship between the therapist's orientation, stance and intention in conventional music therapy" (2010, p. 54) structures the reported case studies. One example from each of the theoretical approaches—psychodynamic, humanistic, and behavioral (or cognitive-behavioral)—is offered. Goals, treatment approach, and evaluation are presented with reference to songs written with each of the adolescents during therapy.

MUSIC THERAPY IN CYMHS

The setting I work in is the Child and Youth Mental Health Service (CYMHS) in a major pediatric hospital. The service has various teams, and I am employed across three of these: consultation-liaison (CL), inpatient ward (IW), and day program (DP). This chapter focuses on my work in the CL team. Consultation-liaison psychiatry is a model that responds to the needs of people with a combination of physical and psychiatric symptoms. Research evidence indicates that more than 25% of children and adolescents presenting to pediatric medical clinics have comorbid mental health issues (Woodgate & Garralda, 2006). Consultation liaison staff can provide direct patient care as well as training for general hospital staff in the detection and treatment of psychiatric problems. Positive outcomes of this approach include improved staff attitudes toward patients with mental illness and greater staff confidence in "addressing emotional distress expressed by patients or patients' relatives" (Academy of Medical Royal Colleges, 2009, p. 22).

The CL team I am employed in works with inpatients and outpatients of the medical wards and clinics within the hospital. The team is multidisciplinary, comprised of two psychologists, one occupational therapist, one clinical nurse consultant (mental health trained), two consultant psychiatrists, a psychiatric registrar, a music therapist, and an administrative assistant. Each staff member has a unique approach depending on their discipline, training, individual experience, and interest. Consultant psychiatrists have ultimate clinical responsibility for patients while the team leader, a psychologist, provides operational and administrative management.

MUSIC THERAPY AND THE QUESTION OF ORIENTATION

The practice of music therapy in mental health encompasses a variety of modalities. Luce (2001) asked the question "is music therapy a primary modality, or a treatment approach to be applied within a particular paradigm?" He concluded that music therapy was still not established enough to call itself a primary modality. Consequently, he believed we must relate to "pre-existing concepts and constructs" because "adopting a particular paradigm . . . facilitates communication with treatment team members and other professionals through vocabulary, language and acculturation" (p. 96). Twyford and Watson (2008) stated a similar opinion, arguing that we have much to gain from and offer to other professionals and that the act of doing so does not dilute our practice but rather enriches it.

However, many music therapists either do not identify with a particular theoretical orientation or at least do not state that they do. Choi (2008) argues that this may be because most music therapists are principally eclectic in approach, employing a variety of techniques and interventions to create "meaningful musical experiences" for their patients (p. 103). Her research suggested that orientation did not determine attitudes related to value, importance, amount of music, and satisfaction in work. Furthermore, Silverman's (2011) survey of 53 psychiatric music therapists indicated that participants who identified themselves as having cognitive behavioral and psychodynamic or humanistic orientations, although espousing some differing views, held many issues in equal importance. This is an interesting finding considering these three philosophies are often presented as disparate in goals and methodology. Silverman (2011) relates this finding to Choi's study, concluding that music therapists have far more similarities than differences, regardless of orientation.

EVIDENCE FOR THE EFFICACY OF MUSIC THERAPY IN CHILD AND YOUTH MENTAL HEALTH

The question of theoretical orientation is also significant in the debate about treatment efficacy. Many studies in the field of mental health have attempted to ascertain which form of therapy is best for which group of patients with specific disorder(s). Although cognitive-behavioral approaches for children and adolescents with psychopathology have a large number of published research trials, Weersing and Dirks (2007) argue that most of this research has been in laboratory settings rather than real-life clinical settings, making generalization of results problematic. Furthermore, research studies directly comparing two forms of therapy have consistently failed to show the superiority of one theoretical orientation over another (Miller, Wampold, & Varhely, 2008).

This outcome is commonly referred to as "the dodo verdict," coined in relation to a quotation from *Alice in Wonderland* where the Dodo announces that "everyone has won and all must have prizes" (Budd & Hughes, 2009, p. 511). Although this verdict can be contested, it has not been categorically disproved. Therefore, there is no defensible position that can argue for the application of one bona fide form of psychotherapy over another. As a result, it is hardly surprising that everyday psychotherapeutic practice is most commonly eclectic, drawing on strategies that meet a specific patient's need at a particular point in time (McFerran, 2010; Weersing & Dirks, 2007).

The evidence base for music therapy in child and youth mental health also supports an eclectic approach. A meta-analysis published in 2004 by Gold, Voracek, and Wigram summarized results from eleven studies relevant to child and youth practice. Data extracted and analyzed to examine overall efficacy indicated that "music therapy has a medium to large positive effect on clinically relevant outcomes that was statistically highly significant and statistically homogenous" (p. 1054). Results were more conclusive for behavioral and developmental disorders than mood disorders, though the authors acknowledged that changes in mood are more difficult to measure and may, therefore, yield less significant results. In terms of theoretical approach, the authors concluded that interventions appeared to be most effective when techniques from different approaches were combined.

ECLECTICISM: AN INTEGRATED APPROACH

In reference to these findings, Gold, Voracek, and Wigram (2004) hypothesize that eclectic approaches may be effective since they allow for flexibility in treatment planning so that interventions can be adapted to suit individual or group needs. McFerran (2010), with specific reference to working with adolescents, infers that "a blended, eclectic model is both best practice and a true representation of music therapy practice" (p. 45). She concludes that music therapists should have a range of methods available in order to focus on the situation at hand and the therapeutic needs of the patient at the time. Nonetheless, she strongly argues that "clarity of intention is essential" (p. 46). Thus, varying approaches may be used depending on the needs and goals of the adolescent, but the music therapist should be clear which approach is being used and why.

In her book, McFerran (2010) provides a concise and insightful map of the "relationship between the therapist's orientation, stance and intention in conventional music therapy" (p. 54) and further outlines a "map of how music therapy can be with adolescents" (p. 55). The three traditional approaches used in mental health are explained in terms of their primary focus of fostering understanding (psychodynamic), offering acceptance (humanistic), or facilitating development (behavioral). A later chapter in her book is devoted to songwriting, outlining its application within these three modalities.

THERAPEUTIC SONGWRITING WITH ADOLESCENTS

Songwriting can be a powerful therapeutic tool when working with adolescents. Songs can provide teenagers with a familiar and reassuring structure, allow them to "use everyday language imaginatively," and engender a sense of achievement and self-confidence (Derrington, 2005, p. 70). Baker (2013) notes that songwriting may provide patients with a vehicle to communicate experiences that are difficult to convey in conversation, thus assisting the therapist and others in comprehending these experiences.

In McFerran's (2010) review of literature describing the use of music therapy with adolescents, 65% of 110 authors utilized live songs, 63% utilized improvisation, 46% utilized prerecorded songs, and only 12% utilized musical games or movement to music. The predominance of choosing, singing, playing, and writing songs with this cohort attests to the significance of songs during this developmental phase. As McFerran asserts, "At no other time in life does music hold such a central role as it does during adolescence" (p. 60). Songwriting is appealing to many teenagers as a means to communicate through a medium that is significant to them. I draw on McFerran's concept of orientation, stance, and intention to structure the following case studies. One vignette for each of the theoretical orientations is presented to illuminate the contribution songwriting made toward fostering understanding, offering acceptance, or facilitating development respectively.

FOSTERING UNDERSTANDING: A PSYCHODYNAMIC APPROACH

In psychodynamic psychotherapeutic work, the therapist aims to provide a "blank slate for the patient to project upon" by remaining detached (McFerran, 2010, p. 53). Offering containment and stability is core, with the dominant intention being to foster understanding and develop resilience. McWilliams (2004) asserts that the common factor that unites psychodynamic approaches is a commitment to honesty for the purpose of developing satisfying and useful lives. Psychodynamic therapists "share the aim of cultivating an increased capacity to acknowledge what is not conscious—that is, to admit what is difficult or painful to see in ourselves" (p. 1).

The use of musical experiences and the memories, thoughts, and emotions these uncover is similar to the psychodynamic therapist's use of dreams, slips of the tongue, and other associations to explore unconscious material. Outlining the musical equivalent, Nolan (2005) describes a cycle of musical experience, verbal processing, and further musical experience, which can deepen understanding and insight. Espousing a belief similar to McWilliams, he describes this process as assisting in the achievement of mastery through expressing hidden, tension-inducing feelings. Defensive energy is freed, resulting in a reduction of anxiety and an increase in positive emotions and mood states.

I have found that songwriting can be effective in helping uncover material to base further analysis on. McFerran (2010) also outlines the use of songwriting techniques for this purpose, suggesting that insight and contemplation can occur "within the lyrics that are composed, as well as through the discussion that takes place around the song" (p. 111). The following case study tells the story of an adolescent girl who utilized songwriting to explore emotions and thoughts, which were not consciously accessible to her.

CASE STUDY: SARAH

Sarah, an attractive, high achieving 17-year-old girl, came to music therapy with a history of poor engagement in verbal therapies. Her initial presentation occurred after she experienced a dissociative episode in which she lost all biographical memories regarding friends and recent occurrences in her life. Her procedural memory was relatively intact as she could successfully complete simple tasks of daily living and higher order tasks such as mathematical problems. Sarah had also experienced several seizures. She had little insight into her psychological distress, presenting as bright and reactive and reportedly feeling "fine." Sarah could not remember any traumatic events or factors that may have precipitated this episode.

Extensive medical investigations were conducted to establish a cause for Sarah's seizures and memory loss but these yielded no results. Sarah subsequently had an admission to the mental health ward of the hospital for observation and assessment. On discharge, she was referred for therapy with a mental health clinician at a community clinic near her home. Although she attended individual psychotherapy sessions for approximately 12 months, her therapist felt there was little progress. Family therapy sessions were offered, and it was observed that Sarah had difficulty articulating negative emotions and that expressed emotion was generally avoided by the family. After three sessions, the family declined further intervention.

Sarah was referred to music therapy when she was an inpatient in the mental health ward and continued to attend weekly or fortnightly sessions concurrently with her community treatment. Objectives for Sarah were to

- develop rapport and a therapeutic alliance with the music therapist,
- explore possible precipitating events or experiences that may be contributing to her current symptoms, and
- articulate negative emotions and personal challenges she was experiencing.

Sarah engaged willingly and enthusiastically in music therapy, and rapport was established by discussing musical genres and artists. Songwriting was instigated early in the process since Sarah was open and willing to engage in this. Her initial song expressed confusion about her direction in life and her desire for support. She wrote of her difficulty trusting those who offered help on one hand and a need for guidance on the other. Her lyrics asked the question, "If I got lost would you show me the way, or would you lead me astray?" However, at this early point in therapy, Sarah was not ready or able to relate the content of her song to her experiences or symptoms.

After approximately six months of weekly, individual sessions, Sarah began to explore some of her stressors head-on as illustrated by the third song we wrote together. Sarah suggested listening to a cover version of Peter Gabriel's song "Don't Give Up" recorded by Shannon Noll and Nathalie Basingwaith. She said that she loved the structure of the song, which has two voices—a man speaking of his suffering and woman providing reassurance—and would like to write a song like this. The following was the outcome.

Weak Bones

VERSE: Well I have weak bones it seems

I bite my tongue and leave my dreams

You have a confident voice to speak

A thought-filled mind explores unique

VERSE: Being compared to those better than me

Whether by my Mum or on TV

She wants what's best, you have to believe

Take a step back, remember to breathe

CHORUS: I won't cry myself to sleep to make it better

I won't cry myself to sleep, I know I'll make it through the weather

When it rains, it pours; the sun ignores your reasons to be free

Embrace the good, embrace the bad, but be who you're born to be

VERSE: Tread softly as you tread on my dreams

Trap me in but hear my screams

We live in chains, refuse to see

That deep within we hold the key

CHORUS

CHORUS 2: I won't cry myself to sleep to make it better

I won't cry myself to sleep, I know I'll make it through the weather

When it rains, it pours; the sun ignores your reasons to be free

From the iron chain of your pity's rein, you're stuck here in between

The two voices you hear, only one can steer you into activity

Embrace the good, embrace the bad, but be who you're born to be

Psychodynamic strategies were utilized to explore the images and phrases Sarah suggested for this song. I listened closely to Sarah's comments and either requested clarification or paraphrased to indicate that I had understood. Nancy McWilliams (2004) argues that a disciplined, attentive process of listening allows the patient "to figure out their own solutions, to find their sense of agency in the presence of a person who welcomes their increasing confidence and competence" (p. 133). I then made tentative interpretations of themes expressed in Sarah's lyrics. For example, Sarah seemed to be expressing a longstanding sense of weakness or vulnerability ("weak bones") contrasted with a growing ability to challenge self-doubt ("you have a confident voice to speak") and self-regulate ("take a step back, remember to breathe"). I suggested to her that the two voices in the song may actually be her own. She agreed and reflected that she would like to strengthen her self-confident voice.

After developing the lyrics for her song, Sarah presented the melody she had composed. I asked Sarah to sing the melody while I played a basic chord progression on guitar. The piece fit easily into a minor key, using the basic building blocks of harmonic accompaniment. I then provided options for adding harmonic color to reflect the lyrical content of the song, and Sarah chose the suggestions she liked best. After this, Sarah and I used a computer application called GarageBand to explore accompaniment styles for the song. She was clear about the genre she wanted, which was "slightly country," and chose an arpeggiated guitar pattern with a country twang. The process of choosing the musical accompaniment was similar to the initial stages of discussing Sarah's lyrics. I listened carefully as Sarah presented her ideas then asked for clarification where necessary. I reflected her wishes by providing options that I thought may be appropriate, and she made the final decision. This provided further opportunities for Sarah to find her own solutions and experience a sense of agency and competence.

When evaluating the effectiveness of this intervention for Sarah, the three objectives mentioned at the beginning of this section were revisited. Rapport was developed easily, but open, honest dialogue was not developed until six months into the therapy process. This objective was, therefore, partially achieved early in the process and developed over an extended period of therapy. Although Sarah did not identify any specific events that may have precipitated her difficulties, she did explore many experiences that may have contributed. One of these was her sense of being compared to others by her mother, especially to her older siblings and their significant achievements. Sarah managed to admit, through her songwriting process, emotions such as confusion, vulnerability, and sadness. Initially verbal discussion and analysis around these emotions was difficult, but over 12 months of therapy, Sarah was able to use the process to acknowledge dual aspects of her nature ("embrace the good, embrace the bad") and her desire to change ("be who you're born to be").

OFFERING ACCEPTANCE: A HUMANISTIC APPROACH

McFerran (2010) describes the humanistic approach as offering unconditional positive regard and acceptance in order to assist the patient with identity formation. She suggests this style of therapy is less structured, adopting a "go with it" attitude (p. 53). In his article on the contribution of humanists to the field of psychotherapy, Barton (2000) reflects on significant figures in the movement including Carl Rogers, Viktor Frankl, Fritz Perls, Virginia Satir, and Milton Erickson. He summarized their contribution as threefold: first, to celebrate and acknowledge human beings as fundamentally valuable; second, to see the person as a whole rather than reduce him or her to a diagnosis or set of symptoms; and third, to free the therapist from the role of silent observer and provide alternative, transformative techniques such as empathic listening and unconditional positive regard.

The predominant humanistic music therapy model is resource-oriented music therapy as developed by Rolvsjord (2010). Rolvsjord's main contention is that "therapy can be as much about nurturing resources and strengths as it is about fixing pathology and solving problems" (p. 5). She also presents a critique of the binary view of health and illness, arguing that they should be understood as interacting elements. Humanistic music therapy can offer acceptance through listening closely to the patient's musical and verbal offerings and demonstrating unconditional positive regard by accepting these and working with them. In the following case study, Kathy, a young teenager on the autistic spectrum, was having difficulty with individuation. Songwriting provided her an opportunity to explore her sense of identity.

CASE STUDY: KATHY

Kathy was 13 years old when she and her mother attended the CYMHS CL service for a mental health assessment. Kathy was adopted as a toddler by an older Australian couple who were unable to have children of their own. She showed signs of developmental delay early in life and was later diagnosed as being on the autistic spectrum. Kathy and her mother had a close relationship, which was initially interpreted as Kathy's mother being overprotective. Through further assessment, it was revealed that Kathy had significant anxiety around individuation and relied on her mother to define her own identity. Kathy received individual music therapy sessions while her mother was offered concurrent verbal psychotherapy sessions. The objectives of Kathy's therapy were to

- recognize and acknowledge her own strengths and weaknesses,

- experience unconditional regard and begin to internalize this experience, and

- see herself as an individual, separate from her mother.

During music therapy sessions, Kathy explored her self-image as well as negative messages she had internalized as a result of bullying in various institutions. She was also able to discover a balanced view of herself, one that acknowledged the things she found challenging as well as highlighting her strengths. The following words formed the final version of her lyrics.

Kathy's Song

Hi, my name is Kathy ___.

There are lots of things I'm good at,

Like gymnastics, dancing, and coloring in.

I am trustworthy, loving, and happy and I try to be fair,

But I don't like change and I don't like to wait.

I like doing the same things and sometimes I need help.

I get a bit anxious and sometimes I'm scared.

I feel I need someone to stick up for me but no one will.

Sometimes I forget my manners,

And I want Mum to tell me what I want to do next.

I try to be careful but sometimes I'm clumsy.

I am honest and full of energy,

And I like doing what my friends want to do.

On my own, the voice makes me want to talk to myself.

It's not someone else's voice, it's my voice!

It makes me feel like I've got my own company,

And that feels GOOD!

That's the way I do things—and who I am!

During the first two sessions of a six session program, I supported Kathy to explore ideas for her song through brainstorming. This is a method commonly used by music therapists, especially with patients who have cognitive or communication impairments. In this method, "client[s] are encouraged to contribute ideas and communicate feelings around a pre-determined theme" (Baker, Wigram, Stott, & McFerran, 2009). The theme that related to Kathy's goals was congruent with a humanistic or resource-oriented approach.

In resource-oriented music therapy, the patients' capacity for self-healing is mobilized, and their potential is emphasized rather than their pathology. At the same time, patients are encouraged to "establish a direct, constructive, and active contact with the structured objects of the surrounding reality" (Schwabe, 2005, p. 50). We explored Kathy's strengths, but also the reality of her limitations, through brainstorming. I encouraged her acceptance and eventual regard for both aspects of herself.

The lyrics were created from phrases and concepts that emerged in the brainstorming process. I then utilized GarageBand to provide Kathy with options for the style of accompaniment she would like. I suggested a chord progression and facilitated Kathy's choice of instrumentation, style, and tempo. This allowed Kathy to choose almost every aspect of the piece, further supporting her emerging sense of autonomy.

In evaluating Kathy's progress in reaching her objectives, it was clear that Kathy's song had provided a forum for acknowledging her strengths and weaknesses, exploring the activities she achieved highly in (e.g., gymnastics), and expressing the things she found challenging (e.g., change). The experience of unconditional regard was offered through respecting Kathy's decisions and wishes during each session rather than challenging her. For example, when Kathy chose not to sing her song, I respected this decision. This could have been interpreted as a lack of confidence in her abilities, leading to the goal of developing confidence through singing exercises and rehearsal. Instead, I saw this decision as an assertion of Kathy's creative autonomy and encouraged her to develop her unique piece, not song and not rap, but rather spoken word with musical accompaniment. The finished product was emotive with Kathy placing particular emphasis on the final words "that's the way I do things—and who I am!" These words also attested to Kathy's emerging vision of herself as an individual, separate from her mother.

FACILITATING DEVELOPMENT:
A BEHAVIORAL/COGNITIVE-BEHAVIORAL APPROACH

McFerran (2010) refers to behavioral work with teenagers as facilitating development of skills and abilities in order to obtain competence in a specified domain. She argues that therapists using this approach usually work with a plan, stay one step ahead of the patient, and are more directive than in other approaches. Although McFerran refers only to behavioral therapy, the treatment of anxiety disorders is most commonly combined with cognitive strategies in a cognitive-behavioral approach. Chorpita (2007) states that the behavioral strategy of gradual and repeated exposure to feared stimuli is the core of all successful cognitive-behavioral treatments (CBT) for anxiety and phobic disorders. However, exposure can be supported with cognitive strategies such as "thought exercises, rewards, praise, and differential reinforcement strategies" (p. 44). He suggests that these are the "nice extras" that make exposure more effective.

Behavioral music therapists often utilize music as a reward or reinforcer to encourage patients to participate in therapy or achieve a certain task. However, music therapy can also be used to support cognitive change. While there has been little literature published outlining this approach, Luce (2001) argued that this may be due to differences in language. He suggested that "cognitive therapy principles may have already found a basic place within good music therapy" (p. 102) without necessarily being described as such.

Silverman (2011) outlined the impact of songwriting on knowledge of coping skills and working alliance in psychiatric patients. He contended that "songwriting about coping skills can be as effective a psychosocial intervention as traditional talk-based psychoeducation" (p. 103). In my practice, I have observed that music can support cognitive change through embedding positive coping statements and strategies within songs. These songs can be used as an anchor when patients feel anxious and forget the strategies they have learned in therapy. This is especially useful for adolescents with a learning disability or intellectual impairment who may find reading and writing difficult and therefore have difficulty utilizing traditional strategies. The following case study illustrates such an application.

CASE STUDY: JAYDEN

Jayden was a 14-year-old boy with respiratory problems and a moderate intellectual impairment. Jayden had undergone extensive medical examinations and treatments, as indicated by multiple, thick medical charts that arrived at CL for review prior to Jayden's mental health assessment. Jayden was required to have blood tests often and had developed a significant needle phobia. He was referred to the CL team for psychological support with his phobia. The treating psychologist identified Jayden's love of music early in her assessment. She discussed the possibility of joint psychology–music therapy sessions with me since she felt music may help engage Jayden and make the process less anxiety provoking. The idea was presented to Jayden who was immediately enthusiastic and engaged in discussion about his favorite artist, John Farnham. Objectives for Jayden's joint therapy sessions were to

- establish rapport and assist Jayden to participate in the process of addressing his needle phobia,

- explore Jayden's strengths and interests and identify elements that may be used to motivate him in therapy,

- write a song containing coping statements, relaxation strategies, and distraction techniques that Jayden could memorize and use during exposure tasks, and

- engage in exposure tasks using his song and other strategies to move up his fear ladder.

Jayden's initial song was a parody using the melody from the traditional Australian song "Walzing Matilda." Jayden explored his strengths, his favorite hobbies, and his favorite foods. This song helped the psychologist and music therapist to establish rapport with Jayden and put him at ease before attempting to support him in challenging his needle phobia. Sessions were held with both therapists and Jayden's mother present. After this initial work, we set about identifying Jayden's level of distress regarding needles and developing a "fear ladder" (Chorpita, 2007, p. 47). This approach is used in cognitive-behavioral work in order to support the patient to face their fears in a graduated manner.

Due to Jayden's intellectual impairment, he could not engage in the cognitive strategies usually used with phobic patients such as thought exercises. Songwriting provided Jayden with an alternative strategy for practicing and memorizing positive coping statements and helpful thoughts to help distract him from his anxiety. The song, titled "Go, Jayden, Go!" reminded Jayden that he could use breathing exercises as practiced in therapy sessions, think about things that made him feel happy (e.g., music and John Farnham), and affirmed his inner strength and bravery rather than focusing on fear.

Go, Jayden, Go!

CHORUS: Go, Jayden, go,

Take a breath and take it slow.

Think about the things I like,

Music, drums, guitars, and mics.

VERSE: Imagine Johnny Farnham's band

Is playing just for me!

With Angus on the drums and backing harmony.

CHORUS

BRIDGE: I can be brave, I can be strong,

Just close my eyes and sing along.

CHORUS

CHORUS 2: Go, Jayden, go!

Go, Jayden, go!

The process of writing the song involved talking with Jayden about his interests, exploring his existing coping strategies, and teaching him new strategies such as breathing techniques. I took this information and constructed song lyrics that were presented to Jayden for consideration and revision. After the lyrics were finalized, I composed a melody and accompaniment that mimicked Jayden's preferred musical genre, pop rock, and employed an upbeat, motivating tempo and style. Jayden responded positively to the finished song, particularly enjoying the rhythmic, guitar accompaniment, and use of his name in the lyrics. I recorded a copy of the song and burned it to CD for Jayden to use during homework exercises.

In evaluating the first objective of Jayden's therapy, the establishment of rapport, it was clear that Jayden felt connected to the therapists as a result of engaging in discussion around his musical interests and hobbies. The inclusion of these topics in a song parody of "Walzing Matilda" further developed our therapeutic alliance. It also provided us with information that fulfilled the second objective, to identify strengths and interests that may be used to encourage Jayden to participate in exposure tasks. The song "Go, Jayden, Go!" fulfilled the third objective of embedding supportive strategies in music. It incorporated coping statements such as "I can be brave, I can be strong," relaxation strategies such as "take a breath and take it slow," and distraction techniques such as "think about the things I like." The fourth objective of using this song during exposure tasks was met by assisting Jayden in memorizing the song and singing it with him during exposure tasks. Over time, Jayden was able to sing his song independently and therefore use it whenever he felt anxious or panicked.

CONCLUSION

The role of consultation-liaison (CL) teams is important in providing services that bridge the gap between medical care and specialist mental health care. The CL team I work in includes professionals from a range of disciplines. These clinicians have differing theoretical orientations and apply a variety of therapeutic techniques and interventions depending on the needs and circumstances of their patients. This approach is common among mental health practitioners working with children and adolescents (Weersing & Dirks, 2007).

The value of explaining music therapy practice with reference to well-established psychotherapeutic traditions is that we can communicate more effectively with multidisciplinary teams such as the one I work in. We are then in a position to share their goals and gain insight from their expertise. The reason that many music therapists do not overtly align with a single orientation is perhaps because the majority of us tend toward an eclectic or blended approach. The evidence in music therapy practice in child and youth mental health supports this method as eclectic practices have been shown to be effective in this field (Gold, Voracek, & Wigram, 2004). Nonetheless, taking an eclectic stance does not mean that we can reject the notion of orientation. On the contrary, it means we must be conversant with a range of approaches and be willing and able to identify and explain which we are taking and why.

The case of Sarah shows the use of songwriting and the therapeutic relationship in a psychodynamic context, providing space to explore salient experiences from the past and express emotions that are difficult to verbalize. The case of Kathy illustrates the use of songwriting to enhance identity formation through exploring strengths and weaknesses and encouraging individuation. The case of Jayden demonstrates a collaborative cognitive-behavioral approach using songwriting as a motivator and a method to help recall coping statements and strategies. These case studies illustrate the interrelated nature of music therapy and verbal psychotherapy in my work with adolescents in the child and youth consultation liaison mental health service of a pediatric hospital. I provided examples of McFerran's map for work with adolescents applied in a mental health setting in the hope of assisting other therapists in the debate of where to position themselves in the confusing and seemingly boundless landscape of psychotherapeutic orientations.

REFERENCES

Academy of Medical Royal Colleges. (2009). *No health without mental health: The alert summary report.* Retrieved September 1, 2013, from http://www.aomrc.org.uk/doc_view/58-no-health-without-mental-health-alert-report

Baker, F. (2013). The ongoing life of participant-composed songs within and beyond the clinical setting. *Musicae Scientiae, 17*(1), 40–56. doi:10.1177/1029864912471674

Baker, F., Wigram, T., Stott, D., & McFerran, K. (2009). Therapeutic songwriting in music therapy, part II: Comparing the literature with practice across diverse clinical populations. *Nordic Journal of Music Therapy, 18*(1), 32–56. doi:10.1080/08098130802496373

Barton, A. (2000). Humanistic contributions to the field of psychotherapy: Appreciating the human and liberating the therapist. *The Humanistic Psychologist, 23*(1–3), 231–250.

Budd, R., & Hughes, I. (2009). The dodo bird verdict—controversial, inevitable and important: A commentary on 30 years of meta-analyses. *Clinical Psychology and Psychotherapy, 16,* 510–522.

Choi, G. (2008). Awareness of music therapy practices and factors influencing specific theoretical approaches. *Journal of Music Therapy, 45*(1), 93–109. doi:10.1093/jmt/45.1.93

Chorpita, B. (2007). *Modular cognitive-behavioral therapy for childhood anxiety disorders.* New York, NY: Guilford Press.

Derrington, P. (2005). Teenagers and songwriting: Supporting students in a mainstream secondary school. In F. Baker & T. Wigram (Eds.), *Songwriting: Methods, techniques and clinical applications for music therapy clinicians, educators and students* (pp. 68–81). London, England: Jessica Kingsley.

Gold, C., Voracek, M., & Wigram, T. (2004). Effects of music therapy for children and adolescents with psychopathology: A meta-analysis. *Journal of Child Psychology and Psychiatry, 45*(6), 1054–1063. doi:10.1111/j.1469-7610.2004.t01-1-00298.x

Luce, D. (2001). Cognitive therapy and music therapy. *Music Therapy Perspectives, 19*(2), 96–103. doi:10.1093/mtp.19.2.96

McFerran, K. (2010). *Adolescents, music and music therapy.* London, England: Jessica Kingsley.

McWilliams, N. (2004). *Psychoanalytic psychotherapy: A practitioner's guide.* New York, NY: Guilford Press.

Miller, S., Wampold, B., & Varhely, K. (2008). Direct comparisons of treatment modalities for youth disorders: A meta-analysis. *Psychotherapy research, 18*(1), 5–14. doi:10.1080/10503300701421311

Nolan, P. (2005). Verbal processing within the music therapy relationship. *Music Therapy Perspectives, 23*(1), 18–28. doi:10.1093/mtp.23.1.18

Rolvsjord, R. (2010). *Resource-oriented music therapy in mental health care.* Gilsum, NH: Barcelona.

Schwabe, C. (2005). Resource-oriented music therapy—The development of a concept. *Nordic Journal of Music Therapy, 14*(1), 49–56. doi:10.1080/08098130509478125

Silverman, M. (2010). Areas of concern in psychiatric music therapy: A descriptive analysis. *The Arts in Psychotherapy, 39*(5), 374–378. doi:10.1016/j.aip.2012.06.2002

Silverman, M. (2011). The effect of songwriting on knowledge of coping skills and working alliance in psychiatric patients: A randomized clinical effectiveness study. *Journal of Music Therapy, 48*(1), 103–122. doi:10.1093/jmt/48.1.103

Twyford, K., & Watson, T. (2008). *Integrated team working: Music therapy as part of transdisciplinary and collaborative approaches.* London, England: Jessica Kingsley.

Weersing, V., & Dirks, M. (2007). Psychotherapy for children and adolescents: A critical overview. In A. Martin & F. Volkmar (Eds.), *Lewis's child and adolescent psychiatry: A comprehensive textbook* (4th ed.) (pp. 789–795). Philadelphia, PA: Lippincott Williams & Wilkins.

Woodgate, M., & Garralda, M. (2006). Paediatric liaison work by child and adolescent mental health services, *Child and Adolescent Mental Health, 11*(1), 19–24. doi:10.1111/j.1475-3588.2005.00373.x

A Dance/Movement Therapy Recovery Model

Engagement in Stages of Change

Anne Margrethe Melsom and Jill Comins

INTRODUCTION: DANCE/MOVEMENT THERAPY IN RECOVERY-ORIENTED SYSTEMS OF CARE

Dance/movement therapy (DMT), a process-oriented form of psychotherapy, is a whole-person approach to health care (Serlin, 1993) offered in many acute care hospitals and residential facilities that adopt a multidisciplinary treatment approach. The use of dance/movement to promote engagement provides a vehicle for stabilization of symptoms and mobilization of the person(s) in preparation for change. The authors both work and direct programming in behavioral health services and have extensive experience providing the Chacian DMT approach to persons receiving treatment within recovery-oriented systems of care. Marian Chace, a pioneer of DMT in the United States, emphasized dance as a form of communication and relatedness in her work with mental health populations (Levy, 2005). Principles stemming from her formative work are well suited for the present day recovery-oriented approach to DMT for persons transforming their lives.

Dance/movement therapy is defined by the American Dance Therapy Association (ADTA) as "the psychotherapeutic use of movement as a process to further the emotional, cognitive, physical and social integration of the individual" (ADTA, 2012b, p. 1) and is a natural fit for the recovery framework. Guiding principles of recovery include installation of hope; a person-driven and relational approach; and a strengths-based, peer-supported, and trauma-informed approach to the person in recovery. Relationships, motivation, hope, and resilience are crucial for a person's wellness and journey of recovery (Vecchio, 2013). These are inherently accepted core constructs for nonverbal engagement and exploration in DMT practice. Dance/movement therapists have in this past decade seen a paradigm shift in the overall symptom-focused treatment of people with mental health disorders and substance-use disorders from the medical model systems to the holistic, person-centered recovery framework (Koch & Fischman, 2011). The federal action agenda titled "Transforming Mental Health Care in America" emphasizes a system of care that is evidence based, recovery focused, and consumer/family driven with access for all (U.S. Department of Health and Human Services, 2013a). The current definition of recovery for people living with mental health disorders and alcohol/substance use disorders is: "A process of change through which individuals improve their health and wellness, live a self-directed life, and strive to reach their full potential" (Vecchio, 2013, p. 1). The use of dance, movement, and the body in action is based on the empirically supported premise of the interconnectedness of the body, the mind, and the spirit (ADTA, 2012a).

The authors propose a DMT RECOVERY Model that emerges from clinical practice, principles, core concepts, and methods in the Chacian approach to DMT: guiding principles of recovery, mind-body theories, and evidence-based practices in behavioral health. Constructs of this model are *Relationship* and *Empathy* through movement to foster hope and engagement; the use of *Creativity* as a method; the *Opportunity* to practice change in action; achieve *Vitalization* and *Expression* through movement experiences; and find *Resilience* in recovery through mind/body integration. The approach is humanistic, with focus on the person—*You* in a community. This model is further applied to the evidence-based stages of change model to exemplify the applicability of DMT in the engagement phase of treatment and in the active, intentional change process. Lastly, therapeutic dance is proposed as a vista for dance/movement therapists to embrace by providing support groups in community wellness settings where dance fosters access to recovery with focus on belonging and sense of purpose (Gaumond & Whitter, 2013).

CORE CONSTRUCTS OF THE DANCE/ MOVEMENT THERAPY RECOVERY MODEL

As the field of DMT is transforming to align with current evidence-based practices, the DMT RECOVERY Model seeks to provide guidelines for the clinical approach to recovery-oriented behavioral health services. The DMT RECOVERY Model has at its core the therapeutic relationship as research identifies the success of this alliance as a salient predictor of treatment outcome (Norcross, 2011).

Relationship (R)

Dance/movement therapists engage individuals in a therapeutic movement relationship established through mirroring and kinesthetic empathy, rhythmic group expression, body action, and the use of nonverbal, spontaneous, and symbolic movement expression (Chaiklin & Schmais, 1993). These Chacian principles allow individuals at any level of readiness the opportunity to express, explore, and engage within a strengths-based alliance that promotes a sense of hope for the potential to change.

Empathy (E)

The development of empathy is considered an important element in the therapeutic alliance that proves to be "demonstrably effective" (Norcross, 2011, p. 1). Mirroring, kinesthetic empathy, and embodiment provide different means for fostering empathy. Nascent research of the mirror neuron system (MNS) offers dance/movement therapists a way to understand these nonverbal concepts (Berrol, 2006; Homann, 2010). Specifically, the MNS plays a fundamental role in understanding actions, empathy, and intentions of others through nonverbal cues. The neural network responds when we perform an action and when we observe another body performing the same action, which has implications for how we learn (imitation learning), process, and empathize with others. Kinesthetic empathy is the experience of heightened awareness of the other person, which promotes a connection between the movement expressed and the emotions of those persons moving together (Winters, 2008). Embodiment may occur through the deepening of one's experience by accessing the bodily felt experience (Bloom, 2006). Kinesthetic relatedness occurs as the dance/movement therapist engages the person within his or her movement repertoire and reflects this back to the person, which promotes empathy (Sandel, 1978).

Creativity (C)

The use of creativity allows for safe expression in which defenses are bypassed and engagement spontaneously arises. Creative movement expression serves as a vehicle to uniquely engage individuals who may be withdrawn, despondent, resistant, disorganized, or impulsive. Structured or spontaneous creative movement tasks can create a holding environment analogous to what Winnicott (1971) spoke of as transitional space or play space. When working with creative movement and symbolism, imagery, or metaphors, the individual may experience embodiment of either unconscious emotional content (Lewis, 1993) or may be able to clarify and begin to transform experiences into the here and now. The expression and integration between the conscious and the unconscious can be bridged, and the person can be held and nurtured at the level appropriate to their engagement in the recovery process. This transformational space is where wholeness, healing, hope, and the experience thereof can be achieved.

Opportunity to Practice (O)

The opportunity to practice change, however small or significant, is promoted within the Chacian structure of a session, which includes warm-up, theme development, and closure. It is the theme development portion of a session that allows for significant flexibility in this approach. After a thorough warm-up, mobilization, and assessment of group needs, the dance/movement therapist can choose to guide members in a spontaneous, process-driven expression in which themes organically emerge. Alternatively, members can be led in a very specific evidence-based intervention where the structured movement activity allows for practice of a specific coping skill, be it a pain management/relaxation technique or a trauma-informed approach working on affect regulation and body awareness. The dance/ movement therapist has a choice between process-oriented theme development and skill-based exercise interventions. Group members make choices about their level of movement engagement. They have opportunities to practice new experiences, new relationship skills, new attitudes, and can make discoveries about their ability to feel small changes in the body or movement. The closure portion of a session is tremendously important since the movement content is reviewed and processed verbally. Connections between the here and now and choices made in movement can be compared with old patterns of behaviors or emotional reactions. As members reflect on their experience, emotional insight occurs, providing opportunity for meaning making and cognitive integration.

During sessions, positive risk taking is encouraged in a respectful manner while opportunities to practice and to receive feedback from peers about one's progress are encouraged. Witnessed by others, members acknowledge that each person is on his or her unique individual path, supported to practice the specific change she or he may need. Hope is reinforced as individuals experience more mastery through the opportunity to explore new ways of moving, expanding one's movement repertoire, and making different choices of interactions or coping strategies. Through shared rhythm and an externalization of feelings, the practice leads to integration and increased tolerance of potential discomforts associated with the process of change (Thomson, 1997).

The empathic, therapeutic movement relationship is always the main factor supporting the person's practice within the holding space. The Chacian circle of dancers promotes safe exploration and generation of hopeful interactions. For example, for traumatized women, the engagement and practice of group action in movement can reinforce mobilization and reduce helplessness. This promotes the experience of strength that may support a positive self-concept reflective of the person's increased ability to mobilize and assume control over her physical and emotional self (Leventhal & Chang, 1991).

Vitalization (V)

Dance/movement therapists promote self-efficacy and provide unique means to motivate and guide participants through the processes of change through vitalization. Rhythm can mobilize even the most depressed person exhibiting minimal movement. Through breath work, awareness of body actions can be experienced in the slightest rise or fall of the chest. In this way, the person senses himself or herself energetically and can reflect on his or her own vitality and feeling of aliveness, promoting transformation from stillness to exertion. The experience of a vital and energized body mobilizes the person in an active manner that engages the body-self and can as such support the emotional experience and transformation of the individual.

Expression (E) and Resilience (R)

As expression and resilience are explored and practiced, when engagement has been established, the individual can take steps toward healing and recovery through the immediate feedback from the body in action. Strength-based, spontaneous movement exchanges promote health and wellness. A playful body in motion can reveal choices and new perspectives. New discoveries and transformed narratives are explored through movement repetition, leading to mastery of new skills. Synchrony in a shared and cohesive group action allows individuals to express more difficult emotions as it is contained in a shared experience. Intensity in emotions can be safely transformed, modulated, and regulated as individuals engage at a level of exertion that they are able to sustain (Schmais, 1985). From a trauma-informed perspective, the facilitation of a movement process that fosters awareness through self-expression promotes insight and learning about one's body, its well-being, recuperation, and health. Psychoeducation about the health benefits of affect regulation and self-expression are essential experiences for recovery. Such expressions often emerge during the theme development section of a session, yet a symbolic gesture in a closing ritual can be a potent life-affirming self-expression as well.

Resilience is the process of adapting well to adversity and stressors, emphasizing a so-called bouncing back for the individual. Relationships that are caring and supportive have been found to encourage a person's resilience. For individuals that have experienced trauma or have been stigmatized and excluded from society, one clear benefit of engagement in group experiences is community reintegration. This involves the experience of resilience, recovery, and inclusion through dance and cohesive group expression (Harris, 2007). The ability to manage strong feelings, active engagement, and action planning are additional factors involved in resilience.

The field of neuropsychology has a large body of research on the efficacy and effectiveness of mind–body interventions for post-traumatic stress disorder. Movement and body practices can impact brain imbalances and the immune system (Rossi, 1986), including the smallest level of cell modification through touch (Pert, 1997). Mapping of the mind–body relationship is becoming more widely understood. Clinical DMT practices and principles are emerging with additional evidence from related fields (Homann, 2010). The dance/movement therapist's ability to foster relaxation and support engagement of the parasympathetic nervous system counters the effects of chronic stress and promotes health and healing. Changes in tensions and breathing patterns can assist the individual in making active changes that foster the experience of resilience when practicing and implementing health-enhancing techniques within a supportive therapeutic movement relationship. The psychoeducational role of a dance/movement therapist is teaching the person about the body, its resilience and flexibility, and the physiology involved in stress management, health, and well-being.

You in Community (Y)

This whole-person approach emphasizes self-directedness while the dance/movement therapist travels alongside the person on his or her journey of recovery. The "you" concept of the model considers the person in his or her community. A circle of dancers or movers can support one another in exploration and practice of change processes. The dance/movement therapist promotes health and wellness while joining individuals through dance or movement, fostering hope, engagement with others, and transformation (Dulicai & Shelly-Hill, 2007). The witnessing that occurs by dancing with peers allows the individual to sense his or her impact on others and receive feedback in the here and now. As individuals begin to experience a broader range of movement and emotional expression, they can embody a greater sense of self-potential and work toward connectedness and belonging.

Acceptance, respect, and belief in a person's ability to recover are necessary conditions for change and healing to take place. Hopes and fears about relapse and recovery can be explored as a group experience. For example, a simple prop like a balloon may symbolize recovery, being passed around gently in a nurturing dance, crystallizing fragility and beauty in motion. The dance/movement therapist's modeling and promoting care and playfulness with the balloon can foster significant intimacy and honesty in support of positive risk taking. That the balloon may be dropped is very likely. As with a person's recovery, it can be picked up again. This opportunity to experience the fall, recovery, and bounce back of the balloon is a symbolic representation of the recovery process. Experiencing letdown in front of peers, tolerating failure, and reclaiming success can be practiced in a supportive group. It also allows for problem solving around group dynamics and potential obstacles or triggers should they occur.

USE OF THE THERAPIST-SELF WITHIN THE DANCE/MOVEMENT THERAPY RECOVERY MODEL

When embracing the recovery-oriented framework, the role of the dance/movement therapist is to authentically join the person on his or her path, which involves intimacy and openness at a more profoundly intentional level within the therapeutic alliance (Goodill, 2005; Melsom, 1999). Similarly to working with the medical population, the dance/movement therapist actively holds and supports the transformative space where healing occurs, and this use of the therapist-self calls for resilience and self-awareness of countertransference material on the dance/movement therapist's part. Her or his ability to embody hope is essential to foster an atmosphere that communicates that change is possible. Hope is the emotional essence of recovery and wellness. Through the guidance of the therapeutic movement relationship, the person is empathetically accompanied on a journey of exploration during which practicing new behaviors happens with the body at the center.

EMERGENCE OF THE DANCE/MOVEMENT THERAPY RECOVERY MODEL

Proposing a model that supports a growth process in which concepts, processes, and methods are often fluid and interchangeable requires flexibility and structure that can hold concepts over time (Leventhal, 2008; Meekums, 2006; Schmais, 1985). For the DMT RECOVERY Model, concepts were synthesized and proposed as an evolving model for a recovery-oriented framework of DMT. The model combines the Chacian process-oriented interventions and directed tasks or evidence-based/evidence-informed approaches to facilitate opportunities to practice new experiences. This supports engagement, hope, motivation, and resilience for persons living with and recovering from mental health and substance use conditions. Core constructs included in this approach will be considered as it applies to the change process.

STAGES OF CHANGE AND DANCE/MOVEMENT THERAPY: AN INTEGRATIVE CONCEPTUALIZATION

The transtheoretical model (TTM) of behavior change, commonly referred to as stages of change, is an evidenced-based approach for developing effective interventions to promote intentional health behavior change. TTM focuses on the decision-making process of an individual involving emotions, cognition, and behavior (Prochaska & Velicer, 1997). It is recognized in recovery-oriented systems of care because it espouses an individualized, self-directed treatment approach and is currently applied in the treatment of numerous biopsychosocial problems. This approach is well suited for the Chacian DMT method in which engagement and mobilization allow for the opportunity to practice change and integration on a body–mind level. The TTM, characterized by ten processes of change that occur within five stages, also considers core constructs of decisional balance (weighing pros and cons) and self-efficacy (Prochaska & Velicer, 1997). Importantly, motivation is a necessary and integral component underlying one's ability to generate change (Center for Substance Abuse Treatment, 1999). Each stage, seen as a series of progressions occurring over time, is marked in part by attitudes and behaviors toward making a behavior change. The therapeutic movement relationship supports the motivation to engage in this transformation. Dance/movement therapists are able to meet and engage individuals at any level of vitality and motivation. The stages of change are identified as:

1. Pre-contemplation

2. Contemplation

3. Preparation

4. Action

5. Maintenance

Relapse, often viewed as a regression or a recycling into an earlier stage, is not considered a failure but an opportunity to reevaluate strategies, reassess motivation, and increase promotion of self-efficacy. DMT as a nonverbal medium provides unique opportunities for the person to directly experience and make meaning of this setback from a strengths-based, resilience perspective.

Each stage is matched with specific strategies or processes that help people progress from one stage to the next. Whereas the stages allow us to understand and assess when particular shifts in attitudes, intentions, and behaviors occur, the processes explain how these shifts occur (Prochaska, DiClemente, & Norcross, 1992). The change processes are both experiential and behavioral in nature and can be practiced effectively through DMT interventions to promote intentional changes in health behaviors.

Precontemplation Stage

Precontemplation is the stage in which people are often labeled as resistant or unmotivated. Individuals typically come into treatment because of extrinsic motivators and fail to recognize how personal behaviors impact others. In this stage, there are three experiential processes that are helpful in advancing individuals toward the contemplation stage. They are focusing on increasing awareness (consciousness raising), facilitating emotional experience and connection to the problem (dramatic relief), and promoting affective and cognitive evaluation of the effects of behaviors on the environment (environmental reevaluation) (Prochaska & Velicer, 1997). The therapeutic movement relationship, rhythmic group expression, the body in action, and symbolism are core constructs in the Chacian DMT method that provide dance/movement therapists with tools to engage individuals in the precontemplation stage. Furthermore, DMT supports the change processes through increased body awareness and awareness of self in relation to others. Also, making meaning through movement in a supportive and cohesive group expression promotes safe exploration of one's "growing edges" and provides opportunities for evaluation of one's own impact on the environment.

Self-exploration is fostered by interpersonal relationships, which ideally communicate empathy, unconditional positive regard, authenticity, and safety (Rogers, 1992). Dance/movement therapists' use of empathic reflection of movement and mirroring is a client-centered approach that assists in establishing rapport and trust needed to support this engagement. Rhythmic movement can generate a climate conducive for change and awareness through cohesion and synchrony (Schmais, 1985). Furthermore, rhythmic clashing and attunement can provide group members opportunities to witness the effects of their own behaviors. With empathy, an evaluation of one's movement expression and behaviors can be explored. During this stage, it is fundamental to motivate and engage individuals in physical action, increase connection to a "felt sense," and awaken feelings through kinesthetic awareness. This assists in intrinsically motivating the unmotivated person in recovery. As individuals engage in physical action, release of muscular tension can lead to relief from psychic tension and provide increased body awareness. Postural shifts can support changes in attitude and the individual can reflect on any differences the new posture may produce. Also, expansion of movement repertoire can serve to expand self-concept and perceptions of options and opportunities available to them. When individuals are able to recognize immediate results of their actions and begin to tap into internal resources, self-efficacy is reinforced as they are more likely to realize themselves as the agent of change.

Finally, symbolic movement is often a precursor to self-awareness and identification of feelings as it facilitates externalization of subconscious thoughts and feelings (Chaiklin & Schmais, 1993). Consciousness raising and dramatic relief can also be explored in supportive dyads or creative group dance experiences. Awareness of choices made in movement can promote increased readiness for change.

Contemplation Stage

In this stage, individuals are increasingly aware of advantages to changing a behavior, yet a strong attachment to the problem behavior still exists. Individuals are not yet committed to action and often experience ambivalence. Pros and cons of behavior changes are contemplated as the individuals are weighing their options. This concept of decisional balance is explored through body actions such as shifting body weight, swaying, or balancing. As people are often at risk for getting stuck in chronic contemplation, experiential strategies that assess one's self-image through cognitive and emotional evaluations (self-reevaluation) are emphasized (Prochaska & Velicer, 1997).

Creative and expressive movement can engage individuals emotionally and instill hope of new and positive outcomes resulting from behavior change. Specifically, creative exercises that explore polarities in movement can promote self-reevaluation and assist in recognizing pros and cons of behavior change. For example, movement explorations of freedom versus confinement lead to a visceral knowledge of each quality. For a person feeling confined by his or her addiction, the embodiment of freedom may provide hopefulness about his or her self-value in pursuing recovery. This can help increase cognitive awareness and lead to clarification of one's value system and priorities. This newfound vitalization gained from embodying freedom can also support individuals with depression in recognizing that change in mood is possible, prioritizing steps toward well-being. Exploring polarities assists in tipping the decisional balance in favor of actions that support change.

Also, symbolic action and the use of imagery are effective and nonthreatening techniques that help in shifting one's perception of self in order to align new experiences with one's own evolving values (Prochaska & Velicer, 1997). DMT can assist in this perceptual shift as nonverbal movement expressions transform into active imagination. When individuals begin to experience and imagine themselves in new ways through creativity, a new concept of body-self is integrated and hope can be felt.

Preparation Stage

Preparation is the stage in which individuals intend to take action to change and have taken significant behavioral steps in doing so. The behavioral process matched with this stage is marked by the belief that one can change (self-liberation), which is rooted in hope and confidence, and a commitment to take action is demonstrated (Prochaska & Velicer, 1997). This is the stage in which concrete action plans are constructed and barriers decrease as support for the new behavior is identified and recruited. It is important to prepare individuals to fully participate in the preparation of their action plan. In DMT, this can be achieved through embodiment methods and expressive movement tasks. Research in embodiment proposes that sensorimotor states inform our concept of self (Koch & Fischman, 2011) and that the physical and expressive actions of the body relate to functions of the mind (Homann, 2010). Expressive movement tasks serve to clarify intentions and promote cognitive awareness as an avenue toward a plan of action.

Interventions that subject one to the actual physical and felt sense of commitment lead to embodiment and integration. This can be achieved through movement exercises that engage core strength and foster a vertical and upright posture. This experience of self can become a catalyst for internalization and engagement of the psychological commitment to take action. "If an individual is motivated, finds purpose in his/her life, and approaches life with confidence and self-esteem, it is both a manifestation of Core Support and an inroad to achieving it" (Hackney, 2002, p. 81). The dance/movement therapist's skillful exploration of movement and movement patterning serve to support a sense of mastery and mobilizes the energy needed to take action. This gives rise to the felt experience of "I can do this." The process of psychological and physiological self-liberation prepares one for the next stage of change.

Creative and expressive movement tasks also help to support new behaviors and facilitate the commitment to take action. Intentions and coping styles are communicated through movement (Bartenieff & Lewis, 1980). Because of this, exploration of how movements are expressed, sequenced, or phrased can provide insight into individualized strategies. As individuals prepare to take action, structured experiential tasks help to explore and externalize a plan of action and assist in problem solving while identifying barriers. For example, as individuals are instructed to symbolically walk a path toward recovery, intentions are externalized and different options may become apparent. Symbolism, metaphor, and imagery in even a simple gesture can help to crystallize commitment while exploring and increasing awareness into possibilities. The process of transformation can be actively experienced as group members are instructed to make sequential changes in improvised movements. Verbal processing of this experience can reveal inherent personal psychodynamic qualities needed to support their process.

Action Stage

Individuals are in the action phase of change when they begin to make specific, overt changes in behavior. Because these new behaviors may not be fully integrated, central to this stage are behavioral strategies that focus on setting up conditions for success (stimulus control); learning healthy, alternative behaviors (counterconditioning); providing positive reinforcement (reinforcement management or rewards); and engaging in supportive relationships (social support). Psychoeducational approaches that teach self-monitoring skills, affect regulation, and mastery of movement are vital to affect self-efficacy. Particular feelings may often trigger a response that results in a relapse. As coping techniques such as breathing and relaxation are learned, unhealthy responses are replaced by these healthy alternatives, and counterconditioning and stimulus-control processes are reinforced.

Exertion and recuperation are natural phases in movement that occur to maintain vitality (Hackney, 2002). These can be observed and practiced during the sequential flow of a DMT session throughout the warm-up, theme development, and cooldown or closure. Investigations into how much energy is exerted and maintained in each of these phases, including in what way one recovers from these efforts, can inform how best to maintain modifications in behavior change. For example, does one collapse as a way to regenerate due to overexertion in the beginning or middle phases, or is a steady balance of effort and energy maintained? These phases can be explored as a way to help understand personal strategies for recuperation and self-care and can be helpful when planning for potential pitfalls in the action stage.

Lastly, DMT engages groups of individuals in shared rhythm in which "each member draws from a common pool of energy and experiences a heightened sense of strength and security" (Chaiklin & Schmais, 1993, p. 80). Through this communal dance/movement experience, individuals are able to explore themes of trust, openness, and acceptance and gain social support that is needed to maintain healthy behavior change. Group experiences that involve peer-supported movement actions in a forward-moving sagittal plane promote the reinforcement of embodied action for change.

Maintenance Stage

In this stage, persons in recovery are confident in their ability to maintain behavior change and are less focused on applying strategies. Attention is placed on preventing relapse through promotion of coping skills, reminders, avoidance, and engaging in alternative behaviors or activities (Prochaska & Velicer, 1997). Recovery-oriented systems of care recognize the importance of community support and components of wellness in maintaining recovery. To this end, support groups are highly valuable. Historically, the medical model approach to therapy focused on individual problems, which led to a more prescriptive DMT approach. This is in contrast to spontaneous approaches that consider people within a social context (Bruno, 1990). As a new recovery paradigm has emerged, one that considers individuals within a community, dance/movement therapists can expand their role and skills to reach outside of clinical and behavioral health settings.

Dance/movement therapists are uniquely skilled in bringing out the inherent healing qualities in dance to offer wellness support for individuals maintaining their recovered state. As individuals experience themselves as self-reliant, the spirit of dance can be more easily accessed (Bruno, 1990). Movement that engages play, spontaneity, rhythm, and ritual supports individuals in the maintenance stage and helps promote resilience. Ritual in dance parallels the process of creating lifelong healthy rituals and habits. Rhythmic movement, particularly when experienced in a group, promotes vitality, empowerment, and channels energy (Chaiklin & Schmais, 1993) necessary in continuing positive growth.

Relapse

Dance/movement therapists can assess individuals in each stage of change by engaging nonverbally and sensing kinesthetically their level of intention, exertion, and mastery of movements. Awareness of nonverbal warning signs for relapse guides therapists to focus on frustration tolerance, channeling of emotions that may trigger relapse, and management of impulses through movement. These self-regulation tools and wellness strategies gained from DMT experiences can be included into a person's Wellness and Recovery Action Plan (WRAP). The WRAP, developed by Mary Ellen Copeland, is an evidence-based, individualized self-help tool that assists in maintaining and promoting wellness (U.S. Department of Health and Human Services, 2013b).

INTEGRATIVE CONCLUSIONS: STAGES OF CHANGE AND THE DANCE/MOVEMENT THERAPY RECOVERY MODEL

Efficient self-change depends on doing the right things (processes) at the right time (stages) (Prochaska et al., 1992). Research indicates that experiential and psychodynamic approaches are best suited for the earliest stages while methods in cognitive and behavioral approaches are useful in the action and maintenance stages (Norcross & Prochaska, 2002). The DMT RECOVERY Model proposes integration of these approaches within the Chacian DMT framework. Successful treatment outcomes occur when the therapy relationship along with interventions are tailored to match the stages (Prochaska & Norcross, 2001). Dance/movement therapists can engage and mobilize an individual at any stage through mirroring and kinesthetic empathy. Furthermore, dance/movement therapists can tailor the interventions with more process-oriented theme development at earlier stages and more task-oriented interventions when a person is actively practicing specific change processes.

In predicting and assuring the best possible outcomes of DMT interventions, it is important to assess where the person is in the process of change. The dance/movement therapist employs a variety of approaches for initiating change and uses verbal processing and application of some form of body-based intervention to integrate participant experiences (Comins, 2007) whether it serves to reinforce commitment or provide insight into discrepancies. Throughout recovery, a person's progress is assessed, explored, clarified, and confronted as connections are made between movement behaviors, movement patterns, qualities of movement, and verbalizations. In this way, functional and expressive movement serves as a catalyst to move forward from any stage as self-directedness is internalized and a sense of hope and optimism about change is embodied.

APPLICATIONS OF THE DANCE/MOVEMENT THERAPY RECOVERY MODEL

The Substance Abuse and Mental Health Services Administration (SAMHSA) asserts that recovery-oriented frameworks include the individual alongside family and community in support of recovery, resilience, health, and well-being (Sheedy & Whitter, 2013). Dance/movement therapists can provide effective services that span the continuum from inpatient clinical settings to outpatient programs as well as health and wellness centers in the community. The dance/movement therapy RECOVERY Model is a conceptual framework with applicability to persons at any point in their recovery journey. The use of the Chacian process-oriented DMT interventions combined with evidence-based and evidence-informed structured tasks allows for a more tailored approach throughout the change process. Chacian principles of body action, therapeutic movement relationship, rhythm, and symbolism facilitate recovery-oriented practice guidelines for DMT interventions. Chacian structures such as the use of the circle, a warm-up, theme development, and closure with verbalization support engagement of experiential and behavioral processes involved in change.

The nonverbal therapeutic alliance creates the holding environment in which individuals are engaged and can practice and embody new behaviors and experiences. The experience of kinesthetic empathy also leads people to experience hope and resilience in a vitalized, mobilized, and expressive body. Spontaneous, creative, and communicative expressions of self in a supportive group of movers can progress one's momentum for growth, healing, and transformation. As life quality improves, a new narrative of one's self in recovery from behavioral health disorders is nurtured. Also, as movement toward recovery continues in the community, therapeutic dance experiences in support groups can provide the person with access to embodied health and wellness, relatedness, and a sense of purpose.

The application of the dance/movement therapy RECOVERY Model to the stages of change is promising, and the continued development of specific assessment tools for stage-specific movement data is encouraged. The dance/movement therapy RECOVERY Model can provide clinical practice guidelines as well as potential methods or strategies informing the ongoing acquisition of DMT outcome research related to the measurement of inherent healing qualities in dance. The authors suggest the dance/movement therapy field engage in a parallel process of becoming an evidence-based practice and embracing its roots with focus on the healing, transformative nature of community dances. The development of this Dance/Movement Therapy RECOVERY Model bridges these concepts.

REFERENCES

American Dance Therapy Association (ADTA). (2012a). About dance/movement therapy. Retrieved June 25, 2012, from http://adta.org/About_DMT

American Dance Therapy Association (ADTA). (2012b). The benefits of dance/movement therapy. Retrieved June 25, 2012, from http://adta.org/

Bartenieff, I., & Lewis, D. (1980). *Body movement: Coping with the environment*. New York, NY: Gordon and Breach Science.

Berrol, C. (2006). Neuroscience meets dance/movement therapy: Mirror neurons, the therapeutic process and empathy. *The Arts in Psychotherapy, 33*(4), 302–315. doi:10.1016/j.aip.2006.04.001

Bloom, K. (2006). *The embodied self: Movement and psychoanalysis*. London, England: Karnac.

Bruno, C. (1990). Maintaining a concept of the dance in dance/movement therapy. *American Journal of Dance Therapy, 12*(2), 101–113. doi:10.1007/BF00843885

Center for Substance Abuse Treatment. (1999). *Enhancing motivation for change in substance abuse treatment*. Rockville, MD: Substance Abuse and Mental Health Services Administration.

Chaiklin, S., & Schmais, C. (1993). The Chace approach to dance therapy. In S. L. Sandel, S. Chaiklin, & A. Lohn (Eds.), *Foundations of dance/movement therapy: The life and work of Marian Chace* (pp. 75–97). Columbia, MD: American Dance Therapy Association.

Comins, J. (2007). *Understanding the use of the body in dance/movement therapy practice: Therapists' perspectives* (Unpublished master's thesis). Drexel University, Philadelphia, PA.

Dulicai, D., & Shelly-Hill, E. (2007). Expressive movement. In L. L'Abade, (Ed.), *Low-cost approaches to promote physical and mental health: Theory, research, and practice* (pp. 177–200). New York, NY: Springer Science + Business Media, LLC.

Gaumond, P., & Whitter, M. (2013). Access to Recovery (ATR) approaches to recovery-oriented systems of care: Three case studies. *Journal of Drug Addiction, Education, and Eradication, 9*(4), 287–311.

Goodill, S. (2005). *An introduction to medical dance/movement therapy: Health care in motion*. London, England: Jessica Kingsley.

Hackney, P. (2002). *Making connections: Total body integration through Bartenieff Fundamentals*. New York, NY: Routledge.

Harris, D. (2007). Dance/movement therapy approaches to fostering resilience and recovery among African adolescent torture survivors. *Torture, 17*(2), 134–155. Retrieved from http://www.ncbi.nlm.nih.gov/pubmed/17728491

Homann, K. (2010). Embodied concepts of neurobiology in dance/movement therapy practice. *American Journal of Dance Therapy, 32*(2), 80–99. doi:10.1007/s10465-010-9099-6

Koch, S., & Fischman, D. (2011). Embodied enactive dance/movement therapy. *American Journal of Dance Therapy, 33*(1), 57–72. doi:10.1007/s10465-011-9108-4

Leventhal, F., & Chang, M. (1991). Dance/movement therapy with battered women: A paradigm of action. *American Journal of Dance Therapy, 13*(2), 131–145. doi:10.1007/BF00844142

Leventhal, M. (2008). Transformation and healing through dance therapy: The challenge and imperative of holding the vision. *American Journal of Dance Therapy, 30*(1), 4–23. doi:10.1007/s10465-008-9049-8

Levy, F. (2005). *Dance movement therapy: A healing art.* Reston, VA: American Alliance for Health, Physical Education, Recreation and Dance (AAHPERD).

Lewis, P. (1993). *Creative transformation: The healing power of the arts.* Wilmette, IL: Chiron.

Meekums, B. (2006). Embodiment in dance movement therapy training and practice. In H. Payne (Ed.), *Dance movement therapy: Theory, research and practice* (2nd ed), pp. 167–183). New York, NY: Routledge.

Melsom, A. (1999). *Dance/movement therapy for psychosocial aspects of cancer and heart disease: An exploratory literature review* (Unpublished master's thesis). MCP Hahnemann University, Philadelphia, PA.

Norcross, J. (2011). *Conclusions of the task force.* Society for the Advancement of Psychotherapy. Retrieved from http://www.divisionofpsychotherapy.org/continuing-education/task-force-on-evidence-based-therapy-relationships/conclusions-of-the-task-force/

Norcross, J., & Prochaska, J. (2002). Using the stages of change. *Harvard Mental Health Letter, 18*(11), 5–7. Retrieved from www.Health.Harvard.edu

Pert, C. (1997). *Molecules of emotions: Why you feel the way you feel.* New York, NY: Scribner.

Prochaska, J., DiClemente, C., & Norcross, J. (1992). In search of how people change: Applications to addictive behaviors. *American Psychologist, 47*(9), 1102–1114. doi:10.1037/0003-066X.47.9.1102

Prochaska, J., & Norcross, J. (2001). Stages of change. *Psychotherapy, 38*(4), 443–448. doi:10.1037/0003-066X.47.9.1102

Prochaska, J., & Velicer, W. (1997). The transtheoretical model of health behavior change. *American Journal of Health Promotion, 12*(1), 38–48. doi:10.4278.0890-1171-12.1.38

Rogers, C. (1992). The necessary and sufficient conditions of therapeutic personality change. *Journal of Consulting and Clinical Psychology, 60*(6), 95–103. doi:10.1037/0022-0006X.60.6.827

Rossi, E. (1986). *The psychobiology of mind-body healing: New concepts of therapeutic hypnosis.* New York, NY: W. W. Norton.

Sandel, S. (1978). The process of empathetic reflection in dance therapy. In S. Sandel, S. Chaiklin, & A. Lohn (Eds.), *Foundations of dance movement therapy: The life and work of Marion Chace* (pp. 98–111). Columbia, MD: The Marion Chace Memorial Fund of the American Dance Therapy Association.

Schmais, C. (1985). Healing processes in group dance therapy. *American Journal of Dance Therapy, 8*(1), 17–36. doi:10.1007/BF02251439

Serlin, I. (1993). Root images of healing in dance therapy. *American Journal of Dance Therapy, 15*(2), 65–76. doi:10.1007/BF00844028

Sheedy C., & Whitter, M. (2013). Guiding principles and elements of recovery-oriented systems of care: What do we know from research? *Journal of Drug Addiction, Education, and Eradication, 9*(4), 225–286.

Vecchio, P. (2013). *SAMHSA's Working definition of recovery updated.* Retrieved May 11, 2013, from http://blog.samhsa.gov/2012/03/23/defintion-of-recovery-updated/

Thomson, D. (1997). Dance/movement therapy with the dual-diagnosed: A vehicle to the self in service of recovery. *American Dance Therapy Journal, 19*(1), 63–79. doi:10.1023/A:1022375418060

U.S. Department of Health and Human Services. (2013a). *A life in the community for everyone.* Retrieved May 17, 2013, from http://www.samhsa.gov/Pubs/MHC/MHReport_060606.pdf (page discontinued)

U.S. Department of Health and Human Services. (2013b). *Wellness recovery action plan.* Retrieved July 6, 2013, from http://nrepp.samhsa.gov/ViewIntervention.aspx?id=208

Winnicott, D. (1971). *Playing and reality.* New York, NY: Penguin Books.

Winters, A. (2008). Emotion, embodiment, and mirror neurons in dance movement therapy: A connection across disciplines. *American Dance Therapy Journal, 30*(2), 84–105. doi:10.1007/s10465-008-9054-y

The Evidence Base for Dance/Movement Therapy in Mental Health

Moving the Body of Knowledge

Sherry W. Goodill

INTRODUCTION

The span of research on dance/movement therapy (DMT) is impressive with many studies in the post-positivist/quantitative and constructivist/qualitative traditions and a growing number of studies published that draw on mixed methodology, program evaluation, participatory action approaches, and artistic inquiry. The demand for scientific evidence of the effectiveness of dance/movement therapy from policy makers, research funders, and insurance plans is increasing and requires a robust response from the field. This chapter will frame the DMT outcome research in this context, describe the evidence for DMT effectiveness with a focus on and examples of quantitative outcome studies, and offer suggestions for advancing this aspect of DMT research globally.

It is beyond the scope of this chapter to review all dance/movement therapy research in health and mental health, and so for the present purposes certain delimitations are accepted and identified. Specifically, this review is built from the experience of a single American academic dance/movement therapist. Thus, the review is far from exhaustive—studies published in languages other than English are generally not referenced in this discussion, and there are many good studies published in English that have been omitted. In addition, given the focus on evidence for efficacy of DMT, our rich body of work in assessment research, qualitative research, and artistic inquiry will not be included herein.

Dance/movement therapy will be understood according to the definition put forth by the American Dance Therapy Association (ADTA) as "the psychotherapeutic use of movement to further the emotional, cognitive, physical, and social integration of the individual" (ADTA, n.d.). Studies published in the United Kingdom and other countries may refer to dance/movement psychotherapy (DMP), which is defined similarly as "a relational process in which client/s and therapist engage in an empathic creative process using body movement and dance to assist integration of emotional, cognitive, physical, social and spiritual aspects of self" (Association for Dance/Movement Psychotherapy UK, 2013), and some earlier studies may refer to *dance therapy* or *movement therapy*. For this review, if the intervention under study was delivered by a therapist with professional education and training in the theories and clinical methods of DMT, and if the intervention was described sufficiently to determine that it fits the definitions here, it was considered DMT.

It may be useful here to briefly describe the clinical discipline of DMT. The work is informed by theories of embodiment, human development, creativity, and movement studies as well as a full spectrum of psychotherapy and counseling theoretical approaches. These are manifest in DMT practice according to the training and education of the therapist, the assessed needs of the individual patient or client, and the prevailing theoretical paradigm of the treatment facility. In 1974, Schmais articulated the following premise for the work of DMT: "Significant changes occur on the movement level that can effect total functioning" (Schmais, 1974, p. 10). This seminal and potent theoretical proposition continues to inform practice and drive scholarship on the mechanisms for change in DMT.

Elsewhere in this volume, the specific application of DMT in the context of the RECOVERY Model is described (see Chapter 11). In addition, as summarized by Goodill and Dulicai (2007), the literature records a broad scope of practice including work with infants and their parents, young children, school-age children, those with learning differences and autism spectrum disorders, teens at risk, those with substance abuse disorders, anxiety disorders, eating disorders, and psychiatric diagnoses. Clinical reports of DMT also describe work with those who have experienced domestic violence, homelessness, physical and sexual abuse, and war-related trauma. In addition, as noted above, dance/movement therapists address psychosocial aspects of medical conditions such as cancer, other chronic illnesses, pain-related and musculoskeletal problems, and in palliative care applications (Goodill & Dulicai, 2007, p. 124).

The World Health Organization's (WHO) definitions of health and mental health are aptly broad with overall health described as "a state of complete physical, mental and social well-being, and not merely the absence of disease" (WHO, 2015a) and mental health as "a state of well-being in which every individual realizes his or her own potential, can cope with the normal stresses of life, can work productively and fruitfully, and is able to make a contribution to her or his community" (WHO, 2015b). The American Psychiatric Association's (APA) *DSM IV* states "there is much 'physical' in 'mental' disorders and much 'mental' in 'physical' disorders," and that the distinction is "a reductionistic anachronism of the mind/body dualism" (APA, 1994, p. xxi). Dance/movement therapy, as a mental health specialty discipline, is a mind–body integrated approach that is consistent with these holistic and biopsychosocial perspectives. Consequently, studies on the psychosocial aspects of what are commonly classified as primary medical conditions are included herein, along with those focusing on what are categorized as primarily behavioral, educational, and psychiatric challenges.

Research will be defined broadly as systematic inquiry. Research projects all include the basic components of a research question, procedures for data collection and data analysis, and a derivation and presentation of findings or conclusions. The reader is referred to the Cruz and Berrol (2012) text for a thorough reference on the wide range of research design options and approaches for DMT.

As with all professional disciplines, DMT can be construed as a dynamic, triadic integration of theory, research, and practice, with each pillar informing the others over time in iterative and bidirectional cycles. Theory can inform DMT research by providing a framework in which research questions can be formed and asked. Observations from clinical practice can stimulate research questions and sometimes become the data for research studies. Research can test theoretical assumptions, generate new theories, explain clinical phenomena, and systematically demonstrate clinical outcomes.

The terms *efficacy*, *effectiveness*, and *outcomes* are often used interchangeably in research on the benefits of treatments, interventions, or programs, including DMT. They are however defined differently, and the American Music Therapy Association provided clarity concerning efficacy and effectiveness:

> The main difference relates to objectives and motivation for the trial. The objective of an efficacy trial is to demonstrate that the intervention works under optimal circumstances while that of an effectiveness trial is to test how it works under usual or typical practice circumstances. (Else, Simpson, & Farbman, 2006, p. 6)

According to the U.S. Agency for Healthcare Research and Quality (AHRQ),

> Outcomes research seeks to understand the end results of particular health care practices and interventions. End results include effects that people experience and care about, such as change in the ability to function. In particular, for individuals with chronic conditions—where cure is not always possible—end results include quality of life as well as mortality. By linking the care people get to the outcomes they experience, outcomes research has become the key to developing better ways to monitor and improve the quality of care. (AHRQ, n.d.)

The term *outcomes* is also a synonym for research results or findings and used frequently in reports of individual studies. Efficacy, effectiveness, and outcomes are all represented in the body of DMT studies, and so this discussion will use all three terms.

Research designs that are used to investigate treatment outcomes include the well-known group designs: randomized controlled trial (RCT, or the true experiment), and the quasi-experimental designs (e.g., the controlled clinical trial with one or more control groups). Time series studies and $N = 1$ experiments with one or more replications can also be used to show efficacy, but on a smaller scale, and findings from these studies are not generalizable. Examples will be given later in this chapter.

SYSTEMATIC REVIEW AND META-ANALYSES

In addition to variety of research designs, there is a great variety of clinical populations, dependent/outcome variables, intervention factors (dosage, specific DMT methods, etc.), and cultural differences represented in this collection of studies. To draw conclusions about the overall effectiveness of DMT, or any treatment, it is necessary to conduct systematic review (SR). Systematic review is itself a well-respected research method that synthesizes findings from several studies, and it may or may not include meta-analysis (Vogt, 2005). Meta-analysis is a statistical procedure that integrates results from multiple studies, and it relies upon the statistic effect size (ES), which is "essentially the magnitude of the obtained experimental effect" (Cruz & Sabers, 1998, p. 101). Four meta-analyses of DMT effectiveness (Bradt, Goodill & Dileo, 2011; Cruz & Sabers, 1998; Koch, Kunz, Kolter, Lykou, & Cruz, 2013; Meekums, Karkou, & Nelson, 2012) are pertinent to this discussion.

The 1998 Cruz and Sabers meta-analysis constituted a correction of statistical errors in an earlier published review by Ritter and Low (1996). They included 16 studies with a total N of 601 participants and reported ES for four clusters of studies (Cruz & Sabers, 1998). Their interpretation of magnitude of effect followed Cohen's guidelines for the ES r statistic and is shown in parentheses. Three clusters of studies focused on outcome variables: for anxiety, ES $r = .54$ (a large effect); for self-concept, ES $r = .15$ (a small to medium effect), and for body awareness, ES $r = .20$ (a medium effect). The aggregated ES for studies with psychiatric participants was reported as ES $r = .37$ (a large effect; Cruz & Sabers, 1998, pp. 102–103). Finally, Cruz and Sabers compared the DMT effects (with ES ranging from 0.15 to 0.54) to those published at the time on other mental health interventions and found the ES of DMT comparable to those for verbal psychotherapy, cognitive behavioral therapy (CBT), meditation, exercise, and some pharmaceuticals. This and the recent meta-analysis by Koch and colleagues (2013) used a broad scope, including studies with a full range of outcome variables and clinical population samples.

The 2013 Koch et al. meta-analysis includes 23 studies of both dance and dance/movement therapy interventions. Studies represent a broad range of clinical populations with a total N of 1,078 participants. The researchers used the standard mean difference (SMD) statistic to synthesis findings and report results. They grouped outcome variables into clusters, each shown herein with the respective SMD. Four clusters were interpreted as having a small positive effect: body image (SMD = .27), mood/well-being and affect (SMD = .30), quality of life (SMD = .37), and a sub-analysis for depression (SMD = .36). The following clusters were reported with moderate positive effect: overall clinical outcomes (SMD = .44) and a sub-analysis for anxiety (SMD = .44). An additional cluster, interpersonal competence, did not show consistency across the included studies (Koch et al., 2013).

There are two additional recent meta-analyses of DMT conducted for the Cochrane Collaboration (see www.cochrane.org). Systematic reviews by the Cochrane Collaboration include only RCTs. Cochrane reviews employ rigorous scientific standards for assessment of study design, risk of bias, and the strength of the evidence produced by each included study. Meta-analysis is conducted when the findings for identified variables or sub-populations exist across one or more included studies. The Bradt et al. review (2011) of DMT for cancer patients included two RCTs of DMT (Dibbell-Hope, 1989, 2000; Sandel et al., 2005), both of which focused on women with breast cancer. These two studies represented a combined total of 68 participants and shared one outcome variable—body image (which is a focus of concern in several medical and psychological conditions). Thus, meta-analysis for body image outcomes was conducted. The combined effect was too small to support the claim that DMT is effective for body image, and the review concludes with recommendations for studies with larger samples and the use of power analysis to determine and ensure adequate sample size. The review will be updated in accordance with Cochrane Collaboration schedules and will include studies conducted since early 2011.

As of this writing, Meekums et al. (2012) are in the protocol stage of a new Cochrane review that focuses on DMT outcomes for depression. The scope of this systematic review includes studies on children and adults, comparing DMT to waiting list controls, standard care (also known as treatment as usual, or TAU), other psychotherapies, physical interventions (such as exercise or yoga), and pharmaceuticals.

LEVELS OF EVIDENCE AND EXAMPLE STUDIES

To determine the strength of evidence produced by research studies, most health professions rely on some derivation of Sackett's levels of evidence (Center for Evidence-Based Medicine [CEBM], n.d.), which were initially developed to inform evidence-based practice in medicine. There is a relatively solid global consensus that in the realm of scientific research on health and mental health interventions, certain designs yield stronger evidence and others weaker. This way of assessing and ranking research studies is decidedly aligned with the post-positivist paradigm and is frequently referenced by policymakers and regulatory entities when choosing which human services to fund or promote. Sackett's levels of evidence address the strength of evidence from both treatment outcome and assessment/diagnostic research, but the discussion here will cover only the material related to outcome studies. To show DMT research in relation to the levels of evidence, one or two examples of each are briefly summarized in Figure 12.1. The pyramid schematic is commonly used to rank various research designs for quality of evidence. It visually suggests that there are more studies in the Level 4 and 5 categories and fewer of the Level 1 and 2 types. This is true in many health professions (see Chapter 9) and in DMT as well. The reader will notice that no study types are shown for Level 3. This is because the CEBM and many other authorities list only observational study types at Level 3 (e.g., longitudinal cohort studies or case-control studies) and not treatment outcome designs.

Level 1: Randomized Controlled Trials and
Systematic Review of Randomized Controlled Trials

Two studies conducted in Germany serve as examples of the RCT. Bräuninger (2012) conducted a multisite RCT of DMT for stress reduction and stress management with a sample of 162 adults who self-identified as suffering from stress. Intervention group

Figure 12.1   Levels of evidence for studies of treatment efficacy.

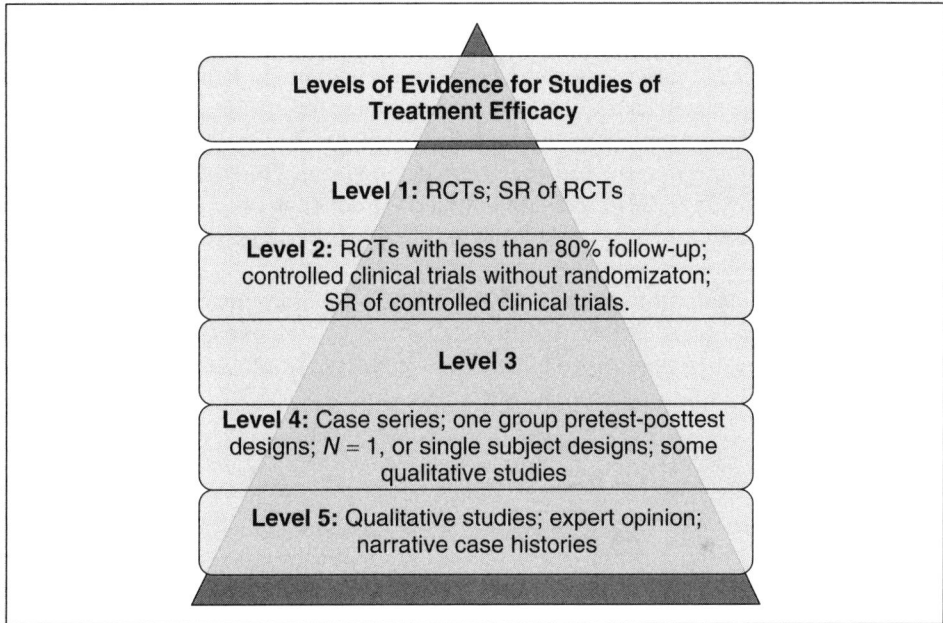

Levels of Evidence for Studies of Treatment Efficacy

Level 1: RCTs; SR of RCTs

Level 2: RCTs with less than 80% follow-up; controlled clinical trials without randomizaton; SR of controlled clinical trials.

Level 3

Level 4: Case series; one group pretest-posttest designs; *N* = 1, or single subject designs; some qualitative studies

Level 5: Qualitative studies; expert opinion; narrative case histories

Adapted from 1. Dileo, C., & Bradt, J. (2009). On creating the discipline, profession, and evidence in the field of arts and healthcare. *Arts & Health,* 1(2), 168–182. 2. National Network of Libraries of Medicine (n.d.) Levels of Evidence Pyramid. Retrieved November 22, 2014, from http://nnlm.gov/training/evidencebased/PICO/pyra midhandout.pdf

participants received ten 90-minute group DMT sessions over a three-month period. Standardized measures were used at pretest, posttest, and six-month follow-up. Results showed significant improvements in the intervention group compared to the control group in stress management at both posttest ($p < .005$) and follow-up ($p < .05$) with statistically significant reductions in depression, anxiety, phobic anxiety, positive symptom distress, and obsessive-compulsive behaviors at posttest (Bräuninger, 2012, pp. 447–448).

Investigating the effects of a single-session dance intervention, Koch, Morlinghaus, and Fuchs (2007) randomized 31 participants with depression to either a group circle dance experience or one of two relevant control conditions—exercise and music listening. When compared to the music listening group, the circle dance group increased in vitality scores ($p < .05$) and decreased in depression scores ($p < .001$), and when compared to the exercise group, the dance group had significantly less depression ($p < .05$).

There are many more RCTs of dance/movement therapy, but space limits do not permit a full review. Some additional studies using the RCT design, some of which have been used in the meta-analyses described herein, are mentioned elsewhere in this chapter or listed in the appendix.

Level 2: Controlled Clinical Trials
Without Randomization (Quasi-Experimental)

The program evaluation study by Koshland and Wittaker (2004) included a comparison of nonrandomized, nonequivalent groups. The 12-week DMT program conducted in a school setting focused on violence prevention with goals to decrease aggressive behaviors and increase prosocial behaviors. The intervention group (n = 54) that received the program were the first-, second-, and third-grade classrooms. Fourth-, fifth- and sixth-grade classes, which did not receive the program, served as controls. The study operationalized reduction of aggressive behaviors by documenting the frequency of reports to the principal's office about aggressive incidents. The number of reports of aggressive incidences about children in the intervention group classrooms decreased significantly more than did the reports of aggressive incidents for children from the control classrooms (Koshland & Wittaker, 2004). Other components of this program evaluation used the one group pretest–posttest design with just the intervention group, and these elements would be considered Level 4 evidence; still other components used qualitative data and analysis.

Level 3: Case Series Designs

It is possible to study DMT effectiveness by studying several participants in a single subject design framework. Moore (2006) systematically collected data from 16 participants who had experienced domestic violence and who received an average of 28 DMT sessions. Fifteen of the participants completed the Beck Depression Inventory (BDI) and the Brief Symptom Index (BSI) at the beginning and end of therapy and a self-report questionnaire about their DMT experiences. In addition, clinical observations and movement analyses using Laban Movement Analysis were systematically recorded. Changes on the BDI and the three subscales of the BSI (Global Severity, Positive Symptoms Distress, and Positive Symptoms Total) were reported at the individual case level and t-test comparisons were computed to compare all pretest with all posttest scores. For all four measures, improvements were statistically significant ($p < .005$ for all four comparisons) in the direction of improved psychological health (Moore, 2006, p.111). The study concluded that DMT can benefit women traumatized by domestic violence but that findings were not generalizable. Moore concluded also that further study with larger samples, male clients, and independent movement raters is warranted.

Level 4: One-Group Pretest–Posttest Design

There are many examples of this design in the DMT literature. In the one-group pretest–posttest design, there is no control group for comparison, and consequently one cannot claim that observed changes before and after DMT are due to the intervention (Mertens, 2009). These are best seen as initial studies and ideally can be followed with the more robust controlled clinical trials or RCT. An example is Harvey's (1989) study of 56 children in the second and fourth grades in a suburban public school in the United States. Harvey described the sample as "from middle and lower-middle class working families, predominantly white" (Harvey, p. 89) and typically developing. The children received integrated creative arts therapy (CAT) sessions (including dance/movement therapy, music therapy, and art therapy) twice weekly over three months, seen in their intact existing classroom groupings. Sessions were cofacilitated by the three CAT professionals, each of whom had graduate level training. Dance/movement therapy methods "facilitated gestural, postural, and facial expressions of affect, dyadic and group mirroring, physical sculpturing, and the development of individual and group dances expressing feelings . . . [including] anger, happiness, sadness, fear and confusion" (Harvey, 1989, p. 90). Standardized pretest and posttest measures assessed on creative thinking, reading comprehension, self-concept, and motivation for learning. Repeated measures analysis of variance statistical tests found significant gains from pretest to posttest in reading comprehension and the following dimensions of creative thinking: verbal originality, figural originality, verbal creative composite, and figural creative composite. In the absence of a control group, Harvey compared the changes in reading comprehension scores (as percentiles) to the published norms for children in the second and fourth grades. He observed that in the two and a half months of the CAT intervention, the children in his sample averaged a six and a half month gain in reading comprehension.

It is interesting to note that within this study Harvey also examined relationships between the creativity and academic variables measured, using the data to explore more theoretical and process questions about the creative skills and academic skills. This observational design component of the study was not compromised by the lack of a control group.

SUMMARY OF EVIDENCE FOR DANCE/MOVEMENT THERAPY

The body of work investigating the efficacy of DMT is impressive, considering the numbers of trained, credentialed practitioners globally, the age of the professional discipline, and the fact that there are very few academic DMT positions in colleges or universities dedicated to the conduct of research. There are trends emerging, but more work is needed. Importantly, all meta-analyses published to date have recommended that future clinical studies employ designs and procedures that will strengthen the quality of evidence reported. As the DMT research agenda moves forward, there are several priorities to consider and the following recommendations address just a few of them.

RECOMMENDATIONS

Multicultural considerations are paramount. Too many of the published studies do not provide enough information about the race, culture, class, or other characteristics of study participants. As DMT practitioners, educators and researchers integrate multicultural perspectives to clinical work and training, our research activity also must align with principles of social justice and multiculturalism (see Caldwell & Johnson, 2012). Mertens' (2009) transformative paradigm for research in education and the social sciences is a good model and framework for this. While it may initially seem that quantitative research for establishing DMT efficacy is incompatible with the transformative paradigm, there are ways to integrate both approaches. For example, instruments selected for measuring outcome variables need to be culturally congruent for the diverse populations served by DMT. Researchers need to transparently consider the interplay of power and privilege in the research dynamic and develop recruitment and data collection procedures that acknowledge and respect cultural values and norms. In addition, post-positivist researchers can and should engage in reflexivity to examine their subjective relationships to their research topics and participants. This can be done without compromising the objectivity required for good outcome studies; in fact, it can strengthen both internal and external validity by compelling researchers to consider all possible aspects of context and potential influences on the study. Mertens (2009) argues that the research paradigms can be merged, and it is this author's opinion that all research should integrate transformative paradigm considerations and elements.

Based solely on this author's impressions, there appear to be themes emerging in the outcome research that suggest areas for a research agenda. Trends in DMT studies seem to point to benefits with mood/emotion parameters (e.g., reducing anxiety, depression, stress, and fatigue, and increasing vitality and positive emotions). Studies with cancer survivors suggest themes of body image and social support parameters. This observation leads to one idea for an overarching DMT research agenda: to focus studies, groups of studies, and aggregation of study findings on outcome variables as opposed to the focus on specific clinical populations. The global communities of DMT researchers may be wise to concentrate on mood/emotion variables and relationship variables, for which good outcomes are already documented, to increase the power of the studies and thus the overall strength of the evidence for DMT effectiveness.

It is this author's view that although DMT master's thesis research projects have occasionally yielded publishable and useful outcomes (e.g., Erwin-Grabner, Goodill, Schelly-Hill, & Von Neida, 1999) it is not sufficient to build the research evidence for DMT with master's level studies. We need more dance/movement therapists educated at the doctoral level who can conduct large, robust, excellent studies, preferably with adequate funding. Many dance/movement therapists have published their doctoral dissertations, but few have gone on to continue the research trajectory started in the doctoral work. This has led to a number of interesting first studies in the literature, and we need to create the conditions for researchers to build on those studies in elaborated research programs or themes. One remedy for this is to advocate for more academic DMT positions that focus on research.

Another recommendation is to encourage collaborations with experienced, funded researchers in closely related disciplines; these studies might conduct the comparative effectiveness research, which is important for policy making around insurance coverage for DMT services. A very good example is the 2012 RCT out of the Netherlands (Cima et al., 2012) on the quality of life and reduction of symptoms associated with tinnitus ($N = 492$). This collaboration with researchers in audiology and psychology integrated DMT into CBT programming and documented statistically significant decreases in tinnitus severity and tinnitus impairment when compared to treatment as usual. The specific contribution of the movement therapy intervention, which was provided by trained dance/movement therapists, was not investigated in the analysis. Nonetheless, this is a powerful study published in a prestigious journal and shows how interdisciplinary collaboration can bring findings about the utility of DMT to wider professional audiences.

Another option is to engage in more international DMT research collaborations, which by bringing together diverse areas of expertise, access to research participant groups, or aggregating data sets—to name a few examples—could facilitate a more productive use of both human and monetary research resources.

Finally, we need to think and act more on the ways in which research informs not only practice but policy. An example of this is the 2010 recommendation from the U.K. National Collaborating Centre for Mental Health on the value of creative arts therapies for people with schizophrenia. The report includes systematic review of several creative arts therapy studies and sophisticated cost effectiveness estimates favoring the use of CAT services in the public health system. As of this writing, the American Dance Therapy Association is in the process of compiling an outcome research bibliography. For this project, 79 studies of DMT effectiveness with various research designs have been collected to date, including RCTs as well as quasi-experimental designs, DMT program evaluations, and single-subject designs. Many of these studies used a mixed method approach as well, incorporating a qualitative research design element. One intended use for the development of this resource is for advocacy with governmental policymakers and in the pursuit of research funding. This use of our research has far reaching potential for making DMT accessible to more participants, families, and communities.

REFERENCES

American Dance Therapy Association. (n.d.). *About dance/movement therapy*. Retrieved July 20, 2014, from http://www.adta.org/About_DMT

American Psychiatric Association. (1994). *Diagnostic and Statistical Manual-IV*. Arlington, VA, USA: American Psychiatric Publishing.

Association for Dance/Movement Psychotherapy UK. (2013). *Home*. Retrieved February 25, 2015, from http://www.admt.org.uk

Bradt, J., & Dileo, C. (2009). On creating the discipline, profession, and evidence in the field of arts and healthcare. *Arts & Health, 1*(2), 168–182. doi:10.1080/17533010903046984

Bradt, J., Goodill, S., & Dileo, C. (2011). Dance/movement therapy for improving psychological and physical outcomes in cancer patients. *Cochrane Database of Systematic Reviews, 2011*(10): CD007103. doi:10.1002/14651858.CD007103.pub2.

Bräuninger, I. (2012). Dance/movement therapy group intervention in stress treatment: A randomized controlled trial (RCT). *The Arts in Psychotherapy, 39*(5), 443–450. doi:10.1016/j.aip.2012.002

Caldwell, C., & Johnson, R. (2012). Embodying difference: Addressing issues of diversity and social justice in dance/movement therapy research. In R. Cruz & C. Berrol (Eds.), *Dance/movement therapists in action: A working guide to research options* (2nd ed., pp. 121–140). Springfield, IL: Charles C. Thomas.

Cima, R., Maes, I., Joore, M., Scheyen, D., Fefaie, A., Baguley D., . . . Viaeyen, J. (2012). Specialised treatment based on cognitive behaviour therapy versus usual care for tinnitus: A randomised controlled trial. *Lancet, 379*(9830), 1951–1959. doi:10.1016/S0140-6736(12)60469-3

Cruz, R., & Berrol, C. (Eds.). (2012). *Dance/movement therapists in action: A working guide to research options* (2nd ed.). Springfield, IL: Charles C. Thomas.

Cruz, R., & Sabers, D. (1998). Dance/movement therapy is more effective than previously reported. *The Arts in Psychotherapy, 25*(2), 101–104. doi:10.1016/S0197-4556(98)00015-X

Dibbell-Hope, S. (1989). *Moving toward health: A study of the use of dance-movement therapy in the psychological adaptation to breast cancer* (Doctoral dissertation). California School of Professional Psychology, San Diego, CA.

Dibbell-Hope, S. (2000). The use of dance/movement therapy in psychological adaptation to breast cancer. *Arts in Psychotherapy, 27*(1), 51–68. doi:10.1016/S0197-4556(99)00032-5

Else, B., Simpson, J., & Farbman, A. (2006). *White paper: AMTA research priority*. Silver Spring, MD: American Music Therapy Association.

Erwin-Grabner, T, Goodill, S., Schelly-Hill, E., & Von Neida, K. (1999). Effectiveness of dance/movement therapy on reducing test anxiety. *American Journal of Dance Therapy, 21*(1), 19–34. doi:101.1023/A:1022882327573

Goodill, S., & Dulicai, D. (2007) Dance/movement therapy: A whole person approach. In I. Serlin, J. Sonke-Henderson, R. Brandman, & J. Graham-Pole (Eds.), *Whole person healthcare, volume 3: The arts and health* (pp. 121–141). Series editor, I. Serlin. Westport, CT: Praeger Press.

Harvey, S. (1989). Creative arts therapies in the classroom: A study of cognitive, emotional and motivational changes. *American Journal of Dance Therapy, 11*(2), 85–100. doi:10.1007/BF00843773

Koch, S., Kunz, T., Lykou, S., & Cruz, R. (2014). Effects of dance movement therapy and dance on psychological outcomes. A meta-analysis. *Arts in Psychotherapy, 41*(1), 46–64.

Koch, S., Morlinghaus, K., & Fuchs, T. (2007). The joy dance: Specific effects of a single dance intervention on psychiatric patients with depression. *The Arts in Psychotherapy 34*(4), 340–349. doi:10.1016/j.aip.2007/07/001

Koshland, L., & Wittaker, J. (2004). PEACE through dance/movement: Evaluating a violence prevention program. *American Journal of Dance Therapy, 26*(2), 69–90. doi:10.1007/s10465-004-0786-z

Meekums, B., Karkou, V., & Nelson, E. (2012). Dance movement therapy for depression. *Cochrane Database of Systematic Reviews, 2012*(6):CD009895. doi:10.1002/14651858.CD009895.

Mertens, D. (2009). *Research and evaluation in education and psychology: Integrating diversity with quantitative, qualitative and mixed methods* (3rd ed.). Thousand Oaks, CA: Sage.

Moore, C. (2006). Dance/movement therapy in the light of trauma: Research findings of a multidisciplinary project. In S. Koch & I. Bräuninger (Eds.), *Advances in dance/movement therapy: Theoretical perspectives and empirical findings* (pp. 104–115). Berlin, Germany: Logos Verlag.

National Collaborating Centre for Mental Health. (2010). *Core interventions in the treatment and management of schizophrenia in adults in primary and secondary care* (Updated edition). National Clinical Guideline Number 82. London, England: The British Psychological Society & The Royal College of Psychiatrists.

Ritter, M., & Low, K. (1996). Effects of dance/movement therapy: A meta-analysis. *Arts in Psychotherapy, 23*(3), 249–260. doi:10.1016/0197-4556(96)00027-5

Sandel, S., Judge, J., Landry, N., Faria, L., Ouellette, R., & Majczak, M. (2005). Dance and movement program improves quality-of-life measures in breast cancer survivors. *Cancer Nursing, 28*(4), 301–309. doi:10.1097/00002820-200507000-00011

Schmais, C. (1974). Dance therapy in perspective. In K. C. Mason (Ed.), *Focus on dance VII: Dance therapy* (pp. 7–12). Washington, DC: AAHPERD/NEA.

Vogt, W. (2005) *Dictionary of statistics and methodology: A nontechnical guide for the social sciences* (3rd ed.). Thousand Oaks, CA: Sage.

World Health Organization (WHO). (2015a). *Health topics: Mental health*. Retrieved on February 25, 2015, from http://www.who.int/topics/mental_health/en/

World Health Organization (WHO). (2015b). *Mental health: A state of well-being*. Retrieved on February 25, 2015, from http://www.who.int/features/factfiles/mental_health/en/

APPENDIX

Selected Additional Studies of Dance/Movement Therapy Effectiveness Using an RCT Design

Berrol, C., Ooi, W., & Katz, S. (1997). Dance/movement therapy with older adults who have sustained neurological insult: A demonstration project. *American Journal of Dance Therapy, 19*(2), 135–160. doi:10.1023/A:1022316102961

Bojner-Horwitz, E., Theorell, T., & Anderberg, U. (2003). Dance/movement therapy and changes in stress-related hormones: A study of fibromyalgia patients with video-interpretation. *The Arts in Psychotherapy, 30*(5), 255–264. doi:10.1016/j.aip.2003.07.001

Brooks, D., & Stark, A. (1989). The effect of D/MT on affect: A pilot study. *American Journal of Dance Therapy, 11*(2), 101–111. doi:10.1007/BF00843774

Goodill, S. (2005). Research letter: Dance/movement therapy for adults with cystic fibrosis: Pilot data on mood and adherence. *Alternative Therapies in Health & Medicine, 11*(1), 76–77.

Jeong, Y., Hong, S., Lee, M., Park, M., Kim, Y., & Suh, C. (2005). Dance movement therapy improves emotional responses and modulates neurohormones in adolescents with mild depression. *International Journal of Neuroscience, 115*(12), 1711–1720. doi:10.1080/00207450590958574

Krantz, A., & Pennebaker, J. W. (2007). Expressive dance, writing, trauma, and health: When words have a body. In I. A. Serlin, J. Sonke-Henderson, R. Brandman, & J. Graham-Pole (Eds.), *Whole person healthcare, volume 3: The arts and health* (pp. 201–229). Westport, CT: Praeger.

CHAPTER 13

Applied Theater
for Mental Health

Literature Review and Evidence-Based Research

Andrea Baldwin

The word *drama* comes from the Greek word *dran*, meaning "to act or do." Like *act*, the term *drama* expresses the dual nature of dramatic performance. On the one hand, drama is a projection of the imagination—a form of make-believe, a way of playing or pretending (Cattanach, 1994). On the other hand, the act of drama is entirely real—the performers use their real bodies, brains, faces, and voices in real space, interacting with other real people. Acting is a way to embody and make visible things that do not have bodies and cannot be seen—ideas, emotions, moods, conflicts, aspects of one's own and other people's personalities, and future possibilities. It is this dual nature of drama—its capacity to bridge imaginative representations of "what is" and "what could be" through the real body of the performer—that makes it such a powerful tool for personal and social change.

This chapter is primarily grounded in Boal's (1995) contention that the essence of theater is the human being observing itself:

> Theatre is born when the human being discovers that it can observe itself; when it discovers that, in this act of seeing, it can see *itself*—see itself *in situ*: see itself seeing. Observing itself, the human being perceives what it is, discovers what it is not and imagines what it could become. (p. 13)

Boal's theory implies that if a person can act (enact herself) and watch herself acting (reflect on the enactment), she can choose to change. Through theater, she can rehearse possible changes and reflect on them in a continuous cycle, empowering herself ultimately to enact herself in the real world as she wishes to be.

Walsh (2013) has pointed out the close correspondence between Boal's insistence on the importance of theater as a means of self-reflection and the mirror stage that forms the basis of human subjectivity in Lacanian psychoanalysis (p. 12). Lacan (1949/2006) describes the mirror stage—the moment of recognizing one's own image in a mirror and thus acquiring a sense of self—as "a drama . . . that forces the child to realise that she is separate from her mother and divided within herself, and condemned to seek wholeness in the world of images for the rest of her life" (p. 5). According to Lacan, acquiring the ability to observe ourselves is the beginning of an inherently psychopathological existence; Boal argues that it is also the tool by which we are able to heal our psychopathology. The close relationship between theater and therapy discussed by authors from both disciplines (e.g., Schrader, 2012; Walsh, 2013) embodies this understanding of theater as mirror. Practitioners of theater as therapy consider that theater promotes self-knowledge and enables change because it supports the seeker to enact and reflect on self in the world: "Man can see himself in the act of seeing, in the act of acting, in the act of feeling, in the act of thinking. Feel himself feeling, think himself thinking" (Boal, 1995, p. 13).

DEFINITIONS

Theater and Drama

There is a sense, though not a consensus, that *theater* implies the presence of an audience separate from the performers, whereas *drama* can be enacted for the benefit of the performers/participants alone (Nicholson, 2005). Landy and Montgomery (2012) point to the Greek etymology of the words *drama* and *theater*: *drama* meaning an action taken and *theater* meaning a place for observing an action. However, the term *applied theater* is commonly used for any dramatic enactment intended to progress educational, psychotherapeutic, and social objectives, whether or not an audience is present. Landy and Montgomery (2012) adopt the term *theater for change*. Throughout this chapter, I will use the more inclusive term *drama* to refer to drama activities with or without an external audience.

Drama Therapy and Social Theater

Several chapters of Sue Jennings' book *Dramatherapy and Social Theatre* (2009) explore the idea of social theater embracing community-based theater, theater for development, popular theater, and theater in education. Similarly, Landy and Montgomery's book *Theatre for Change* (2012) has sections on drama and theater in education, social action, and therapy. Jennings rejects the suggestion that drama therapy should be included under the rubric of social theater since drama therapists are specifically trained professionals whose work focuses strongly on the individual while most forms of social theater focus on the group as a means of promoting both individual learning and social change. Landy and Montgomery (2012) explore the similarities and differences between what they term *drama therapy* and *applied theater* in some depth (pp. 171–175). For current purposes, I will differentiate drama therapy from other forms of social theater.

Participants

There is a sensitive question of terminology concerning whether people who experience or have experienced severe disruptions to their mental health prefer to call themselves consumers, service users, patients, clients, or survivors. To some extent, obviously, the choice is individual. For an author, however, each of these terms carries a wealth of connotation and is founded in ideological beliefs and assumptions about the nature of mental illness, the role of the mental health system, and the relationship between the individual and service providers. It is important to acknowledge that everyone faces challenges to their mental health and that at any given time some people are living with more severe and potentially disabling problems than others. Since this chapter is mostly concerned with people engaging in dramatic activity, I will adopt the term *participant* where practicable. At other times I will use the term *person with mental illness* since this formulation (like *person with disability* or *person living with HIV/AIDS*) affirms the primacy of the person without diminishing the significance of the challenges they live with. Similarly, I feel the term *client* empowers the person and respects the client–service provider relationship within the appropriate context.

FORMS OF DRAMA PRACTICE IN RELATION TO MENTAL HEALTH

The focus of this chapter is on drama as a wellness-enhancing activity in which a person with mental illness may engage. Drama is also be used in mental health education, health promotion, and advocacy, but these applications are beyond the scope of this chapter.

Without attempting an exhaustive review, the following section provides an overview of some forms of drama practice commonly found in the literature. In practice, many of these forms overlap or share boundaries. Each form mentioned below is worthy of exploration in its own right; some have chapters, books, and journals devoted to them. The descriptions and examples given here are necessarily brief and are not intended to capture all the nuances of these practices.

THEATRICAL THEATER

Theater About Mental Health Issues

Theater about mental health issues takes mental health issues as its content material. Typically it is scripted by a professional playwright, performed by professional actors, staged in theaters or recognized theatrical spaces, and seeks to entertain a mainstream audience while challenging stereotypes and deepening understanding of mental illness. Examples of published plays in this category abound, including Louis Nowra's (1992) *Cosi* and Alan Bennett's (1991) *The Madness of George III*.

Theatre Royal Plymouth Young Company is, at the time of writing, producing a monologue by Claire Dowie about "how a young woman's life can spiral downwards into mental illness," which the director sees as giving the young company members an opportunity to engage with challenging material (Haller, 2010; see Appendix 1).

Theater Based on Lived Experience

Theater based on lived experience is more immediately based on the true story of a person or a group of people living with mental illness. It may be performed in theaters or in nontraditional venues, including residential institutions, community festivals, and public spaces. It is most commonly performed on an amateur or profit-share basis, though some professional companies exist throughout the world. Teatro Patologico (n.d.) is an Italian theater company made up of people with mental illness that produces professional shows in Italy and off Broadway.

The objectives of theater based on lived experience may include promoting social inclusion, enabling people with mental illness to tell their own stories, encouraging confidence, developing theatrical skills, challenging audiences toward more informed and positive understandings of mental health, reducing stigma, and influencing mental health policy and practice. There may also be financial benefits for the artists involved.

The Minotaur in Me, Paul Whittaker's play about his experiences of bipolar disorder, was performed at the Sherman Theatre in Cardiff in 2006 (Theatre Wales, 2013). Our Own Voice Theatre Troupe (n.d.), based in Memphis, Tennessee, is a "nonprofit organization working to empower people marginalized by mental illness, and striving to engage our community in dialogue about mental health." The company devises and performs plays about mental illness for a mainstream audience. Stepping Out Theatre, based in Bristol, England, describes itself as the United Kingdom's leading mental health theater group (Stepping Out, 2010). It has produced a wide range of work on mental health themes and is open to people who have used mental health services and their allies. The group runs drama, writing, dance, and music workshops. It offers mental health service users the opportunity to work alongside people with professional experience of writing, directing, and acting, some of whom are service users themselves.

Canonical Theater Performed by People With Mental Illness

The idea that performing classic, canonical works of theater can be a therapeutic activity is well established, particularly in the United Kingdom. Louis Nowra's (1992) semiautobiographical play *Cosi* is based on the efforts of a group of inpatients, supported by a well-meaning professional director, to stage Mozart's opera *Cosi fan tutti*. There is a strong tradition of staging Greek tragedies such as *Oedipus Rex*, canonical plays such as Beckett's *Waiting for Godot*, and works by Shakespeare in prisons and mental health institutions where the themes of these works are seen as speaking to issues relevant to participants (Cox, 1992; Landy & Montgomery, 2012). The Educational Shakespeare Company (n.d.) in Belfast, Northern Ireland, develops drama and film with prisoners and ex-prisoners based on Shakespearean texts. One of its best-known productions is the film *Mickey B*, based on *Macbeth*.

Theater for Social Action With a Mental Health Component

This category of theater represents an overlap between the kind of theater often described as community theater or theater for social action and more specifically "therapeutic" drama forms. While it is beyond the scope of this chapter to explore the many applications of theater for social action, this type of theater typically addresses important social issues for a community or a group within a community. Landy and Montgomery (2012) provide examples such as a play performed by child laborers in the Philippines, which led to the reexamination of laws and the raising of funds to support the children's education, and a play performed by ethnic minority Hakka women in Taiwan to draw attention to their stories of displacement and abandonment (p. 127).

On occasion, theater for social action aims to help communities or groups recover from traumatic events. Much community theater in Northern Ireland in the 1990s and 2000s, for example, attempted to help individuals on both sides of the conflict to express, explore, and move on from The Troubles. Since so many people had been personally involved in the violence and/or lost friends and family members, this kind of theater recognized the traumatic nature of these events and included an agenda for psychological healing (see Jennings & Baldwin, 2010).

Standing Tall was a theater project undertaken with nine-and ten-year-old school children who had witnessed the 9/11 attacks on the World Trade Center. With the support of a drama therapist, teaching artists, and classroom teacher, the children participated in a workshop and created a play that they performed for an audience of peers, teachers, parents, and community members. One child participant epitomized the psychotherapeutic aims of the project in the comment, "I don't know what I'd do without the drama . . . without the drama, I would just be . . . dead in my mind" (Landy & Montgomery, 2012, p. 144).

DRAMA AS SOCIAL EXPERIENCE

Visiting Performances

Visiting performances are usually intended to engage residents or clients of an institution in vivid and valuable learning experiences. The degree of interaction between performers, audience members, and staff may vary. Sue Jennings (2009) was asked to perform her one-woman adaptation of *Romeo and Juliet* for women at Broadmoor Hospital by a psychiatrist who said that "the play raised issues about mothering and abandonment . . . it was important for some of the female patients in the secure hospital" (p. 6). Jennings says, "The performance opened up areas of discussion with myself and the women about the Nurse's role as mother substitute and the mistakes she made" (p. 7) and also notes that the performance and discussion forced her to confront her own sense of failings as a mother.

Participatory Drama

Participatory drama uses the techniques of drama in education but repurposes these for mental health treatment settings rather than school settings. Geese Theatre Company (n.d.) runs participatory theater workshops in prisons and secure mental health settings. Respect Yourself Drama Education (RYDE) is an improvisation-based program designed to help adolescents with mental health problems explore, enjoy, and respect their own creativity.

DRAMA AS THERAPY: PSYCHODRAMA AND DRAMA THERAPY

It is worth exploring in some detail the practices known respectively as psychodrama and drama therapy. The summary tables convey a sense of the similarities between these two forms, but from a practitioner point of view, they are distinct bodies of practice with different theoretical roots, certification requirements, and processes.

Psychodrama

Psychodrama was founded by Jacob L. Moreno M.D. in the 1920s (Fox, 1987). It is a form of psychotherapy in which a person enacts personal issues rather than simply talking about them. Psychodrama can be conducted on an individual basis or in a group. While the focus at any given point in time will be on an individual—the protagonist—other people in the group (auxiliaries) help the protagonist to enact the story by taking on the roles of other people or other aspects of the protagonist's thoughts and feelings or by simply bearing witness. The therapist, termed the *director,* facilitates the therapeutic process.

The enactment of dramas based on the protagonist's life and internal conflicts implies a level of reliving through which both protagonist and audience experience emotional catharsis. Following Freud, Moreno adopted the Aristotelian idea of catharsis—a release of deep feelings, which Aristotle saw as a purging or purification of the senses and the soul (Jones, 2007). By stating that the function of tragedy was to induce this emotional and spiritual state of catharsis, Aristotle formalized an idea that recurs throughout the history of writing about the healing potential of theater. Psychodramatic scenes usually aim to induce catharsis and so tend to be deeply emotional, dealing with painful memories, childhood trauma, unresolved conflict, and critical life events. In psychodrama, healing is supposed to occur as the protagonist faces and relives these events, understanding them differently through the distance provided by the dramatic form and the assistance of others (Emunah, 1994).

Drama Therapy

Drama therapy is a much broader term that is now viewed as including psychodrama as one specific form. While Peter Slade used the term in his 1959 pamphlet "Dramatherapy as an Aid to Becoming a Person" and had been using drama for therapeutic purposes since the 1930s, the movement is also traced to virtually independent developments by Sue Jennings and Gordon Wiseman in the 1960s (the Remedial Drama Centre in London) and Billy Lindkvist in the 1970s (the Sesame organization; Jones, 2007).

Jones (2007) provides a comprehensive and fascinating history of the development of modern drama therapy, showing how this new field of practice emerged over the twentieth century from areas as seemingly disparate as the study of human development and children's play, education, psychology, anthropology, experimental and political theater, and actor training. A key idea emerging from this history is that drama facilitates change—participation in drama helps individuals and groups to learn, grow, and do things differently.

MODELS OF DRAMA THERAPY

Meldrum (1994) describes four current models of drama therapy: theater models, therapeutic drama, role models, and anthropological approaches. Meldrum points out, however, that these are only four models of drama therapy that can be identified in an eclectic body of practice, which ranges from "an intellectual pursuit of metaphor in Shakespearean text and its meaning for the individual, to the use of touch and simple mime" (p. 25).

Theater Models of Drama Therapy

Sue Jennings views drama therapists not as psychotherapists but as creative artists, and drama therapy as a system founded in theater. Jennings says the therapeutic effect of drama therapy requires the presence of another person and a special place (Jennings, 1990). Meldrum also emphasizes the importance of the theater space: "Metaphor is the medium of theatre, drama and dramatherapy and rituals are played out in the empty space" (Meldrum, 1994, p. 22).

Drama therapists who use theater models see the therapist as a facilitative director and an empathic facilitator. Mitchell's theater model emphasizes the way in which the therapist helps the client shift the everyday problems of life into a theatrical reality, "to capture the appropriate image and make it both emotional and cognitive" (Meldrum, 1994, p. 23).

Meldrum's model focuses on the way in which a drama therapy session can be seen to parallel a theatrical production, allowing the participants/actors to use their physicality, develop their characterizations, and engage their intellect. The client uses projective techniques to give voice to feelings and desires through drama, and the therapist and other group members become what Boal (2000) calls "spectators"—both spectators and actors. As the spectators watch the drama of others, they see in their stories multiple mirrors of themselves (Meldrum, 1994, p. 24).

Therapeutic Drama Models of Drama Therapy

Therapeutic drama models do not limit themselves to the client's own story but make use of myths, legends, folktales, and classic texts, as well as the forms of stories. Gersie and Lahad are two drama therapists who ask clients to draw, enact, or tell a story based on some basic elements: a landscape, a dwelling place, a main character with a mission or task, an obstacle, a helper, and a resolution. Lahad listens for the overtone of the story, the kind of language the client uses, and the coping mechanisms expressed. Gersie focuses on the helper character, exploring how clients can make better use of the various helpers and resources available to them. Jenkyns, with a different approach, encourages clients to use an existing text (such as Shakespeare's *The Tempest*) as a projective or metaphorical technique to explore their own personal story (Meldrum, 1994).

Role Models of Drama Therapy

In these models, the therapeutic goals of the drama therapist are to help clients increase the number of roles they have, not to be engulfed by or stuck in one or two roles, and to be flexible in their ability to move from one role to another. "Role theory invites the dramatherapist to look at the healing aspects of the client rather than their psychopathology" (Meldrum, 1994, p. 24). A resolution is successful "when the client has recognised the existence and significance of the healing part of himself [*sic*] and has acted toward himself as the therapist has acted toward him" (Landy, 1992, p. 103).

Anthropological Models of Drama Therapy

Meldrum briefly examines an emerging trend in drama therapy, which follows director Jerzey Grotowski's vision of the actor as shaman. Drama therapists such as Johnson (1992) extend this metaphor to the therapist. Johnson describes the shaman as going into a trance state, exchanging roles with the client, and creating "a symbolic enactment of the malady and its roots" (Johnson, 1992, p. 235). Johnson (1992) says that the drama therapist should be comfortable with the role of actor/shaman, enacting images in the drama while the client watches as audience.

However, many drama therapists take issue with this development, considering it inappropriate for the therapist to take the role of actor with the client as spectator. According to this view, the client's embodiment of his or her own story is central to the therapeutic intervention. Like models of hospital theater from the 1950s, in which staff performed plays for the entertainment of patients, the idea of therapist as shaman is felt to reinforce unhelpful power relations in which staff are seen as capable and patients fit only to receive (Jones, 2007). Jones is also critical of the appropriation of the idea of shamanism from traditional societies:

> This way of interpreting past history or the practices of non-western cultures . . . has a tendency to impose inappropriate contemporary notions and concepts upon practices and forms . . . a distortion can occur as a tradition or practice is given a false contemporary interpretation. (p. 25)

THE DIFFERENCE BETWEEN DRAMA AS THERAPY AND DRAMA AS SOCIAL EXPERIENCE

Many theater professionals use drama to help participants achieve change of some kind without seeing themselves as therapists or their work as a form of therapy. Geese Theatre, a company that works with offenders and people at risk, offers an interesting discussion in its handbook. They point out that "drama and psychological therapy have been professionally linked since as long ago as 1797, when the Abbé de Coulmier used theater productions as a method of therapy for patients at his asylum at Charenton, near Paris (Jones, 1996). Nevertheless, it is important to stress that therapy is separate and distinct from drama, and its boundaries should be respected." Further, they explain that

> in the broadest sense of the word, however, drama can be therapeutic, just as all art, education and social interaction have the potential to be psychologically challenging and life enhancing. Nevertheless, when we apply drama intending to

challenge participants' ideas and encourage positive change, and we do not have specific therapy training, we should know what constitutes the boundary between work that is broadly social/educational as opposed to that which is directly psychotherapeutic. This means having some insight into where the path might lead, so that we are aware when we are moving from the relatively safe ground of social experience—concentrating mainly on the social functioning of the participant—into the realm of therapy, which is purposely aimed at surfacing deeply personal material, tracing behavioural and emotional patterns back to their origins, and, where appropriate, working through life experiences. (Baim, Brooks, & Mountford, 2002, p. xv)

Perhaps the main difference between drama as therapy and drama as social experience is that drama therapy requires the presence of a person specifically trained, qualified, and employed as a therapist. Despite the collaborative nature of therapy, which is explicitly emphasized in most models of drama therapy, the therapist carries a heavy burden of responsibility and expectations. The therapist is expected to be familiar with the client's needs, to have a rationale for the activities undertaken, to maintain safety, to conduct the session in an ethical manner, and—usually—to report periodically on the client's progress in therapy. These expectations come from the client, the client's family, the treatment setting, the treatment setting's wider context (for example, the state-run health service or the nongovernment organization operating the setting), and the therapist's professional organization and/or registration board.

Of course, theater practitioners such as Geese Theatre instructors are also expected to conduct activities in a safe and ethical manner with a clear rationale for what they do. Perhaps the activities of a company such as Geese can best be seen as further along the continuum on some of the aspects that distinguish drama therapy from psychodrama. Moreno developed a form he called *sociodrama*, in contrast to psychodrama, because Moreno focuses on enactments of issues pertaining to the group as a whole, rather than an individual's personal situation (Emunah, 1994). Participants assume social roles in hypothetical situations related to issues they share but do not play roles specific to their own personal lives. Moreno saw roles as having both private and collective components; psychodrama addresses the private components, sociodrama the collective. Groups of people who are highly threatened by personal self-disclosure can benefit by interactively exploring their issues with the greater distance, or disguise, offered by sociodrama (Emunah, 1994). It may be useful to consider the work of companies that seek to help groups address difficult issues, without focusing intensely on the real-life experiences of individuals, as a form of sociodrama.

The second concept to look at on a continuum in relation to drama as social participation versus drama as therapy is the concept of change. In the discussion above, the Geese Theatre handbook states that "drama can be therapeutic, just as all art, education and social interaction have the potential to be psychologically challenging and life enhancing" (p. xv). According to Meldrum, a process of therapy begins with the assumption that one is sick or wounded and needs to heal. The term *psychologically challenging* as used by Geese implies the notion of being psychologically stuck in a pattern or way of being, and change to this way of being will constitute healing. Lahad, interviewed in Jennings (1994), articulates this "stuckness" as a narrowing down of pathways the client perceives as being available for them to take: "Suicidal adolescents. . . . don't even believe there is *one* way" (p. 181).

Participation in drama is seen as a way of opening up pathways, helping the client experience the possibility of alternatives (e.g., Diamond-Raab & Orrell-Valente, 2002).

But what of a process that does not begin from an assumption that healing is needed but rather an assumption that change would be life enhancing, helpful, good for you—"therapeutic" in the sense used by Geese? This starting point is implied in the phrase "work that is broadly social/educational." Such a view of drama is closer to drama in education than drama therapy—the idea that building knowledge, attitudes, and skills through drama is a form of personal growth that will help the client to overcome problems and meet challenges in real life.

The group of professionals variously known as leisure therapists, diversional therapists, or recreation therapists work to help their clients enrich and enhance their lives through pleasurable and challenging activities. For example, adventure therapists make use of the disequilibrizing effects of experiences, such as jumping off a pamper pole, to help clients cultivate trust in themselves and others. Recreation therapists are not usually trained as psychotherapists or drama therapists per se. However, some recreation therapists seek to enhance their social drama skills through appropriate training in order to offer drama activities directly to groups of clients. Others refer their clients to drama activities in the community. In either case, these professionals recognize the processes theorized as supporting mental health recovery, outlined in the section "Community-Based Theater."

Working with drama in the interests of personal growth does not necessarily require a therapist. People with mental illness may organize themselves, with or without the support of professional theater makers, to create theater for the purpose of making changes they are interested in, personal and social (*Barking Mad: The Musical* is one Australian example). It is perhaps this form of drama as a social experience that most fully embodies the notion of drama for recovery—people feeling empowered to use the resources at their disposal in collaboration with others to enjoy the creation of drama for the realization of their own goals.

HOW DOES PARTICIPATION IN DRAMA SUPPORT RECOVERY?

There have been many attempts to identify the "core processes" (Jones, 2007) of drama practice that help to support mental health and well-being. Different theorists identify different processes as these active ingredients of dramatic practice. For example, Jones' (2007) analysis of the core processes in drama therapy emphasizes intrapersonal effects while Faigin and Stein's (2010) analysis of the core processes, in what they call community-based theater, highlights communal and social effects.

Drama Therapy Core Processes

Dramatic Projection

Projection refers to the process by which participants project aspects of themselves and their experiences into theatrical or dramatic materials or into enactment, thereby externalizing their internal conflicts (Crenshaw, 2006; Meekums, 2000). The externalized material, which might previously have been unconscious or seemed unspeakable, is then available for the participant, therapist, and group to see and work with.

Empathy and Distancing

Empathy encourages emotional resonance, identification, and involvement with dramatic work (Boal, 2000). Distancing is the process by which emotion is contained and the participant is able to orient toward thought, reflection, and perspective (Jones, 2007). In Brecht's terminology, distancing allows the participant to function as a reader of material (Boal, 2000). Both processes can apply to a participant as actor or as audience, and both are needed for dramatic work to have the power to drive change.

Role Playing and Personification

Jones (2007) identifies three kinds of roles most often taken on in drama therapy: the participant taking on a fictional identity, the participant playing themselves in a situation from life outside the therapy context, and the participant deliberately isolating an aspect of their identity. There is also role reversal in which the participant plays the role of a significant other in a situation that is causing him or her problems. Personification means the act of representing something or some personal quality or aspect using objects (Jones, 2007). Role playing and personification can help the participant to look at a situation in new ways and to explore a repertoire of responses outside her own normal patterns of response. Evreinov (1927) saw role playing as inherently therapeutic both because of the "transfigurative energy" involved in enacting a different role (p. 125) and because creating a new role is a way of engaging with real life differently: "Play a role well, and you will live up to it" (p. 125).

Interactive Audience and Witnessing

Witnessing is the act of being an audience to others or to oneself (Jones, 2007). The act of witnessing, and of being witnessed, expands awareness of and validates one's emotions, crystallizes awareness of one's behaviors, and opens up the opportunity for exploration of aspects of experience that otherwise remain unconscious or denied.

Embodiment: Dramatizing the Body

Drama therapist Lili Levy reflects on an interaction with a client in drama therapy thus: "By talking, she *tells* me how she feels, but by embodying the characters she has the experience and *feels* it in the 'here and now'. Embodying allows her to get in touch with her emotions and to express her wildest fantasy" (Jones, 2007, p. 225). The body is the main tool of communication and expression in drama and drama therapy. Jones says that individuals in drama therapy may have new experiences of the body and identity, discover new behaviors and new languages of gesture and expression, gain an increased awareness of the body's range and potential, experience altered perceptions and sharpening of the senses, find others relating to the individual's body and identity in new ways, and gain self-awareness (p. 239).

Playing

Most key figures in the development of modern drama therapy have been interested in the developmental functions of children's play (Bolton, 1984; Cattanach, 1994; Slade, 1954).

Jones (2007) argues the creation of access to playfulness is often therapeutic in itself for clients who may be cut off from the ability to engage spontaneously with self, others, and life (p. 165). In Jones' view, drama enables groups and individuals to "engage creatively . . . with problematic material where before they have only been able to remain stuck and uncreative in response to problems" (p. 165). Evreinov (1927) said of children's play that "all children have the ability to create a new reality out of the facts of life" (p. 36). Play provides children and adults with a means to master and come to terms with events, to assimilate and accommodate reality, and to make meaning of their lives (Oon, 2010).

Life–Drama Connection

Drama therapy is founded on the principle that life and drama are intimately connected; one's performance within a drama is both real and not real, and one's discoveries through drama are about the nature of one's relationship with life. What one learns through drama one is therefore able to apply to life, whether consciously or otherwise. Jones (2007) points out that in some work the life–drama connection is constantly acknowledged, as for example when working with clients whose relationship with reality is confused or tenuous. For other clients, it might be important to work in a way that has little direct acknowledgment of the life–drama connection, for example where self-disclosure is overwhelmingly anxiety provoking but the client is able to work comfortably at a metaphorical level. Jones provides several studies of young people with autism for whom this is the case (e.g., pp. 185, 198, 242–249; see also Oon, 2010).

Transformation

Transformation refers to positive changes in state that the client experiences through engagement in drama. Jones (2007) feels these changes are facilitated by the transformative nature of drama—the way life events are transformed into enacted representations of those events, people encountered in everyday life are transformed into roles or characters, and objects are transformed into representations and given significances beyond their concrete properties. Since to make drama, the person must engage with this fluid and dynamic process of multiple transformations, it is perhaps impossible to remain unchanged. Evreinov (1927) was one of many theorists who believe the change enabled by drama is inherently change for the better because of the human instinct toward self-actualization: "He selects, so to speak, a part for himself. And then he begins to play this part" (p. 27). In Jones's words, people transfigure reality by imagining difference, and thus effect the transformations they imagine and wish for (p. 33).

Community-Based Theater

Group Cohesion and Affiliation

Faigin and Stein (2010) call attention to the fact that people living with mental illness are often socially isolated. Interacting with others to produce drama, whether in a workshop context or for a theater performance, engenders and requires the operation of socially cohesive forces—trusting and being trustworthy, personal and communal risk taking, feeling safe and maintaining the safety of others, and working as a team.

Openness and Inclusion

The setting in which service users participate in community-based theater is usually characterized by a sense of openness, inclusion, permission, leaving no one out, and enlisting everyone's strengths. Such a philosophy tends to activate and acknowledge the personal capabilities of individual group members and enables drama to form a bridge between personal development and community integration.

Common Experiences

Typically, a group of people with mental illness engaged in creating drama will share and draw on some common experiences. These are likely to include both positive and negative experiences with the symptoms and challenges of mental illness, experience of hospitals and service systems, medication, medico-legal proceedings, relationships, sources of support, and so on. The sharing of these experiences, and the use of performance to transform such experiences into aesthetic products that can be processed in a different way, supports both personal growth and group cohesion.

Expanded Sense of Self

Participating in drama can result in an expanded sense of self (Faigin & Stein, 2010, p. 307) as a result of acting in public a valued social role (actor, performer, entertainer, artist, director, musician, writer, stage manager, and so on). The skills a person develops and hones through the process of meeting the demands of these roles can be useful in facing other life challenges and are likely to lead to greater self-esteem, self-confidence, and self-efficacy in novel situations. To experience such growth in one's identity as a creative and capable person can be extremely powerful, affirming, and life enhancing.

Flexibility

Many forms of mental illness are characterized by a level of mental rigidity or "stuckness." Drama encourages flexibility of thought, feeling, and expression. The community-based theater context typically balances structural demands for flexibility with the provision of adequate support to achieve this flexibility. It fosters a sense that it is acceptable to take risks and make mistakes; indeed, a constant process of risk taking is necessary if performance is to occur at all, and drama therefore encourages the development of complex and fluid problem solving skills.

Opportunities for Community Connections and Integration

While people are performing the valued social roles associated with dramatic practice, they are likely to experience various opportunities for community connections and communication. This is perhaps especially the case in public performance, which provides an opportunity for advocacy, destigmatization, and raising levels of awareness and understanding of mental illness in the community. It is common for audience members to converse with cast members either through formal sessions structured into the show or through informal conversation afterwards. The person with mental illness is thus cast in the role of expert and is empowered to connect with the wider community as educator, advocate, and person of worth.

Ownership

Finally, Faigin and Stein (2010) emphasize the empowerment that comes from a sense of ownership of personal and social change processes. Community-based theater encourages a sense of personal ownership toward everything from the skills one is exercising to the character one is playing onstage, the theater troupe of which one is a member, and the audience for which the theater troupe performs. This sense of personal ownership is likely to enhance self-efficacy, encourage pride in the creative activities being undertaken, and strengthen identity as a powerful and capable individual.

EVIDENCE OF EFFECTIVENESS: HOW PARTICIPATION IN DRAMA SUPPORTS RECOVERY

Arts-based therapies are still determining how best to assess their own claims of therapeutic efficacy. On the one hand, health sciences privilege quantitative data collected through the framework of scientific enquiry as the desired evidence base for psychosocial interventions. On the other hand, many therapists (and clients) reject what they consider a reductionistic approach to assessing the impact of therapy on the client's life. How, for example, does one operationalize and measure an expanded sense of self? Instead, these researchers see evidence of effectiveness in the way detailed case studies, therapists' notes, and clients' reflections demonstrate the operation of processes that are predicted by theories of psychological change or transformation. Journals such as *Dramatherapy: The Journal for the Association of Dramatherapists*, *The Arts in Psychotherapy*, and the *Journal of Group Psychotherapy, Psychodrama and Sociometry* make a concerted and sustained effort to report on the clinical experiences of practitioners working with a range of populations and to document outcomes for individuals and groups.

Drama educator Brad Haseman (2006) champions another understanding of what constitutes evidence in applied theater research. He notes the distinction between quantitative and qualitative data and adds the category of "performative data" to assert that evidence of change in clients' lives and functioning can be seen in their performances, what they *do*, perform, or enact on a stage, in a therapy room, or in a workshop space. In the same way that the complexity of qualitative data cannot be reduced to numbers without losing richness and meaning, so performative data cannot be reduced via qualitative techniques such as text-based description without a similar loss of value—the evidence it provides must be read through the experiencing of the performance.

Basso and Pelech (2008) provide an example of the limitations of quantitative data analysis for assessing the success of drama programs. Their drama program for children coping with juvenile diabetes did not produce significant changes on quantitative measures of the children's knowledge about their illness. However, their parents' qualitative reports indicated that after the drama program the children were more willing to "speak up directly" about their illness and its management. The children were reported as more likely to ask questions, more likely to make suggestions about day-to-day management, and more willing to express their feelings and frustrations related to the illness and its impacts on their relationships. Even more telling are the therapists' observations of the children's actual performances, in which they expressed their ambivalent feelings about dependence on parents and caregivers (including medical staff), feelings of anger and helplessness, the impact of a sense of poor or compromised health on identity and self-image, fears that they were in some way to blame for their illness, and the need to be free from feelings of guilt, shame, and self-recrimination. From the performative data, much more than from the quantitative or even the qualitative data, it was clear that the drama program

> permitted the children to directly address their feelings, issues, and concerns about their chronic illness and provided a safe, topical, and metaphorical avenue for them to express these concerns . . . Creative arts activities supported a comprehensive goal of assisting the children in learning how to assume age-appropriate responsibilities and contribute toward the maintenance of their own health. (Basso & Pelech, 2008, p. 28)

Jones (2007) engages in some depth with the question of whether quantitative methods of data collection can be useful in assessing the impacts of drama work on mental health. He says:

> The arts therapies need not be seen as either art or science. The arts therapies are a product of a link made in a divide present in cultural concepts and practices. They are a sign of a vital connection between areas often seen as divided. (p. 89)

However, it must be acknowledged that the divide is currently more in evidence than the link. Quantitative studies of the impact of involvement in drama on discrete, specific, measurable aspects of clients' lives are few and far between. A Cochrane review of studies using drama therapy and psychodrama for schizophrenia found only five studies of a possible 183 that met the criteria for inclusion in the review and concluded that "due to poor reporting very little data from the five studies could be used and there were no conclusive findings about the harms or benefits of drama therapy for inpatients with schizophrenia" (Ruddy & Dent-Brown, 2007). Jones (2007) recognizes the argument that such studies are philosophically at odds with the process of dramatic transformation and cannot hope to capture or express it. By contrast, there is a rich literature of case studies exemplifying aspects of the theory of therapeutic drama and that support mental health recovery through stories of real clients' experiences (e.g., Crenshaw, 2006; Jennings, 2009; Meekums, 2000). The majority of the literature available through academic sources has been written by therapists and theater practitioners and focuses on the formal therapeutic forms of drama such as psychodrama and drama therapy (e.g., Oon, 2010; Rousseau et al., 2007). Stories told directly by service users of their experiences with drama and documentation of drama activities that support mental health outside formal treatment settings are more difficult to locate but sometimes appear in service newsletters and on websites.

CONCLUSION

As noted at the beginning of this chapter, mental health recovery can be seen as "a journey toward a new and valued sense of identity, role and purpose outside the parameters of mental illness; and living well despite any limitations resulting from the illness, its treatment, and personal and environmental conditions" (Queensland Health, 2005). Dramatic activities provide a kaleidoscope of ways to enact different selves—different identities, roles, and purposes—and different worlds in which to live well. Most major theories of drama in mental health are underpinned by a belief that enacting new possibilities in drama provides a first step toward enacting these possibilities in real life.

Perhaps the question of whether and how involvement in drama can support mental health is as broad as the question of whether and how drama enhances human experience, learning, and growth generally. Evreinov (1927) is one of many writers who claim that drama is a vital aspect of how human beings understand themselves and successfully live in society with one another: "It is something as essentially necessary to man as air, food, and sexual intercourse" (p. 6). Drama enables us to enact and reflect on potentially infinite versions of self and world. Accordingly, it is an invaluable aid in a self-actualizing process of recovery.

REFERENCES

Baim, C., Brooks, S., & Mountford, A. (2002). *The Geese Theatre handbook*. Winchester, England: Waterside Press.

Basso, R., & Pelech, W. (2008). A creative arts intervention for children with diabetes. Part 2: Evaluation. *Journal of Psychosocial Nursing, 46*(12), 25–28. doi:10.3928/02793695-20081201-01

Bennett, A. (1991). *The madness of King George III*. London, England: Faber & Faber.

Boal, A. (1995). *The rainbow of desire*. London, England: Routledge.

Boal, A. (2000). *Theatre of the oppressed*. London, England: Pluto.

Bolton, G. (1984). *Drama as education*. Essex, England: Longman.

Cattanach, A. (1994). The developmental model of dramatherapy. In S. Jennings, A. Cattanach, S. Mitchell, A. Chesner, & B. Meldrum (Eds.), *The Handbook of Dramatherapy* (pp. 28–40). New York, NY: Routledge.

Cox, M. (1992). *Shakespeare comes to Broadmoor: The actors are come hither*. London, England: Jessica Kingsley.

Crenshaw, D. (2006). *Evocative strategies in child and adolescent psychotherapy*. Lanham, MD: Jason Aronson.

Diamond-Raab, L., & Orrell-Valente, J. (2002). Art therapy, psychodrama, and verbal therapy. An integrative model of group therapy in the treatment of adolescents with anorexia nervosa and bulimia nervosa. *Child and Adolescent Psychiatric Clinics of North America, 11*(2), 343–364. Retrieved from http://www.ncbi.nlm.nih.gov/pubmed/12109325

Educational Shakespeare Company. (n.d.). Understanding through film. Retrieved July 11, 2013, from http://esc-film.com

Emunah, R. (1994). *Acting for real: Drama therapy process, technique, and performance*. London, England: Brunner-Routledge.

Evreinov, N. (1927). *The theatre in life*. New York, NY: Harrap.

Faigin, D., & Stein, C. (2010). The power of theatre to promote individual recovery and social change. *Psychiatric Services, 61*(3), 306–308. doi:10.1176/appi.ps.61.3.306

Fox, J. (1987). Moreno's philosophical system. In J. Fox (Ed.), *The Essential Moreno: Writings on psychodrama, the group method and spontaneity* (pp. 3–12). New York, NY: Springer.

Geese Theatre Company. (n.d.). Forensic mental health. Retrieved March 6, 2010, from http://www.geese.co.uk/work/adults/forensic-mental-health/

Haller, B. (2010). *British youth theatre takes on mental health themes in play*. Retrieved March 6, 2010, from http://media-dis-n-dat.blogspot.com.au/2010/03/british-youth-theater-takes-on-mental.html

Haseman, B. (2006). A manifesto for performative research. *Media International Australia Incorporating Culture and Policy*, *118*(118), 98–106. Retrieved from http://www.emsah.uq.edu.au/mia/

Jennings, M., & Baldwin, A. (2010). "Filling out the forms was a nightmare": Project evaluation and the reflective practitioner in community theatre in contemporary Northern Ireland. *Music and Arts in Action*, *2*(2), 72–89.

Jennings, S. (1990). *Dramatherapy with families, groups and individuals*. London, England: Jessica Kingsley.

Jennings, S. (1994). What is dramatherapy? Interviews with pioneers and practitioners. In S. Jennings, A. Cattanach, S. Mitchell, A. Chesner, & B. Meldrum (Eds.), *The Handbook of Dramatherapy* (pp. 166–186). New York, NY: Routledge.

Jennings, S. (2009). *Dramatherapy and social theatre: Necessary dialogues*. East Sussex, England: Routledge.

Johnson, D. (1992). The dramatherapist "in-role." In S. Jennings (Ed.), *Dramatherapy theory and practice 2*. London, England: Routledge.

Jones, P. (1996). *Drama as therapy, theatre as living*. London, England: Routledge.

Jones, P. (2007). *Drama as therapy: Theory, practice and research*. New York, NY: Routledge.

Lacan, J. (2006). The mirror stage as formative of the *I* function as revealed in psychoanalytic experience. In B. Fink (Trans.), *Écrits: The first complete edition in English*. New York, NY: W.W. Norton and Company. (Original work published 1949)

Landy, R. (1992). One-on-one: The role of the dramatherapist working with individuals. In S. Jennings (Ed.), *Dramatherapy theory and practice 2*. London, England: Routledge.

Landy, R., & Montgomery, D. (2012). *Theatre for change: Education, social action and therapy*. New York, NY: Palgrave Macmillan.

Meekums, B. (2000). *Creative group therapy for women survivors of child sexual abuse: Speaking the unspeakable*. London, England: Jessica Kingsley.

Meldrum, B. (1994). Historical background and overview. In S. Jennings, A. Cattanach, S. Mitchell, A. Chesner, & B. Meldrum (Eds.), *The handbook of dramatherapy* (pp. 12–27). New York, NY: Routledge.

Nicholson, H. (2005). *Applied drama: The gift of theatre*. New York, NY: Palgrave Macmillan.

Nowra, L. (1992). *Cosi*. Sydney, Australia: Currency.

Oon, P. (2010). Playing with Gladys: A case study integrating drama therapy with behavioural interventions for the treatment of selective mutism. *Clinical Child Psychology and Psychiatry*, *15*(2), 215–230. doi:10.1177/1359104509352892

Our Own Voice Theatre Troupe. (n.d.). Our Own Voice Theatre Troupe. Retrieved March 6, 2010, from http://www.ourownvoice.org/

Queensland Health. (2005). Sharing responsibility for recovery: Creating and sustaining recovery-oriented systems of care for mental health. Retrieved July 11, 2013, from http://www.health.qld.gov.au/mentalhealth/docs/Recovery_Paper_2005.pdf

Rousseau, C., Benoit, M., Gauthier, M., Lacroix, L., Alain, N., Rojas, M., . . . & Bourassa, D. (2007). Classroom drama therapy program for immigrant and refugee adolescents: A pilot study. *Clinical Child Psychology and Psychiatry*, *12*(3), 451–465. doi:10.1177/1359104507078477

Ruddy R., & Dent-Brown, K. (2007). Drama therapy for schizophrenia or schizophrenia-like illnesses. *Cochrane Database Systematic Review*, *24*(1):CD005378. doi:10.1002/1465185.CD005378.pub2

Schrader, C. (2012). *Ritual theatre: The power of dramatic ritual in personal development groups and clinical practice*. London, England: Jessica Kingsley.

Slade, P. (1954). *Child drama*. London, England: University of London.

Stepping Out Theatre. (2010). Stepping out theatre troupe. Retrieved March 6, 2010, from www.steppingouttheatre.com

Teatro Patologico. (n.d). *Teatro Patologico*. Retrieved July 11, 2013, from http://www.teatropatologico.org/

Theatre Wales. (2013). *Theatre in Wales*. Retrieved July 11, 2013, http://www.theatre-wales.co.uk

Walsh, F. (2013). *Theatre and therapy*. Basingstoke, England: Palgrave Macmillan.

Table 1 Classification of drama/theater forms in mental health practice

Description	Who Writes?	Who Performs?	Who Is the Audience?	What Is the Purpose?
Theater about mental health issues				
Mainstream theater, which addresses mental health issues as interesting story material	Professional writers	Professional actors	Mainstream audiences	Entertainment, challenging audiences to a broader understanding of mental health problems
Theater based on lived experience				
Scripted theater performed for an audience, based in the stories, experiences, and ideas of the group	People living with mental illness and/or a writer who collaborates with them	People living with mental illness and/or actors who collaborate with them	Mainstream audiences or target audiences (e.g., families and friends, mental health professionals)	Sharing true stories of experience, challenging audiences to a broader understanding of mental health problems, destigmatization, advocacy
Canonical theater performed by people with mental illness				
Canonical theater works performed by people with mental illness	Writers recognized as belonging to the canon of theater in English	People with mental illness, often in an institutional setting	Other people from the same institution, staff, family, friends	Engagement with role, exploration of characters and themes that have relevance in the participants' lives, the enjoyment of mastering and demonstrating drama and performance skills
Theater for social action with a mental health component				
Scripted theater created through workshops and play-building processes, usually performed for an audience, based in the traumatic experiences of a group or community which includes performers and audience	People who have experienced the trauma, usually with professional support	People who have experienced the trauma, usually with professional support	Other members of the group or community that has experienced the trauma	Sharing individual stories of traumatic group experience, creating a forum for collaboratively processing traumatic experience, and seeking ways to move on from traumatic events

(Continued)

Table 1 (Continued)

Description	Who Writes?	Who Performs?	Who Is the Audience?	What Is the Purpose?
Visiting performances				
Professional performers stage performances for clients/residents, usually in a nontheater venue such as a residential institution	Professional writers	Professional actors	Clients/residents of the service and staff	To provide aesthetic, emotional and cognitive experiences that may benefit audience members, individually and collectively
Participatory drama				
Usually improvizational or process-drama based	Usually unscripted, relies on the participants' inputs with structure provided by a facilitator	Clients/residents of the service	Usually no audience beyond the participants themselves	To support participants to develop or relearn skills such as self-expression, confidence, teamwork, communication
Psychodrama				
Specialized form of psychotherapy based in psychoanalysis	Not scripted—techniques known by therapist are used by therapist and participant to seek psychological revelation	People with mental illness—individual or group—and therapist	No audience apart from therapist and (in group context) group	Individual learning, healing, and growth
Drama therapy				
Name for a range of psychotherapeutic techniques using drama	Not scripted—techniques known by drama therapist are used by therapist and participant to seek psychological revelation	People with mental illness—individual or group—and therapist	No audience apart from therapist and (in group context) group	Individual learning, healing, and growth

CHAPTER 14

Respect Yourself Drama Education Program in Practice

Andrea Baldwin

INTRODUCTION

This chapter introduces the Respect Yourself Drama Education (RYDE) program, a practical six-workshop series that can be used by facilitators with minimal training in drama. The chapter briefly outlines the theory and practice underpinning the design of the RYDE program and provides an example of a session conducted in an adolescent mental health setting. The RYDE program was originally designed as a resilience-building program for adolescents aged approximately 12 to 15 in Years 8 to 10 at school. It was designed to be compatible with the contemporary state curriculum for health and physical education, addressing curriculum topics within three strands: promoting the health of individuals and communities, developing concepts and skills for physical activity, and enhancing personal development.

RYDE was conceptualized as a drama-based social skills program. Since it was originally intended for use in schools, the language of the program manual is educational rather than clinical. This has proved helpful, enabling the program to be implemented by providers across a range of contexts. To date, RYDE has been delivered as a mental health promotion and resilience-building school holiday program for adolescents, a social skills program for 9-year-old boys with autistic spectrum disorder, and a drama program for young adults with learning disabilities, in addition to the author's use of the program in an adolescent inpatient mental health setting, described in this chapter.

PROGRAM OUTLINE

Aim

To enhance adolescents' general resilience to stressors and difficulties and thereby promote mental health

Objectives

- To build self-confidence by encouraging students to communicate their ideas assertively, using face, voice, and body

- To promote individual imaginative problem solving and creativity

- To encourage teamwork, cooperation, and mutual support among group members

- To reinforce and expand participants' knowledge of basic concepts in social functioning

- To promote practical understanding and use of social skills

- To encourage exploration of humor in social interactions and problem solving

Format

Six lessons, each 45 to 60 minutes in length (can be tailored to fit available time)

Modality

Drama-based games and exercises to be played in groups ranging from pairs to whole class

Content Summary

Session 1: Introduction to improvisation, concepts, ground rules, group-building activities

Session 2: Working in space, expressing and responding to emotions

Session 3: Portraying characters, attitudes, beliefs, values

Session 4: Social contexts, status, self-presentation

Session 5: Trust and teamwork, roles, responsibilities

Session 6: Process drama, bringing it all together

Requirements

Optimum

- Class size of 8 to 12 (or larger with assistance)

- Auditorium or large classroom cleared of furniture, enclosed, carpeted, comfortable temperature, preferably curtained to avoid distractions from outside or embarrassment due to fear of being observed

- Teacher aide or other staff to assist classroom teacher, willing to participate

Necessary

- Teacher trained in RYDE program and improvisational drama rationales and techniques

- Class size manageable by teacher

- Room large enough for class to divide into pairs or small groups for exercises, space to work physically in safety

CLINICAL RATIONALE

As outlined in Chapter 13, drama in mental health settings can be approached as a form of therapy or more broadly as a social/educational experience. While its developer is a qualified psychologist as well as an applied theater practitioner, RYDE is designed to work within the latter category of practice rather than the former; that is, RYDE is intended to help build resilience and social skills rather than to function as therapy. RYDE provides young people with the experience of enacting an enjoyable, cooperative, creative process with other young people, and—in Boal's terms—"seeing" themselves doing this (Boal, 1995, p. 13). Boal's theory predicts that by enjoying this experience in the drama classroom, participants build confidence and competence to engage in cooperative social processes with others in other settings.

For some young people, various life disruptions prevent the accomplishment of developmental tasks at an appropriate age. A young person might experience significant disruptions to schooling and socialization as a result of the family moving multiple times throughout their childhood. Deciding it is not worth the effort of making friends only to keep losing them, the child may quickly lose the skills required to make friends. Not having friends exacerbates feelings of loneliness, isolation, anxiety, and depression, which in turn tends to alienate others so friendships are less likely to be formed.

A similar "spiral of disability" can often be observed among young people who have difficulty with their schoolwork. Forming the belief that he or she is dumb, the young person is less likely to apply himself or herself to schoolwork and so is less likely to succeed, reinforcing the negative self-belief.

These are very simple examples of the "spiral of disability" process. Given that some young people have difficulties in multiple areas of life, they may develop a range of negative self-beliefs, reinforced by the labels, perceptions, judgments, and assumptions of others in their lives including family, teachers, previous clinicians, and peers.

The development of mental health symptoms can severely limit the young person's opportunities to engage with the normal challenges of life, experience success, and achieve appropriate developmental tasks. For example, being too anxious to leave the house will prevent a young person from going to school, working at a part-time job, or going to the movies with friends. The young person is thus deprived of opportunities to learn to use public transport, save and budget earnings, negotiate a social occasion, and so on. He or she loses the opportunity to acquire a range of skills vital to living and working in the world.

Drama can provide challenges and developmental opportunities that may be difficult to access in the real world due to one's mental health problems, hospitalization, or both. It can provide experiences of success that help counteract negative self-beliefs and social interactions that help build or rebuild social skills.

The state government's definition of mental health recovery current at the time of RYDE's design was

the journey toward a new and valued sense of identity, role and purpose outside the parameters of mental illness; and living well despite any limitations resulting from the illness, its treatment, and personal and environmental conditions. (Queensland Health, 2005)

A recovery focus is perhaps especially important for young people and particularly for those who find themselves in an institutional setting. For older people with mental health challenges, resources may be available in the form of life experience, maturity, perspectives, and networks that have developed over time. Without these resources, young people may struggle to experience a sense of hope, meaning, empowerment, social inclusion, and connectedness.

Since the 1960s, there has been increasing concern about institutionalizing people by compelling or allowing them to live in inpatient mental health facilities for long periods of time. Children and young people, in particular, are thought to be at risk of institutionalization if they are confined to a hospital environment for extended periods during their development. The child and youth mental health system in Australia has gradually developed a number of treatment options, including community child and youth mental health services, inpatient units designed for short-term acute admissions, day patient programs, and outpatient services. The various components of the system are intended to work together, to meet the needs of young people without necessitating extended periods of hospitalization.

The RYDE group described in this chapter was conducted in an adolescent inpatient setting. However, as noted above, the program was originally designed for schools and can be implemented in a variety of settings including community and residential facilities.

IMPLEMENTATION

Only minimal adaptations were needed to run RYDE as an after-school activity in the inpatient unit. The TV room became the drama room with the chairs pushed back. Curtains could be drawn to prevent outsiders seeing into the room while the group was in progress; the group usually opted for this level of privacy. A nurse provided the coleader role so the leader could concentrate on running the group while the nurse supported individual participants and encouraged participation. In the case of someone becoming too unwell to continue participation, it was anticipated that the nurse could accompany the young person leaving the room. In the event, however, this never happened.

Maintaining consistent group membership over the six weeks of the program was predictably problematic. Since the unit served an assessment function as well as providing extended care, it was common for new members to join the group after the first week or for people to be discharged before the end. Other appointments, family visits, conflicts with staff or other patients, episodes of being too unwell to participate, and other disruptions prevented most members from participating on a regular weekly basis. Group size therefore varied from four to eight, and only one participant attended more than three of the six sessions.

EXAMPLE SESSION

With such a small number of participants, none of whom who could be considered to have completed the program, no formal quantitative or qualitative evaluation of outcomes could be undertaken. Nor could workshops be filmed to provide performative evidence of learning and therapeutic change (Haseman, 2006) since it was clear that recording the sessions would inhibit the drama. At the level of participant-rated enjoyment of the group, all participants reported enjoying the group "a great deal" (the highest possible rating) and staff noted participants tended to be more settled and positive in mood for a time immediately following each session. However, such anecdotal evidence does not capture what was apparent to staff observers, including the leader: that the participants used the RYDE program to express themselves and to explore social relations within a dramatic framework in much more sophisticated ways than might have been expected given the severity and acuteness of their mental health issues. The following description of a final session, summarized from the leader's notes, provides some evidence of ways in which participants used the drama to explore new roles and possibilities for social behavior.

Participants

The group on this occasion consisted of six young people, two boys and four girls. Two of the girls and one of the boys had participated in at least one of the five workshops that had preceded this one. The other participants were new on that day.

Stimulus

The class commenced with a physical warm-up game, after which the leader introduced the idea of an extended improvisation—an improvised story that could have multiple scenes and characters. The leader offered a choice of topics, from which the group selected, "What if the Christmas story happened in the modern day?"

The leader's main interventions were to ask clarifying questions about the characters and their action, to provide a summary of the action that had occurred in the previous scene, and to encourage the group to decide quickly when and where the next scene should take place. For the most part, the group made story decisions collaboratively. Moments of disagreement over where the story should go next (creative conflict) were not debated but maneuvered through dramatically, the leader using the technique of side-coaching (Johnstone, 1989), which disrupts the flow of the improvisation as little as possible. The group succeeded in creating a coherent narrative by making and accepting offers and expressed a high degree of satisfaction with themselves and with each other at the end of the session.

Characters

All participants' names have been changed.

- Mary: Theresa, 14, a young woman with severe anxiety issues including agoraphobia

- Joseph: Jonathon, 14, a young man with a history of suicidal ideation and oppositional defiant disorder

- Innkeeper, Nurse, Samuel aged 2: Patrice, 16, a young woman with family issues and an eating disorder

- Guard, Social Security Worker, Joseph's South American girlfriend Mark I, Jose: Belinda, 16, a young woman with an acute psychotic disorder who at this time was electively mute

- Police officer, Gynecologist, Social Worker, Joseph's South American girlfriend Mark II: Sheree, 15, a young woman with severe anxiety and depression issues, including rumination, suicidal ideation and attempts, and chronic self-harm

- Cell mate/partner in crime: Daniel, 13, a young man with a history of acting out behavior, along with anxiety and suicidal ideation

- Watch-house doctor, South American aid worker: Leader

- Samuel as a baby: mimed

Summary of the Narrative

Mary and Joseph arrived in Bethlehem in their Torana, which broke down as they reached town. They tried to find accommodation at the Motor Inn, but due to a big convention there was no room for them. Mary revealed she was pregnant. Joseph, who had not been aware of this, became angry and accused Mary of "trapping" him. Mary in turn became angry and said he was very unobservant not to have realized and that it was his fault for refusing to use condoms. Joseph suggested they go to the beach.

On the beach, they lay down to sleep. A police officer arrived and said they couldn't sleep there. Joseph, already surly, tried to fight the police officer and was arrested. The police officer noticed that Mary was about to give birth and called the ambulance. The police officer took Joseph off to jail.

In the Watch House, Joseph was belligerent toward the guard. A cell mate told Joseph to pipe down and he would tell him something. The cell mate said he had a gun and intended to rob the Social Security office. They made a plan that Joseph would get himself released, then help his cell mate escape, and together they would carry out the robbery.

Joseph started singing a sad song and pretending to be depressed, and the guard called for a doctor. The doctor took Joseph from the cell, but on his way to hospital, Joseph escaped and returned to jail. The guard had fallen asleep, so Joseph stole the keys, released his cell mate, and they went off together to rob the Social Security office.

Meanwhile, Mary was in the delivery room at the hospital. She was attended by a nurse and a gynecologist. (Sheree played the gynecologist as a high-status male doctor, more intent on his golfing schedule than his patient, arranging his next game by mobile phone while occasionally telling Mary over his shoulder to "breathe.")

Next we saw Joseph and his cell mate lining up at the Social Security office. They commented on how typical it was that they had to queue up even to rob the place. They then held up the worker at the desk using the cell mate's gun and got away with a million dollars.

Back at the hospital, the baby had been delivered. The name Jesus was suggested, but Mary didn't like it and decided instead on Samuel. The gynecologist had gone off to play golf and Mary was being interviewed by the hospital social worker. Joseph and his cell mate walked in, and Joseph told Mary about the million dollars they had stolen. Mary was furious that Joseph had taken to a life of crime with no consideration for his baby and his responsibility as a father. Joseph in turn was angry, saying he had stolen the money to provide for the kid and what more did she want? Mary told him she was breaking off the relationship as she didn't want her son to have a criminal for a father. Joseph and his cell mate left, stating they were going overseas.

The next scene found Mary caring for the baby in a flat, which the social worker had helped her rent. The social worker was there, supporting Mary, who was feeling down about the breakup of her relationship and the pressures of single parenthood. The social worker left and Mary went to sleep. Joseph and his cell mate broke in and stole the baby. After some abortive attempts to find transport, they bought a boat and went to Africa.

Some time passed in the story. In the next scene, about a year later, we saw Mary who had never given up her struggle to find baby Samuel, supported by the social worker, who had become her friend and housemate. They had finally received a tip-off that Joseph was in Africa. However, when they arrived in Africa, Joseph made a quick getaway.

Joseph and his cell mate started jumping from country to country, pursued by Mary and the social worker. (At this point the leader coached Jonathon, in the role of Joseph, to stay put and allow the confrontation to occur.)

Mary and the social worker were forced to abandon the search as the clues had petered out. They went on holiday together to South America and just happened to walk into Joseph's Bar. The prosperous Joseph came out to greet them, recognized them, tried to run, and then decided to brazen it out. A stormy confrontation followed, with Mary demanding her son back and Joseph saying the child was well and happy and would not even know Mary.

Samuel, now aged around 2, emerged with Joseph's new South American girlfriend (played, at this stage, by Belinda). Samuel called this lady Mummy and clung to her, not recognizing Mary. Mary was heartbroken. The social worker urged her to surrender custody of the child to Joseph for the sake of Samuel's emotional security. Joseph pointed out how prosperous he was and how he could provide Samuel with everything he needed. Mary said she did not think a South American beach resort was a good place to raise a child and insisted on having Samuel back. Samuel clung to the family he knew and expressed his fear of the angry woman shouting at Daddy.

With neither Mary nor Joseph prepared to yield, and the session running way over time, the leader stepped in with an offer. In role as a South American aid worker, the leader brought on stage José (coopting Belinda from the role of Joseph's girlfriend), an orphaned South American child, and asked if Mary would be willing to adopt him in place of Samuel. Mary stated her determination to return home with both Samuel and José.

The situation seemed unresolvable until Sheree stepped from the role of social worker into the abandoned role of Joseph's South American girlfriend. She revealed that she was only 14 and wanted to escape from Joseph, whom she now considered a dirty old man. Mary returned home with all three children, leaving Joseph and his cell mate to enjoy their moneyed lifestyle in South America.

Drama Processes at Work/Play

Clearly, a number of the core processes identified by Jones (2007) as tools for drama therapy were at work in this drama, including dramatic projection, empathy and distancing, role playing and personification, witnessing, playing, embodiment, and the life–drama connection. A therapist seeking to work individually with this material would help the client to reflect on his or her experiences in the drama and how these related to real life experiences. Patrice, for example, herself the child of separated parents who felt herself forced to choose between them, assertively took on the role of Samuel and delivered a moving though brief performance as a 2-year-old caught up in parental conflict. Earlier, as the innkeeper, she took great delight in refusing Mary and Joseph a room, an action far removed from her usual compliant and deferential manner toward people. Jonathon initially seemed determined to maintain Joseph as a high-status role, exhibiting bravado, defensiveness, and avoidance whenever his actions were challenged. The fact that, when coached, he always reluctantly accepted disempowerment—for example, losing the initial fight with the police officer and getting locked up—enabled the story to progress and granted him new opportunities to be clever, funny, and powerful. There would also be rich material for reflection in the dignity and maturity with which he invested Joseph at the end of the story.

But the RYDE program seeks to work not through the individual, reflective, and discursive processes of drama therapy but through the intrinsically social and educational experience of participating in drama. This focus opens up RYDE, as a program based on improvisational drama for use by professionals in areas of education, mental health promotion, counseling, youth work, and social work rather than being the province of trained drama therapists. Many of the processes identified by Faigin and Stein (2010) as typical of community-based theater were evident in this workshop, including group cohesion and affiliation, openness and inclusion, the dramatic exploration of common experiences, expanded sense of self, working with flexibility, and the empowerment that comes with ownership. The group's easy acceptance and inclusion of Belinda, despite her not speaking, was rewarded by her being more responsive and participative in the drama than she had been on the unit since her arrival. The energy and spontaneity with which the story emerged was clearly related to the group's feeling of ownership over the drama, and this sense of empowerment and pride was evident in the general euphoria with which the participants eventually left the drama room.

Of particular interest was the way in which the drama allowed the participants to explore common experiences of authority figures and institutions in a safe, symbolic way. Initially, the story was dominated by a theme of authority figures taking control of the characters' lives, often against their will. By the end, the story had transformed into a family conflict successfully handled by the individuals involved. By stepping out of the social worker role (which had long-since morphed into that of a family friend, anyway), Sheree removed the last remnants of external authority. The leader was struck by the parallel between this shift in the drama (to the characters working out their own resolution) and what was happening at the level of the class (the participants insisted on finding their own way to the end of the story, resisting the leader's attempt to offer them an ending).

LONGER-TERM EFFECTS

It is always difficult to attribute therapeutic effects to a specific intervention when participants are simultaneously experiencing a wide range of interventions intended to promote similar outcomes. Members of this participant group were engaging with various combinations of twenty-four-hour multidisciplinary health care, special schooling, the therapeutic milieu, individual therapy, group therapy, family therapy, and pharmacotherapy. However, anecdotally, it appeared that RYDE participants did benefit in some of the ways predicted by the program. Specifically, following the group, staff members noted increased verbal communication by several group members, more positive relationships among group members, and greater expression of humor.

CONCLUSION

Drama is often seen as an activity that people can engage in when they are living in the community and/or when their illness is settled or not acute. The experience of delivering RYDE in an inpatient setting demonstrated the power of drama to provide a context in which people can take control, take risks, work with others, succeed, and derive great satisfaction, even when significantly unwell.

While a drama therapy approach could focus on the content of material generated by the young person through dramatic play—the themes, dynamics, thoughts, feelings, beliefs, and attitudes enacted by the participant in imaginative interaction with others—such an approach relies heavily on the clinician to observe this content, reflect it back to the person (either in the course of the drama workshop or later in individual therapy), and assist the person to make sense of what they have created within the broader context of their real life. People with severe and complex mental health issues may not always have the patience, concentration, motivation, or verbal skills to participate productively in such formalized reflective processes.

This chapter has focused on the value of drama in itself as an activity to support recovery. From this perspective, the emphasis is not on the clinician's process of helping the person to make the unconscious conscious, to articulate and integrate the experiences of dramatic play with the experiences of everyday living. Rather, the emphasis is on the person's own engagement in the dramatic play and the experiential learning that occurs consciously or otherwise through the act of collaborative enactment.

REFERENCES

Boal, A. (1995). *The rainbow of desire: The Boal method of theatre and therapy*. A. Jackson (Trans.). New York, NY: Routledge

Faigin, D., & Stein, C. (2010). The power of theatre to promote individual recovery and social change. *Psychiatric Services, 61*(3), 306–308. doi:10.1176/appi.ps.61.3.306.

Haseman, B. (2006). A manifesto for performative research. *Media International Australia incorporating Culture and Policy, 118*(118), 98–106. Retrieved from http://www.emsah.uq.edu.au/mia

Johnstone, K. (1989). *Impro: Improvisation and the theatre*. London, England: Methuen.

Jones, P. (2007). *Drama as therapy: Theory, practice and research*. New York, NY: Routledge.

Queensland Health. (2005). *Sharing responsibility for recovery: Creating and sustaining recovery-oriented systems of care for mental health*. Brisbane, Australia: Queensland Government. Retrieved July 11, 2013, from http://www.health.qld.gov.au/mentalhealth/docs/Recovery_Paper_2005.pdf

Digital Storytelling for the Self-Advocacy of Marginalized Identities

Theory and Practice

Sonja Vivienne

To thine own self be true.

—Polonius, in *Hamlet*,
William Shakespeare (1600)

People often say that this or that person has not yet found himself. But the self is not something one finds, it is something one creates.

—*The Second Sin*, Thomas Szasz (1974)

INTRODUCTION

This chapter explores understandings of well-being and identity as framed in digital story-telling practice. I describe workshops in which vulnerable people, in recovery from social marginalization,[1] learn to use digital media tools in order to create and share their personal stories. I argue that, in examples of nuanced workshop facilitation, the agency storytellers acquire in constructing their digital self-representations and the ownership they take in distributing them among networked publics afford empowerment and greater social engagement and, in turn, improved well-being.

The quotes that commence this chapter allude to contrasting yet commonly held understandings of selfhood. Shakespeare, via Polonius, suggests people are guided by an internal moral compass or inner truth, evoking a certain essentialism that theoretically fell from favor with social constructionism. This view, however, still holds sway in popular culture, broadly reflected in many self-help guides. Szasz (1974), on the other hand, ever alert to the social discourses that frame mental illness, argues that the self is something of our own making. In the tradition of positive psychology and drawing on Maslow's concept of self-actualization, participant-centered epistemologies regard well-being as a byproduct of social and self-acceptance. This binary schism in ontological philosophy—whether self-image is a stable given or something negotiated with others and somewhat reflective of context—is crystallized in digital storytelling workshops that encourage participants to hone in on a personal story of significance, to describe an anecdote, memory, or belief with what is often painful and revealing honesty. Put simply, digital stories represent *both* essential personal truths and a deliberate articulation of self that is influenced by social context. The fact that they are made for audiences, whether that be a few family members or unknown audiences online, requires storytellers to publicly affirm what are sometimes fragile self-beliefs. For vulnerable storytellers who regard themselves as being marginalized or disenfranchised in some way, this step toward social exposure and engagement can seem very risky and represents a profound step in recovery. At its best, digital storytelling is a process that enhances positive self-image and social connections that are built on acceptance of a core identity, framed and articulated by the storyteller.

Digital stories are most often around three minutes long and are composed of family photos or personal artworks edited together with music and narrated in the first person. Workshops are often tightly scheduled for three or four consecutive days with a high ratio of experienced facilitators to participants who typically have little or no media-making skills. A typical workshop commences with a story circle in which people take turns to share personal anecdotes and experiences, some of which may eventually develop into a digital story. While digital stories are clearly a construction, they invariably distill vast lived experience and numerous points of view into a compact beginning, middle, and end. Often participants feel overwhelmed, reflected in statements like "I have nothing important to say" or, the opposite, "I have so many stories—which should I tell?" Icebreaker exercises include sharing a story about your name or a favorite object. Once the burden of telling something "important" is relieved, many storytellers discover that even an apparently superficial story can serve as a starting point for important self-revelations—for example, why a name has been modified to better suit personality or why a favorite object is a kind of metaphor for identity. Group norms of mutual respect, confidentiality, and considered, constructive feedback are established and, further, participants are encouraged to abandon comfort zones. For example, if they are habitually shy they are prompted to "step up"; if they are accustomed to holding the floor, they are encouraged to listen and support others in speaking.

As a facilitated workshop-based practice, digital storytelling grew from roots in therapeutic community arts programs in the United States in the 1990s (manifest in the work of Joe Lambert and the Center for Digital Storytelling[2]) and spread to the United Kingdom where it was slightly repositioned as an exemplar of ordinary people finding voice in the public sphere. In the first instance, primary audiences might be expected to be family and friends whereas the potential to broadcast to unknown and imagined audiences (evident in the "Capture Wales" initiative pioneered by Daniel Meadows[3]) exerts a different influence on the content canvassed by participants. This amplification of stories for larger audiences and, later, the longevity of stories posted online have brought new and largely unanticipated dimensions to digital storytelling practice, including the necessity of negotiating understandings of privacy and publicness.

Social convergence or context collapse describes the modern experience of disparate audiences that intersect across face-to-face and online spaces. Any representation of identity that is shared online—whether that be a Facebook update, blog post, tweet, or digital story—has searchable and persistent qualities that give it resonance far beyond the circumstances of its original creation and upload. It is available to multiple audiences, known and imagined, both now and in the future, and this heightens the ramifications of personal revelations. Further, digital storytellers must consider the consequences not only for themselves but for friends and family members who are also identifiable in their story. Thus, storytellers speak to networked publics that they are *a part of* (intimate, familiar circles) as well as those that they are *apart from* (unknown and imagined circles). As they deliberate over the narrative arc of their tale, they also negotiate self-representation with these networked publics, sometimes in actual discussions and sometimes by imagining how various people might respond. In this way, as per the feminist dictum, the personal is also political. In the case of marginalized storytellers, these negotiations bridge differences in values and beliefs alongside class, race, gender, and sexuality. By sharing a personal tale, storytellers seek social acceptance and affirm self-acceptance. I call this labor "networked identity work" (Vivienne, 2013; Vivienne & Burgess, 2012) and argue that it is central to any recovery from social marginalization—a recovery that might also be more emphatically framed as "digitally enabled citizenship" (Papacharissi, 2010).

Self-representations made in public spaces, whether face-to-face or online, carry with them a social expectation of coherence, consistency, or what some may refer to as truthfulness. Giddens refers to the desirability of maintaining "a consistent narrative" that "must continually integrate events which occur in the external world, and sort them into the ongoing 'story' about the self" (Giddens, 1991, p. 54). The autobiographical nature of traditional digital storytelling practice tends to align itself with discourses of authentic self-expression. (I regard *authenticity* as a problematic term plagued by subjective moral connotations. Rather than focus on first person authorship, narration, or technical assembly as bona fides, I prefer to evaluate the storytellers' own description of their agency in the process and ownership of their end product.) Theoretically at least, the storyteller's voice is privileged over all other voices, including those of facilitators and, more importantly, the many other actors that may merit a speaking role in the storyteller's anecdotes. In practice, for a variety of reasons, this does not always occur.

While the process of story–self construction can be empowering, it can also be problematic. A storyteller's representation might be contentious among his or her intimate publics or express beliefs that are socially inadmissible. Not all life stories are consistent or coherent. In particular, mental illness and trauma is often associated with dramatic shifts in self-concept and fractured identity narratives (Citron, 1999; Radden, 2004). Narrative theorists point to the problematic prevalence of the "coherence paradigm":

> The coherence paradigm generally implies that (i) good and competent narratives always proceed in a linear, chronological way, from a beginning and middle to an end, which also constitutes a thematic closure; (ii) the function of narrative and

story-telling is primarily to create coherence in regard to experience, which is understood as being rather formless (which may be understood as a merit or disadvantage of narrative); (iii) persons live better and in a more ethical way, if they have a coherent life-story and coherent narrative identity (or, in contrast, narrative is understood as being detrimental because it creates such coherence). (Hyvärinen, Hyden, Saarenheimo, & Tamboukou, 2010, p. 2)

Conventional digital storytelling facilitation does not countenance the difficulties of social convergence and coherence (or truth rendered problematic by postmodern theory). Indeed, these concerns are not always central for storytellers. However, the social consequences of incoherence or fractured self-narratives are worthy of consideration, especially when ramifications can be severe. Social derision can lead to loss of relationships, self-esteem, employment, and—in some extreme cases—death through assault or suicide.

In 2011, the case of 14-year-old American teen Jamey Rodemeyer became news worldwide as the first of too many teenagers to commit suicide after coming out online (ironically, via "It Gets Better"), only to face increased bullying in his face-to-face school environment (Hughes, 2011). While online social movements like "It Gets Better" have no doubt contributed to increasing social acceptance of diverse gender representation and sexual preferences, they do not address the difficult gaps between online self-disclosure and face-to-face networks of support. To some extent, the spin-off campaign "Make it Better" attempts to shore up vulnerable individuals with support networks through organized GSAs (Gay Straight Alliance Network).

Congruence, in contrast to coherence, may accommodate divergent descriptions of self across place and time and is centered in the storytellers' ownership of their articulations of self rather than an audience's judgment of the same. Some of the narrative techniques (e.g., remembering and definitional ceremonies) I describe later can support this ownership and counter the difficulties of coherence.

Storytellers who wish to challenge social norms frequently report having to weigh up the benefits of "speaking out" against the risks of further marginalization. Articulating a consistent or coherent story can be problematic in representations of fluid identity as vehemently expressed new incarnations may not always be accurate. This scenario was deftly navigated by Karen, a transgender storyteller, who mapped her origins as a "normal little boy" before becoming a woman and a sister. When I caught up with Karen some time after making her story, she had decided—for a range of complex reasons—that she would live as a man again. Her gender explorations, she noted, were the cause of many lost relationships with family members and friends, both new and old. I asked whether she felt the need to retract or modify her story, and she explained that any new incarnation of self would inevitably reflect aspects of previous selves:

I believe that it's a little bit like a history record . . . it comes from the perspective of the writer. . . . You ask different people about that history and they'll see it differently but it was true to the writer. . . . Also, that story didn't finish at that point, in fact that was the beginning of a journey in many ways. . . . But it doesn't diminish the truth of that story and experience at that time.

The experience of fluidity is not the exclusive domain of queer people; it is shared by a broader population of young people becoming adults, adults becoming retirees, and people whose health status and consequent self-concept shifts radically. In particular, young people exploring performance of identity in online spaces are frequently warned of the consequences of irreconcilable, incoherent self-exposure; for example, drunken party photos posted to Facebook may have serious implications for future job prospects.

Throughout this chapter I use *queer* to encompass a broad spectrum of sexualities and gender identities including gay, lesbian, bisexual, transgender, transsexual, intersex, and same-sex attracted—often represented in the acronym GLBTTQIS. While *queer* is also useful for its theoretical alignment with queer scholarship, I acknowledge that it is not necessarily a descriptor used by the individual participants I describe. In specific examples, I use the terminology chosen by participants to describe themselves.

OVERVIEW OF CASE STUDIES

These case studies took place in Adelaide, South Australia, between 2009 and 2012. I facilitated two digital storytelling workshops (one face-to-face and one online) that were provided by SHine SA (a government-funded sexual health information and education service). A DVD compilation of eighteen stories and a facilitator's guide was produced in order to raise awareness of diverse sexualities and gender representation. This resource was intended for use by social service providers, educators, and trainers working in a variety of contexts. A third workshop, with a smaller group of four participants, was provided by the AIDS Council of South Australia (ACSA) to raise awareness of living with HIV. Widely cited figures from a variety of sources estimate that queer people are overrepresented in statistics on bullying, drug use, self-harm, depression, homelessness, and suicide (Hillier et al., 2010; Ministerial Advisory Committee on Gay and Lesbian Health, 2002; Pitts, Mitchell, Smith, & Patel, 2006; Waidzunas, 2011). In both case studies, digital storytelling was regarded as a creative and preventative intervention into the social phenomena that underpin these issues—homophobia, transphobia, heterosexism, and attending social alienation.

I engaged in these workshops as a facilitator, ethnographic researcher, and digital storyteller with a background in documentary filmmaking. My research interests lay in exploring the complexities of voice, queer identity, and networked publics among a cohort of everyday activists broadly encompassing gay, lesbian, bisexual, transgender, transsexual, intersex, and same-sex attracted—or queer—identifying people. I use *everyday activist* to describe people who, while not necessarily engaging in more organized forms of activism, are nevertheless motivated to catalyze social change through sharing their personal stories in public spaces.

Participants in the case studies broadly identified with a social change agenda and ranged in age from 17 to late 50s and across socioeconomic and cultural backgrounds. Recruitment took place via pamphlets and emails distributed via social service providers and queer community groups as well as direct canvassing of people who steering committee members thought might have an interest. While the finished stories all referred to queer identity in some regard, many dealt primarily with a sense of difference from perceived social norms. A young fair woman spoke about her invisible Aboriginality and additional social burden of having two mothers. Several people spoke of conflict between sexuality and spirituality, both Christian and Muslim. A wheelchair-enabled man spoke about his degenerative disorder and the queerness of disability. Transgender participants spoke in some instances of losing biological family while gaining a family of friends, and parents of a transgender child spoke of her inspirational faith in her own identity. HIV-positive participants spoke about generational changes to AIDS and sexual health.

Analysis of approaches to production and modes of sharing revealed a typology of privacy and publicness: visible, bounded, and pseudonymous approaches to images, narration, and text, and targeted, ad hoc, and proxy strategies to distribution.

Throughout the digital storytelling process, participants consider who will see their story and imagine what meaning these people might make. While some storytellers choose to be wholly visible and target their audiences directly, others carefully manipulate, demarcate, or code their stories so as to deliver only a certain amount of personal information to a finite audience. Many storytellers reconsider their strategies as they understand the process better, and some continue to modify their self-representation for years after their stories are locked off (for example by changing privacy settings in the online spaces in which their stories are shared). This typology has been developed further elsewhere (Vivienne & Burgess, 2012, 2013); however, in the context of this chapter, the management of privacy and publicness is pertinent to how marginalized storytellers overcome social risks to advocate for themselves. In the following section I discuss facilitation strategies that support storytellers in these endeavors while acknowledging the mediating influence of workshops regardless of whether they take place face-to-face or online.

NARRATIVE PRACTICE AND EMPOWERMENT

Narrative practice constitutes a raft of story-oriented techniques that "privilege the preferred identity" (Freedman & Combs, 1996) of the storyteller. It has evolved from anthropology, influenced by the likes of Barbara Myerhoff (1982) and Jay Ruby (1991), and

Figure 15.1 Privacy and publicness negotiated throughout digital storytelling process.

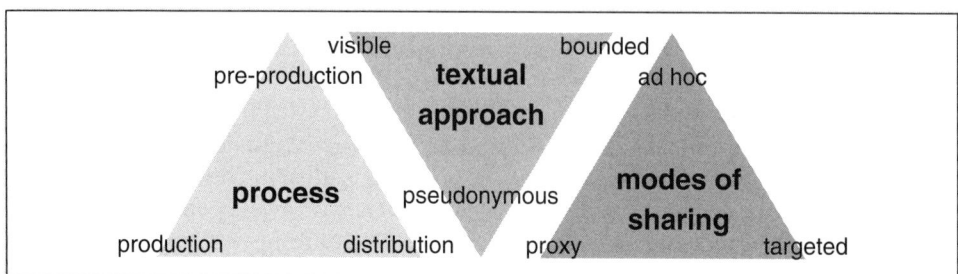

has connections with narrative theory, therapy, and analysis. Narrative therapy was shaped by psychoanalysts Michael White and David Epston (1990) and is used in various forms by social workers, psychologists, and counselors. Narrative therapy rests on the premise that the client is the expert in their own lives (rather than the therapist) and that problems are external to identity rather than defining of identity. This is characterized in the motto "the person is not the problem, the problem is the problem." In its application to digital storytelling, it offers not only some useful strategies for facilitation but also an awareness of storytelling as a meaning making process and a framework for considering the digital story product as one among many alternative stories.

Traditional digital storytelling workshops are led by a primary facilitator who orchestrates group norms, storytelling circles, and technical instruction in the use of editing software (like MovieMaker, Sony Vegas, iMovie, and Final Cut Pro) as well as some of the thornier ethical considerations of authorial voice and copyright. Additional facilitators support participants with technical difficulties and creative solutions to privacy and publicness. John Hartley (2008) draws attention to the asymmetric dynamics of the workshop format, suggesting that proficient facilitators counter hierarchy by acknowledging the cultural aptitude of participants who are expert in their own experiences (p. 205). While there may be an integral structure to the workshop format (with facilitators positioned as helpful experts) when it comes to the nuances of listening, guiding, and framing praxis, group leaders can benefit from utilizing the tools of narrative practice. Penn and Sheinberg (1991) argue

> for the therapists to resist declarative language and to stay in a questioning and speculative mode . . . acts as a counterweight to the inherent properties of language that represent reality as though it were independent of our construction of it. . . . Maintaining this position also protects the therapists from assuming a hierarchical posture and reconfigures the idea of the therapist as an expert. (p. 32)

Penn and Sheinberg point not only to the social construction of a therapist–client (or facilitator–participant) power dynamic but difficulties in naming story tropes or identities. If a facilitator distills a rambling or complex narrative it is likely that a participant will incorporate this version of events and, recognizing that this is how at least one other person understands the story, may come to conflate this version with the original experience. Rather than summarize or define, narrative practice suggests decentered listening in which the key words of the storyteller are carefully preserved and further gentle questioning uncovers depth in a story. Similarly, loitering around important turning points or themes allows a certain richness to evolve. This is in contrast to what can often be a tightly packed three or four consecutive day schedule, dominated by the technical logistics of digital storytelling. Spreading workshops over an extended period also allows participants periods of reflection (and negotiation with their intimate publics who are frequently the supporting cast) that can significantly influence the content of a personal story and the meaning that is made of it. Strategies that reinforce storytellers as the center of their production and distribution process are significant if they are to emerge with a sense of heightened well-being and social connection.

Other useful tools, such as the concept of re-membering, employed in narrative therapy, can be traced back to origins in the work of anthropologist–filmmaker Barbara Myerhoff.

> To signify this special type of recollection, the term "Re-membering" may be used, calling attention to the reaggregation of members, the figures who belong to one's life story, one's own prior selves, as well as significant others who are part of the story. Re-membering, then, is a purposive, significant unification, quite different from the passive, continuous fragmentary flickerings of images and feelings that accompany other activities in the normal flow of consciousness. (Myerhoff, 1982, p. 111)

Here, Myerhoff suggests a meaning-making version of storytelling that invites reflection upon the significance of people and events within a larger life narrative. This process of reexamination and analysis also suggests the possibility of restorying the past, for example, recognizing the valuable life lessons that were gained through adversity or acknowledging complicity in events that were previously attributed wholly to others. Myerhoff continues in a vein that sharply parallels the process of digital storytelling:

> The focused unification provided by Re-membering is requisite to sense and ordering. A life is given a shape that extends back in the past and forward into the future. It becomes a tidy, edited tale. Completeness is sacrificed for moral and aesthetic purposes. Here history may approach art and ritual. (Myerhoff, 1982, p. 111)

A digital story is quite literally a "tidy, edited tale," but Myerhoff also touches upon the networked identity work that underpins the process. Often participants describe broaching difficult subjects with loved ones, discussing taboo issues or misunderstandings, thereby catalyzing reconciliation. Negotiations undertaken with friends, family, and even imagined, unknown publics allow storytellers to make connections, to feel socially engaged, and to shape new meanings that "extend back in the past and forward into the future."

Myerhoff derived her analysis from case studies located in an elderly Jewish community in Venice, Florida. She worked with members of a community center over an extended period of time, gathering their stories in formal interviews and informal ethnography, or what Geertz (2001) coined as "deep hanging out." These stories eventually became a the-atrical production and later formed the backbone of a documentary and book, both titled *Number Our Days*. Myerhoff drew on Victor Turner's work on social dramas and Goffman's understanding of spoiled identities to highlight the importance of what she called defini-tional ceremonies. Clearly, like the term *marginalized* that connotes a center of activity from which one is marginal, *spoiled* implies a norm. Sharing digital stories allows individu-als the opportunity to speak back to these alienating social constructs.

> When cultures are fragmented and in serious disarray, proper audiences may be hard to find. Natural occasions may not be offered and then they must be artificially invented. I have called such performances "Definitional Ceremonies," understanding them to be collective self-definitions specifically intended to proclaim an interpretation to an audience not otherwise available. . . . The latter must be captured by any means necessary and made to see the truth of the group's history as the members understand it. (Myerhoff, 1982, p. 105)

Myerhoff synthesized the stories of the elders in multiple outward-facing forms—a theater piece, documentary, and book—providing opportunity for recognition and acknowledgment. Similarly, digital storytelling offers disenfranchised storytellers an opportunity to revisit the framing narratives of their past and to renegotiate these stories with multiple publics. Further, definitional ceremonies, whether they be orchestrated as theatrical screenings, corporate training, TV, or web spaces, and regardless of whether storytellers are copresent with audiences, afford collective self-definition. Marginalized storytellers can consolidate their preferred identities and move forward as digitally enabled citizens. As proactive creative interventions, these processes are also preventative of social isolation, offering resilience to bigotry and disillusionment.

STORYTELLING AS PRAXIS

In this section I describe three examples of digital storytelling participation and the nuances of workshop facilitation that illuminate the obstacles and opportunities for storytellers in recovery from social marginalization. I consider a variety of approaches to production and distribution and draw on interviews that I undertook with storytellers soon after they finished their stories and then again up to a year later. Revisiting questions like "has sharing your story shifted they way you think of yourself or the way others think of you?" after a significant period of time has lapsed allowed storytellers to thoroughly digest the experience and later repercussions. They broadly summarize these experiences as self-empowerment, demonstrating an acquisition of agency and ownership of self/identity through digital storytelling praxis.

Notice One

When I first invited Kirsten to share her story, I called her on her mobile while she was travelling on a train. I told her a little about the workshops and SHine SA's objectives (at that stage framed as "stories and strategies for overcoming homophobia"). Kirsten is an artist and had already experimented with some digital storytelling, but she had some reservations with the subject matter. She explained (somewhat awkwardly given the public context of her conversation) that the story she'd like to make was not really about homophobia so much as her experience with depression and mental illness. I realized that even our call for participation was influencing the prospective content of the stories and suggested to the Shine SA steering committee that, rather than prescribing themes, we offer space to see what participants created. The compilation of stories would in this way provide insight into diverse experiences and nevertheless could be offered an interpretive frame by accompanying promotional materials, including the facilitator's guide.

When a *product* is commissioned as well as a *process*, there is a possibility that this final deliverable, wholly created by disparate community forces, may not fulfill organizational goals or funding criteria. In the case of the third case study, provided by ACSA, there was a clearly stated objective to promote awareness of HIV and sexual health among a younger target group. As devil's advocate, I asked the steering committee how they would respond to a hypothetical story that spoke of HIV as a gift rather than a burden. This provocation generated much discussion over the complex storying of life events in contrast to the binary positive/negative, healthy/ill, good/bad frameworks of many social-well-being marketing campaigns. These negotiations with overseeing agencies are significant because often marginalized people feel that they are patronized by well-meaning social service providers and this can perpetuate a sense of helplessness.

Meanwhile, the mediating influence of organizational agendas echoes throughout the facilitation process—even choosing examples of digital stories to screen for a group exerts an expectation of what a digital story looks and sounds like. Group discussions of what is acceptable content for public consumption and what remains private or morally taboo also influence individual decisions of what to share and what to contain. However, at a facilitation level, the constrictions of framing discourses can be tempered by acknowledging the presence of the frame and affirming the primacy of the storyteller's voice or preferred self-representation. This is in line with narrative practice in which a therapist may make a point of highlighting how their own life experience (e.g., as a white privileged male) may influence their participation in counseling.

Kirsten went on to become a valuable workshop participant; her experience allowed her to be generous in her technical support of other participants and she was steadfast in her own creative expression. Unlike most digital stories, hers is told without voiceover in a rapid and expressionistic montage of personal artworks, photographs, and superimposed text. She tells the story of being an angry and out-of-control child who grew into a troubled adult: "My blood is black . . . I know because I have seen it." Her statement of intent, accompanying the final DVD, describes her ambition to "make the viewer feel the chaos that I lived for almost four decades." In a later interview she revealed

> I have many scars from years of self-harm and have only recently worn short
> sleeves in public. Telling my story has made this easier, though I am often still self-
> conscious. . . . I think now I am generally less worried about being myself, feeling
> now that I am not the monster I thought I was.

While Kirsten's final story product bears only the slightest of references to her sexuality, her story, offered in context with others and aligned with a facilitator's guide, makes an important contribution to a larger story of social marginalization. She considers that sharing her personal yet painful story with networked publics (audiences that included her mother, siblings, and strangers) has played in her improved well-being. Further, *Notice One* (available to view at http://rainbowfamilytree.com/video/notice-1) is a work of art in itself, an enigmatic and fast-paced evocation of childhood anxiety and the overwhelming desire to fit in a strange social context.

My Secret Story

My Secret Story (view at http://rainbowfamilytree.com/video/my-secret-story) is an example of a story told pseudonymously—that is, removing any overtly identifying information (while acknowledging that people close to the storyteller would nevertheless recognize particularities). Frank, a pseudonym, speaks of a warm Catholic upbringing, followed by a devastating realization of same-sex attraction. Later he goes into the intimate and explicit details of falling in love with an HIV positive man, breaking up, having drunken make-up sex, and seroconversion.

While Frank participated enthusiastically in the workshops he was able to attend, his involvement was hampered by geographic isolation, work commitments, and erratic Internet access. He later revealed that these complications were compounded by his fears that making this story public for the first time would jeopardize some important friendships. Additionally, while he is out as gay in his rural community, only a select few know of his HIV status. Frank considered that, should his employers know of his status, there was a very real possibility that he could lose his job. He is acutely aware of the subtle nuances of discrimination on an everyday basis, both actual and potential.

> Part of me thinks they [neighbors and acquaintances] would be ok with it but then instead of them thinking oh that's the gay guy on the corner . . . they'd be thinking oh that's the HIV pos guy . . . So you go to the pub and have a sip from your schooner and you wonder whether they'll be looking at your schooner going "how do they wash that schooner?" . . . Everything becomes much more slow motion.

On numerous occasions I was concerned about Frank's well-being and whether the onus of storytelling was placing unreasonable stresses upon him. During the extended workshop schedule (in this case over eighteen months) I called and emailed often and, when I failed to make contact, on one occasion I asked another workshop participant with whom Frank was close to get in touch. Frank, due to limited time and the aforementioned logistic difficulties, ended up working closely with an experienced editor on his project, producing a story that is slickly professional yet bears the raw hallmarks of first person storytelling.

Frank's distribution strategy is what I call *proxy*, that is, it is enabled by others—in this case digital storytelling peers, organizational representatives, and the general public. The ACSA compilation was launched at a public screening and discussion forum during the FEAST Festival (Adelaide's annual GLBTTQIS cultural festival). While Frank's workshop peers sat on stage and facilitated discussion, Frank chose to remain in the audience. During drinks and nibbles after the event, he chatted with people about the stories without acknowledging that he had made one of them. However, because Adelaide has a relatively small positive community and because Frank had narrated the story himself without concealing his voice, he was never quite sure whether people knew. This was difficult for him but nevertheless part of a process he describes as becoming liberated from his story: "The issues haven't gone away but if I need to tell that story again it's there, nicely wrapped in a box, but organised, explored and honest." This comment evokes a fundamental tenet of narrative therapy—that is, helping people externalize their issues allows them to see different ways they might respond to them, rather than feeling overwhelmed or defined by problems.

Despite Frank's choice to conceal his identity in personal photographs and to observe rather than participate in the public launch, he participated actively in the Rainbow Family Tree website and community. This space was initially established to facilitate an online digital storytelling workshop and later became a hub for storytellers to exchange creative strategies, ask technical questions, and post anecdotes about everyday activism. Frank set up a profile with his real name but chose not to link it to his story. In this way he was able to track comments posted as feedback to his story and play a role in distributing other people's stories (e.g., by sharing them on his Facebook page or sending links as emails to friends). His careful management of pseudonymity and proxy sharing is an example of the kind of agency and ownership that digital storytelling, when carefully facilitated, can provide participants.

> I feel more confident and at peace for having made the short film. I don't feel apologetic for being gay and the depth of the religious hang up seems diminished, so I think it has helped me settle. . . . Having worked out where I stand on keeping my HIV status to myself and why, was also useful.

Balancing the overarching priorities of a community development or community education process with the complicated and evolving privacy needs of participants can be difficult for organizations, especially when funds and time are finite. However, if storytellers feel like their story is taken out of their hands in a final cut or distributed in ways they haven't specifically approved, there is a risk that the process can undermine agency and ownership.

Greg's Sermon

Conventional digital storytelling practice focuses on the significance of story ownership codified in the fact that the storyteller is solely responsible for the creation of the product. However, this is not always what storytellers prefer, and for those who are dogged by ill health or logistic difficulties, their storytelling may be thwarted by technical frustrations when strategic and sensitive hands-on support might be more useful. What eventuates in practice is most often a complex co-creative overlapping of skills and cultural knowledge between participants and facilitators. Participants are often eager to play a directorial role while nevertheless gaining a better understanding of story construction, logistics, and a broad base of technical aptitudes. As I have already highlighted in various illustrations of mediating influences, a rigid adherence to first person hands-on editing does not guarantee authorial control. In any case, while some people gain sufficient skills to work autonomously, the specificity of hardware and software combinations, not to mention the emotional labor involved, mean that only the very keen and proficient venture into further personal digital story creation following the workshop.

Greg participated in the ACSA workshops and had a strong desire to explore several divergent themes. One story was an homage to his parents who had supported him and many other HIV positive men throughout the devastating 1980s when the virus wreaked havoc on the gay community. The other story was first scripted as a somewhat bitter vent at young gay men who seemed to think that "AIDS is only for old men!" After some attempts to interweave the stories, Greg decided to develop the ideas as two discrete stories that allowed exploration of tonal and stylistic differences. He also engaged in quite different production processes for the two pieces. Greg assembled photographs, video excerpts, artworks, and voiceover for *Me, Mum and Dad* (view at http://rainbowfamilytree.com/video/me-mum-and-dad) on his own laptop before handing the project over to an editor to complete the finishing touches. Meanwhile, because he didn't think a tirade would have the desired influence on his target audience, Greg worked to lighten the vehement tone of the second story. With deadlines drawing closer, another editor offered to cut the narration to music as a first step. They discussed musical styles and the editor returned to the next meeting with a spoken-word-does-disco reworking that added levity and prompted humorous visuals. With trust clearly established between the two, they retreated into an office to shoot some cutaways and Greg handed over a USB stick with some of the images he thought might work somewhere. The final product, *Greg's Sermon* (view at http://rainbowfamilytree. com/video/greg-s-sermon), was produced largely by the editor between workshops but has all the hallmarks of Greg's creative input. It is an upbeat dance floor video clip that entreats its audience to "love yourself!" amid ironic asides ("Since when is a virus ageist? Is herpes? Or the flu?") and features Greg as an officious mortgage broker, a DJ, and a seminaked chef. Greg admits the final product is something he couldn't have achieved by himself but believes the energetic editing and music make the message more appealing to a target audience of young gay men. He has been very engaged in distributing the story, screening it at AIDS retreats, posting it to Facebook groups, and would love to see it on mainstream TV. He uses both targeted (sending DVDs to specific people and festivals) as well as ad hoc sharing strategies (in this case, embracing opportunities for speaking and writing about the project). He says *Greg's Sermon* "makes me feel a little bit of a 'star' in my own lunch box" and goes on to reveal,

> This is possibly one of the few projects that I have been involved with, put on by an AIDS council, where I have finished the project feeling empowered as opposed to sad or sort of feeling like a victim.

The question of whether facilitators speak for, about, with, or alongside participants has been canvassed by scholars in a variety of disciplines (Leadbeater, 2009; Ruby, 1991) as well as consultants and entrepreneurs working in areas of community and commercial co-creativity. For example, Myerhoff describes her authorship of *Number Our Days* as a kind of co-creative process in which an abstracted "third voice" results—the fusion of her voice with those of her participants, directly attributable to neither. This idea initially appears to parallel those of Bakhtin, particularly "double-voiced discourse" and "reported speech" in which discourse is layered with multiple meanings, combining numerous distinct voices in one final representation. However, in a critique of Myerhoff's proposal, Kaminsky (1994) points out that

> in Bakhtin, who is ever conscious of the power relations among speaking voices that enter into contact, the boundary marking the separation between different semantic intentions is never obliterated. . . . [Myerhoff's] formulation evades the whole problem of the relationship between her discourse and "somebody else's discourse," thus rendering it wildly inappropriate to ask the question that the caterpillar poses to Alice, concerning the meaning of words: the question of who shall be master. (p. 129)

This focus on the discrete semantic intentions of an interviewee and the anthropologist who reports on and contextualizes the interview illuminates the complex negotiation of co-creative terrain. A digital storytelling workshop facilitator, editor, or providing agency may equally be charged with eliding the semantic intentions of participants, thereby undermining their agency and eroding their ownership of the end product. Narrative practice addresses this very charge with concerted effort to privilege the storyteller's voice and to reaffirm semantic intentions with regular check-ins. Similarly, digital storytelling facilitators can make regular opportunities for storytellers to affirm their agency in the process and their ownership of the end product. This counters a dominant paradigm (at least in documentary film production and often in conventional digital storytelling praxis) that prioritizes deadlines, budgets, and perceived audience expectations as final cut is negotiated and locked off.

Digital stories are permanent and inflexible in form; however, they need not necessarily be deemed inconsistent with later iterations of identity, an accusation that potentially renders them inauthentic. Complex, fractured self-narratives and postmodern concepts of identity can be discussed in workshops. They can also be implicit or made explicit in a simple and engaging digital story. Creative solutions from my case studies include the use of superimposed text to counterpoint narration and explanatory statements on process (in an accompanying DVD guide or web space) that offer a more complex interpretation and context. This is evident in "Stealth Crip," made by a disabled man who only realized after finishing his edit that he'd not canvassed the issue of sexuality. He adds clever commentary in superimposed text to address these multiple layers of self-image. (This is available to view at http://rainbowfamilytree.com/video/stealth-crip-1.) Facilitators can canvass the concept of networked identity work to highlight the labor undertaken by storytellers. This occurs first in the cocreation of digitally mediated identity and second in efforts to speak across differences among imagined publics. Workshop discussions should underpin agency in storytelling and ownership of both the final story and its evolving ramifications. A focus on agency and ownership rather than authenticity affords a more sustainable self-concept and can be accommodated by a variety of customized production and distribution processes tailored to suit the individual participants in a workshop.

In summary, a variety of facilitation strategies, derived in part from narrative practice, can support personal recovery and empowerment in digital storytelling:

- First, creating a workshop space where personal connections are forged between participants and facilitators establishes trust and dissipates inevitable fears.

- Second, acknowledging multiple influences on story construction arms storytellers with the power to choose their own reconstruction.

- Third, providing some flexibility in the framing objectives of a workshop allows participants to consider which publics they wish to address and articulate their tales in ways that are meaningful to them.

- Finally, loitering throughout production and distribution allows storytellers opportunities to develop and modify their stories, affirming semantic intentions that may also shift and grow.

These strategies can serve to counter or at least deconstruct the dogmatic framing discourses that influence many kinds of community health interventions. Additionally, they empower participants with capacity to critique the social construction of their identities and civic participation.

CONCLUSION

Nowadays, digital stories can last forever and be seen by many people in many places. With these higher stakes, networked self-representation has increased potential to be both helpful and harmful to vulnerable storytellers. While privacy and publicness, and agency and ownership are not often conceptualized as central tenets of digital storytelling practice, in a context where digital stories have resonance beyond immediate time frames and copresent audiences, these precepts have become increasingly significant.

In traditional workshops, the behind the scenes networked identity work that is implicit in digital storytelling is often regarded as peripheral and afforded very little time or space. Nevertheless, this labor of co-creative self-construction plays a central role in recovery from social marginalization. Greater social participation is underpinned by a sense of well-being and affirmed citizenship. Through careful management of privacy, storytellers reclaim space in public; through strategic self-representation, they affirm their place among social networks that are simultaneously familiar, unknown, and imagined. In short, strategies that support deep listening and empowered narrative construction constitute powerful tools for creative recovery and can easily be incorporated into nuanced digital storytelling facilitation. Further, these tools can be adapted and accommodated in a wide range of mediated creative praxis.

NOTES

1. I use "in recovery" in the most broad and general sense to imply deficits or social exclusion as framed by participants and storytellers rather than in a diagnostic sense.

2. Joe Lambert, alongside artist/educators Dana Atchley and Nina Mullen, are regarded by many as being the pioneers of digital storytelling, and Lambert's (2002) text *Capturing Lives, Creating Communities* is widely referenced and used as a "how to bible" in many workshops.

3. Daniel Meadows is an English photographer and proponent of digital storytelling as participatory media. From 2001 to 2006, he pioneered the BBC "Capture Wales" project and has written extensively about what he calls the amplification of ordinary voices (Meadows & Kidd, 2009).

REFERENCES

Citron, M. (1999). *Home movies and other necessary fictions* (Vol. 4). Minneapolis: University of Minnesota Press.

Freedman, J., & Combs, G. (1996). *Narrative therapy: The social construction of preferred realities*. New York, NY: Norton.

Geertz, C. (2001). *Available light: Anthropological reflections on philosophical topics*. Princeton, NJ: Princeton University Press.

Giddens, A. (1991). *Modernity and self-identity: Self and society in the late modern age*. Cambridge, England: Polity.

Hartley, J. (2008). Problems of expertise and scalability in self-made media. In K. Lundby (Ed.), *Digital storytelling, mediatized stories: Self-representations in new media* (Vol. 52, pp. 197–212). New York, NY: Peter Lang.

Hillier, L., Jones, T., Monagle, M., Overton, N., Gahan, L., Blackman, J., & Mitchell, A. (2010). *Writing themselves in 3: The third national study on the sexual health and well-being of same sex attracted and gender questioning young people*. Melbourne, Australia: La Trobe University. Retrieved from http://www.glhv.org.au/report/writing-themselves-3-wti3-report

Hughes, S. (2011). Jamey Rodemeyer, bullied teen who made "It Gets Better" video, commits suicide [Web log post]. *Washington Post*. Retrieved from http://www.washingtonpost.com/blogs/blogpost/post/jamey-rodemeyer-bullied-teen-who-made-it-gets-better-video-commits-suicide/2011/09/21/gIQAVVzxkK_blog.html

Hyvärinen, M., Hyden, L., Saarenheimo, M., & Tamboukou, M. (Eds.). (2010). *Beyond narrative coherence*. Amsterdam, Netherlands: John Benjamins.

Kaminsky, M. (1992). Myerhoff's "third voice": Ideology and genre in ethnographic narrative. *Social Text, 33*, 124–144.

Lambert, J. (2002). *Digital storytelling: Capturing lives, creating community*. Berkeley, CA: Digital Diner Press.

Leadbeater, C. (2009). *We-think: Mass innovation, not mass production*. London, England: Profile Books. Retrieved from http://books.google.com.au/books?id=ipHhSn00OeQC

Meadows, D., & Kidd, J. (2009). "Capture Wales": The BBC digital storytelling project. In J. Hartley & K. McWilliam (Eds.), *Story circle: digital storytelling around the world* (pp. 91–117). West Sussex, England: Wiley-Blackwell.

Ministerial Advisory Committee on Gay and Lesbian Health (MACGLH). (2002). *What's the difference? Health issues of major concern to gay, lesbian, bisexual, transgender and intersex (GLBTI) Victorians* (Leonard, W., Ed.). Melbourne, Australia: Department of Human Services.

Myerhoff, B. (1982). Life history among the elderly: Performance, visibility and re-membering. In J. Ruby (Ed.), *A crack in the mirror: Reflexive perspectives in anthropology*. Philadelphia: University of Pennsylvania Press.

Papacharissi, Z. (2010). *A private sphere: Democracy in a digital age*. Cambridge, England: Polity.

Penn, P., & Sheinberg, M. (1991). Stories and conversations. *Journal of Strategic & Systemic Therapies, 10*(3-4), 30–37.

Pitts, M., Mitchell, A., Smith, A., & Patel, S. (2006). *Private lives: A report on the health and well-being of GLBTI Australians*. Melbourne: Australian Research Centre in Sex, Health and Society, La Trobe University. Retrieved from http://www.glhv.org.au/report/private-lives-report

Radden, J. (Ed.). (2004). *The philosophy of psychiatry : A companion*. New York, NY: Oxford University Press.

Ruby, J. (1991). Speaking for, speaking about, speaking with, or speaking alongside: An anthropological and documentary dilemma. *Visual Anthropology Review, 7*(2), 50–67.

Szasz, T. S. (1974). *The second sin*. London, England: Routledge & Kegan Paul.

Vivienne, S. (2013). *Digital storytelling as everyday activism: Queer identity, voice and networked publics* (Unpublished doctoral thesis). Queensland University of Technology, Brisbane, Australia.

Vivienne, S., & Burgess, J. (2012). The digital storyteller's stage: Queer everyday activists negotiating privacy and publicness. *Journal of Broadcasting & Electronic Media, 56*(3), 362–377. doi:10.1080/08838151.2012.705194

Vivienne, S., & Burgess, J. (2013). The remediation of the personal image in queer digital storytelling. *Journal of Material Cultures, 18*(3), 279–298. doi:10.1177/1359183513492080

Waidzunas, T. (2011). Young, gay, and suicidal: Dynamic nominalism and the process of defining a social problem with statistics. *Science, Technology & Human Values, 37*(2), 1–27. doi:10.1177/0162243911402363

White, M., & Epston, D. (1990). *Narrative means to therapeutic ends*. New York, NY: Norton.

Index

About the Editors

Philip Neilsen, MA, PhD, ASA, is both a senior academic and an internationally acclaimed author and poet. He founded the creative writing program at the Queensland University of Technology where he is currently adjunct professor, and teaches poetics at the University of Queensland. He has published five books of poetry, including *Without an Alibi* (2008), five novels/novellas, and has been widely anthologized in Australia and the United States. His creative work has been translated into German, Chinese, and Korean. As an academic, he has contributed scholarly works on literature and on the use of creative writing as mental health therapy. Philip has been president of PEN International for Australia North, has served on the Australia Council for the Arts, and is coeditor (with Professor David Morley, University of Warwick, United Kingdom) of *The Cambridge Companion to Creative Writing*.

Robert King is a clinical psychologist and professor in the School of Psychology and Counselling at Queensland University of Technology. He is a fellow of the Australian Psychological Society and a member of the College of Clinical Psychology. Professor King holds a MA (Clinical Psychology) from the University of Melbourne and a PhD from Monash University. Robert's primary areas of research focus include the impact and effectiveness of online delivery of counseling and psychotherapy services; the role of creative therapies in mental health; development and evaluation of models of mental health service delivery; and the mental health workforce (training, structure, organization and management). Robert publishes extensively in Australian and international peer-reviewed journals. He is associate editor for the U.S.-based journal *Administration and Policy in Mental Health and Mental Health Services Research* and was for many years the peer review editor for *Psychotherapy in Australia*.

Felicity Baker is a music therapist, associate professor in music therapy, and currently an Australia Research Council future fellow (2010–2015) based at the University of Melbourne. She is currently associate editor the *Journal of Music Therapy* and immediate past president of the Australian Music Therapy Association, Inc., the peak body of the discipline in Australia.

Felicity has established herself as an international leader in music therapy and is regularly invited to teach in institutions through Asia, the United Kingdom/Northern Europe, and the United States. Felicity is recognized for her research expertise in therapeutic songwriting and in neurorehabilitation. Her text *Songwriting Methods: Techniques and Clinical Applications for Music Therapy Clinicians, Educators and Students* (Jessica Kingsley Publishers) is a best seller that has sold over 4,000 copies and has been translated into Korean and Italian. Felicity is a member of a research consortium involving music therapy researchers from nine international universities from the United States, United Kingdom, Norway, Denmark, Finland, and Australia with international recognition of being at the forefront of music therapy research. Her innovative research has attracted significant media attention. She has achieved a strong publication record (four books, 17 book chapters, and more than 70 peer-reviewed journal articles) and developed a recognized capacity for cross-disciplinary research.

About the Contributors

Kate Aitchison is a registered music therapist with ten years' experience providing services for infants, children, adolescents, and adults. She completed her graduate diploma in music therapy in 2005, and a master's of mental health majoring in psychotherapy in 2013. She maintains professional registration with the Australian Music Therapy Association. In 2006, she established a music therapy program at the Jacana Acquired Brain Injury Unit, Queensland Health. In 2008, Kate began employment with the Mater Children's Hospital (MCH) Child and Youth Mental Health Service (CYMHS) in Brisbane. She transferred to the Lady Cilento Children's Hospital when the MCH merged with the Royal Children's Hospital in late 2014. At this time, she also began employment with the newly established CYMHS day program in North Brisbane.

In her role with CYMHS, Kate works with children from birth to 17 years of age. In 2009, she ran a pilot project for children under the age of four and their primary caregiver focusing on healthy attachment and bonding in conjunction with the community-based program "Sing & Grow." The program received funding from Heart Kids and earned extremely positive feedback from participants. In 2012, Kate wrote a grant proposal obtaining funding from the Mater Foundation to run a follow-up research project titled "Music Together." The following year, she wrote a successful application for funding to purchase recording and music equipment to establish a portable recording studio within CYMHS. Kate balances her time working part-time at CYMHS with looking after her two young daughters.

Andrea Baldwin works at the nexus of arts and health. She has over 20 years' experience as a registered psychologist, teacher, researcher, facilitator, and community theater practitioner. She holds PhDs in both psychology and creative writing and a master of arts in drama. While employed as a senior psychologist working with adolescents, and based on her experience as performer and teacher of improvisation forms created by Keith Johnstone, Andrea developed the Respect Yourself Drama Education (RYDE) program. The program has been successfully implemented with groups of young people with autism spectrum disorders, learning disabilities, and severe mental health issues. Dr. Baldwin has developed a number of other drama-based programs for adolescents and adults including Queer Theatresports, a community development/sexual health promotion program for the gay and lesbian community; Amir/Amira, a leadership development program for young Australian Muslims; and Streetwise, a program for adolescents at risk of becoming involved in the criminal justice system. As director of RealWorld Consulting, in collaboration with the Queensland University of Technology, Andrea instigated the Life Drama project, a seven-year project in Papua New Guinea using community theater for sexual health education. Under the same collaborative arrangement, Andrea has conducted other consultations in the Pacific, examining effective strategies for behavior change communication.

She continues to work in arts health, community capacity building, education, and practice-led research. She has served on the editorial boards of journals *Cognition* and *Music and Arts in Action* and has published in the areas of clinical psychology, applied theater, behavior change communication, youth arts, creative writing, and evaluation.

Jill Comins, MA, BC-DMT, LPC, is a graduate of Drexel University's Creative Arts in Therapy program. Working as a dance/movement therapist in an acute inpatient behavioral health hospital in Philadelphia, she is experienced in assisting individuals in discovering their innate power to heal themselves and restore wholeness. Jill helped to implement the first recovery-oriented care unit in the hospital in 2010, whose guiding principles include a person-centered approach to treatment and a focus on wellness. As the supervising director, she supported changes in the structure and delivery of expressive arts services that paralleled the transformation process of the hospital's philosophy of recovery and trauma-informed care. Jill has since integrated recovery-based dance therapy programming throughout multiple units in the hospital including general adult, women's, and older adult units, guiding individuals with various mental health disorders, trauma, and/or addiction in their process of change. Jill is a member of the Pennsylvania Counseling Association (PCA) and American Dance Therapy Association (ADTA) where she holds an elected office as program coordinator for the Pennsylvania chapter. She has presented for ADTA and PCA conferences, emphasizing how techniques and methods utilized in dance/movement therapy parallel and support the guiding principles of recovery set forth by SAMHSA (Substance Abuse and Mental Health Services Administration), a division of the U.S. Department of Health and Human Services. Additionally, Jill enjoys sharing her recovery and wellness-based approach as a supervisor to dance/movement therapy graduate students.

Sandra Drabant, MA Art Therapy, completed her master's in art therapy at the University of Illinois and worked in Chicago for eight years. She returned to Australia in 2005, where she worked with at risk children and their families. Currently, Sandra works as a senior art therapist at the Lady Cilento Children's Hospital in the Child and Youth Mental Health Service Day Program South. She coordinates the art therapy program at the Mater Cancer Care Centre and lectures in the School of Medicine at the University of Queensland, Brisbane. Sandra can be contacted by email at sandra@arteverafter.com.

Claire Edwards. After gaining a BA (Hons) in art history and English, Claire Edwards trained as an art therapist in London in 1984 and migrated to Australia in 1989. Claire helped establish art therapy training (Master's of Mental Health—Art Therapy) at University of Queensland in Brisbane in 2004 and has had lecturing and coordinating roles in this program. She has maintained a clinical practice throughout, working with adults, young people, and children in child safety, mental health, private practice, and drug and alcohol services for over 30 years. Claire completed a research master's at the University of Western Sydney in 2005, investigating art therapy with women with eating issues. She completed a qualifying master's of social work in 2013.

Patricia Fenner is a registered art therapist, the course coordinator of the Master of Art Therapy program at La Trobe University, and has an ongoing commitment to developing graduates with strong practice skills. Patricia is a researcher with a particular focus on art-based research, art making, and mental health recovery in Australia and the Asia Pacific, as well as art therapy in cancer care. Prior to working in the university sector, she worked in diverse contexts including public mental health, education, and in aged care, as well as a community artist in both Melbourne and Berlin.

Sherry W. Goodill, Ph.D., BC-DMT, NCC, LPC, is a clinical professor and chairperson of the Department of Creative Arts Therapies at Drexel University in Philadelphia, teaching at both the master's and PhD levels, and is also the immediate past president of the American Dance Therapy Association. She holds a doctorate in medical psychology with a concentration in mind/body studies and has 30 years of experience as a clinician, researcher, and educator in dance/movement therapy and the creative arts therapies. She serves on editorial panels for the journals *Arts in Psychotherapy: An International Journal* and the *Journal of Creativity in Mental Health*. Dr. Goodill received one of the U.S. National Institutes of Health Office of Alternative Medicine (now the NCCAM) initial research grants to study the benefits of dance/movement therapy for adults with medical conditions. Her 2005 volume *An Introduction to Medical Dance/ Movement Therapy: Health Care in Motion* was the first book devoted entirely to this topic.

Anne Margrethe Melsom is a board-certified dance/movement therapist and a licensed professional counselor that has focused her clinical work on the process of change and transformation through dance and creative expression for people in recovery from serious mental and medical illness, substance use, trauma, and homelessness. She is the director of a creative arts therapy department at a behavioral health hospital, where she provides direct care to adults in inpatient, residential, and wellness programs. She chairs recovery-oriented initiatives and develops, directs, and implements recovery-oriented creative arts therapy programming.

Ms. Melsom is a faculty member at Drexel University's Creative Arts Therapy Department and she maintains a private supervision practice for professionals seeking board certification in dance/movement therapy (DMT) as well as counseling licensure. Ms. Melsom serves on the American Dance Therapy Association Committee on Approval, reviewing and approving master's programs in dance/movement therapy and counseling in the United States.

Decades of clinical work and recent collaborations with her colleague has informed and shaped the DMT RECOVERY Model. The Chacian DMT approach is the essence of the model, lending itself to a spontaneous here-and-now process and including evidence-based/evidence-informed structures. Interventions can target particular change processes, meeting individuals at their level of readiness for practicing change. Empathy, cohesion, and mobilized movement experiences support the integration of embodied recovery and hope. The DMT pillars of the model are outlined in the acronym RECOVERY: relationship, empathy, creativity, opportunity to practice change, vitality, expressions, resilience, and a person-driven focus on the "you"—the person in his or her community.

Tom O'Brien is a foundation fellow of the Australian College of Social Work. He is a senior lecturer in the School of Medicine at the University of Queensland and principal psychotherapist at Mater Children's Hospital Child and Youth Mental Health Service (CYMHS) in Brisbane. His appointment as the foundation coordinator of the Master of Mental Health—Art Therapy program at the University of Queensland (2004–2006) was the opportunity to work with an enthusiastic and creative group of art therapists. This led to important developments in his professional, clinical, and personal practice for which he is grateful.

Margot J. Schofield, M.Clin.Psych., PhD, MAPs, is a clinical psychologist and professor of counselling and psychotherapy in the School of Psychology and Public Health, La Trobe University, Melbourne, Australia. The current research focuses on counseling and clinical supervision, development of psychotherapists and counsellors, creative therapies in mental health, art-based approaches in cancer recovery, family violence, elder abuse, and women's health. Margot has received over $14 million in research grants and has published extensively in international peer-reviewed journals. She serves on the editorial boards of *Counselling Psychology Quarterly* and *Counselling and Psychotherapy Research*, and regularly reviews grants for the Australian Research Council.

Claire Stephensen is a registered music therapist (RMT) and neurologic music therapist (NMT) who provides mental health services and family-centered therapy for those who present with complex needs. Claire graduated from the University of Queensland in 2008 with a master's of music therapy and completed training in neurologic music therapy in 2012. Based in Brisbane, Australia, Claire works from her private practice—Press Play Music Therapy—and in psychiatric, medical, and community health settings. She regularly presents her work at national and international conferences and facilitates lectures and workshops on music therapy in psychiatry and mental health.

Claire is passionate about the capacity for music and creativity to connect individuals, families, groups, and communities, not only at a social and emotional level but also at a neurological and subcortical level. Through listening to music, engaging in conversations, and creating music, she is most interested in working with people with backgrounds of trauma, self-injury, and addictions. Claire has experience working from multiple psychological frameworks, such as cognitive behavioral therapy, trauma model therapy, dialectical behavior therapy, solution focused therapy, and narrative therapy. She actively engages in ongoing professional development in fields of music therapy, mental health, neurobiology of trauma, neuropsychotherapy, creative arts therapies, sensory modulation therapy, and talking therapies. Claire's key research interests are in creativity, mental health recovery, psychological trauma, and emotion.

Sonja Vivienne lectures in digital media at Flinders University of South Australia. She balances teaching with practice-led research, everyday activism, and parenting. She is particularly interested in the strategic management of privacy at the heart of Intimate Citizenship 3.0. Recent research, undertaken as a postdoctoral research fellow at the University of Queensland's Centre for Communication and Social Change, includes a survey of free and open-source software and digital citizenship in India and Australia, and development of a hybrid online/face-to-face teaching space exploring information and communication technologies (ICTs), social movements, and development. Sonja's doctorate was based at the ARC Centre of Excellence for Creative Industries and Innovation (CCI) at Queensland University of Technology, where her research explored digital storytelling as a tool for everyday activism, focusing particularly on the problems of voice, queer identity, and networked publics. She is also a graduate of the Oxford Institute of Internet Research (OII) summer doctoral program. In years previous, Sonja worked as writer, director, and producer of drama and documentaries, tackling subjects as diverse as youth suicide, drug culture in Vietnamese communities, and lesbian personal columns. As creative principal of *Incite Storie,* Sonja also produced and co-directed *Wadu Matyidi,* a children's animation and documentary package exploring the rejuvenation of the Adnyamathanha language and culture of the Flinders Ranges.